Environmental Policy in New Zealand

To John Hayward

OXFORD READINGS IN NEW ZEALAND POLITICS: No. 3

General Editor: Martin Holland

Environmental Policy in New Zealand
The Politics of Clean and Green?

Ton Bührs

Robert V. Bartlett

Auckland
OXFORD UNIVERSITY PRESS
Melbourne New York Toronto

Oxford University Press, Walton Street, Oxford OX2 6DP
Oxford   New York   Toronto
Delhi   Bombay   Calcutta   Madras   Karachi
Kuala Lumpur   Singapore   Hong Kong   Tokyo
Nairobi   Dar es Salaam   Cape Town
Melbourne   Auckland   Madrid
and associated companies in
Berlin   Ibadan

Oxford is a trade mark of Oxford University Press

© Ton Bührs and Robert V. Bartlett 1993

This edition first published 1993

All rights reserved. No part of this publication may be reproduced, stored in a retrieval system, or transmitted, in any form or by any means, without the prior permission in writing of Oxford University Press. Within New Zealand, exceptions are allowed in respect of any fair dealing for the purpose of research or private study, or criticism or review, as permitted, under the Copyright Act 1962, or in the case of reprographic reproduction in accordance with the terms of the licences issued by Copyright Licensing Limited. Enquiries concerning reproduction outside these terms and in other countries should be sent to the Rights Department, Oxford University Press, at the address below.

ISBN 0 19 558284 5
ISSN 0967-4144

Cover designed by Nikolas Andrew
Typeset in Adobe Times by Egan-Reid Limited
Printed in New Zealand by GP Print Limited
Published by Oxford University Press
1A Matai Road, Greenlane
PO Box 11-149, Auckland, New Zealand

CONTENTS

Acknowledgements — vii

Introduction: Environmental Policy—Themes and Directions — 1

1. Analysing Environmental Policy: Perspectives, Concepts, Tools — 12

2. Environmental Policy Evolution: Pressures, Demands, Agendas — 37

3. The Greening of New Zealand: Towards a New Paradigm? — 68

4. The Role of the State: From 'State Vandalism' Towards a 'Market-led' Environment? — 90

5. Institutional Reform: Environmental Policy and Management — 113

6. Comprehensive Environmental Policy: Obstacles and Prospects — 135

Conclusion — 156

References — 170

Index — 187

SERIES INTRODUCTION

This is the third publication in the *Oxford Readings in New Zealand Politics* series. The *Readings* are designed to bring together the leading writers on New Zealand politics to produce a series of titles on a variety of important topics. Studies that warrant examination because of their contemporary relevance, as well as significant areas that have been unduly neglected in the past, will be included in the series. The objective is to create a core body of literature essential to the study of political science in New Zealand. Through this it is hoped to stimulate academic debate and to provide students of New Zealand politics with a collection of texts that are interesting, original, and challenging.

Up till now, political science publishing on New Zealand politics has lacked a focus with no single publisher being identified as leading the field. Oxford's international and local reputation will ensure both the high quality of each publication and guarantee exposure and a wide distribution beyond New Zealand.

Previous titles in the series have been *Electoral Behaviour in New Zealand* and *State and Economy in New Zealand*. Further titles envisaged for the future include: *Political Culture*; *Political Parties in New Zealand*; *The Cabinet in New Zealand*; *Health Policy*; and *Women and New Zealand Politics*.

Martin Holland
General Editor

ACKNOWLEDGEMENTS

Many people and organizations have been helpful to us in the writing and publishing of this book. The Centre for Resource Management at Lincoln University has provided a professional home, technical support, and a lively intellectual environment for both of us. We thank all of the Centre staff but especially John Hayward. Bartlett also drew upon the resources provided by the Department of Political Science at Purdue University during his work on this project. The libraries at Lincoln University, the University of Canterbury, and Purdue University were intensively used and the librarians were unfailingly helpful. Administrative and secretarial assistance was provided by Bruna Jones, Carmel Edlin, Shona Wilson, Barbara Bergner, Beth Turner, Marty Dahlstrom, and Claire Windler. Andrew Upfield facilitated electronic communication between New Zealand and the United States.

Crucial financial support of Bartlett for an extended research and teaching visit to Lincoln University and the University of Canterbury in 1990 was provided by a Fulbright Scholarship from the New Zealand–United States Educational Foundation. Supplementary funding for research activities was provided by Lincoln University. Fulbright support for travel about New Zealand to give lectures at various universities made it possible for us to meet and to begin our collaboration on this book. Bartlett offers a special thanks to the Foundation's Executive Director, Laurie Cox, for his helpful and friendly introductions to New Zealand society. Bartlett is also grateful to Purdue University, the Purdue Research Foundation, and the Centre for Resource Management for making possible a second extended research visit to New Zealand in 1992, a sabbatical which was indispensable in completing this book.

We thank the innumerable individuals throughout New Zealand who have taken the time to speak with us and answer questions about New Zealand environmental politics and policy over the past several years. We are humbly aware that social research of this kind is possible only with the help of many other people. In particular, we are grateful to all those people, including politicians, civil servants, and members of interest groups, who have kindly given of their time to inform us about their views or to provide us with information.

A draft of Chapter 3 was originally presented at the 1992 conference of the New Zealand Political Studies Association, and versions of Chapters 4 and 5 were presented at the 1992 conference of the Australasian Political Studies Association. Parts of several chapters were presented by each of us as lectures at the Centre for Resource Management. Several individuals offered helpful questions, criticisms, and suggestions in response to these earlier manifestations. We thank Peter Ackroyd, Priya Kurian, Stefanie Rixecker, Simon Swaffield, Tracy Williams, Walter F. Baber, Martin Holland, Ian McChesney, John Hayward, Hyam Gold, and students of the Centre for Resource Management, for their feedback.

Finally, much of what we know about New Zealand environmental policy we learned with, sometimes from, and often because of our families. We thank Nicole, Eric, Muriel, Sally, Emily, and Helen for their patience and encouragement.

Ton Bührs and Robert V. Bartlett   May, 1993

Introduction
ENVIRONMENTAL POLICY
Themes and Directions

In June 1992, delegates from more than 175 nations gathered in Rio de Janeiro, Brazil, for the United Nations Conference on Environment and Development (UNCED), better known as the 'Earth Summit'. Held twenty years after the first major world conference on the environment in Stockholm, the 'Earth Summit' was a manifestation of ongoing world-wide concern about what can be referred to as 'the environmental problematique'. Two decades after the first wave of environmentalism swept over much of the world, the environment was higher than ever on the international political agenda. Concern for the environment has proved to be neither fashion nor fad, but, rather, a persistent phenomenon.

The UNCED also reflected a widespread feeling that the efforts undertaken during those twenty years to bring environmental problems under control have been grossly inadequate. That feeling is not only shared by people all over the world, in developed and developing countries, who are experiencing threats to and deterioration in the quality of their personal environment. It is also a sign of a growing recognition, spurred by scientific observation and analysis, that the global environment is under serious threat from multiple human-based sources, resulting in such phenomena as global warming, ozone depletion, and a decline of biodiversity (Brown et al., 1984–92; World Resources Institute, 1987–92). On a world scale, 'every major indicator shows a deterioration in natural systems' (Brown, 1991, p. 4). The idea that time is running out, and that drastic action must be taken urgently, is no longer confined to a handful of doomsayers, but has even caught on among politicians. At Rio, world leaders acknowledged that the dramatic changes needed to avoid global environmental and social disaster had not been achieved (*The Press*, 18 June 1992).

Given the perceived urgency of change, the 1990s have been labelled 'the decisive decade'.[1] Yet, despite the growing chorus of those calling for fundamental transformation, there is no guarantee that it will occur. Faced

---

1. Such declarations are, of course, not necessarily an omen of anything, as it should be remembered that the 1970s had been declared 'the environmental decade'.

with the need for such a degree of change, the temptation of denial is very real (Postel, 1992). The attachment to existing ways of life and thinking, and vested interests in the established order, exert formidable counter-pressures to drastic reforms on a national and international level.

New Zealand, however, can be identified as a country where, in recent years, barriers to reform have been overcome. Indeed, the scale of change in New Zealand has been such that hardly anything has been left untouched. Since 1984, reforms undertaken by successive governments have been directed at almost all spheres of public affairs and policy, ranging across the economy, the civil service, Parliament, and local and regional government, to defence, education, health, social welfare, and the environment. As a consequence, not only the State has been reshaped (Boston et al., 1991), but much of New Zealand society has been transformed.

Whether *all* these changes have been beneficial is a question that we will not address. We will ask whether, and if so in what way, changes in New Zealand have improved, or laid a basis for the improvement of, environmental policy. The reforms have been so comprehensive and radical that they can be called unique in the experience of western societies. New Zealand, having taken bold steps in environmental reform, may be an example and a source of inspiration to other countries in the search for new directions in environmental policy.

Analysing Environmental Policy Development

Although attention since the late 1980s has shifted towards global environmental problems and the need for more effective international action to address them, it can be argued that the key to change still lies in the motto, 'think globally, act locally'. A good case can be made for strengthening global environmental governance (Brundtland Commission, 1987; Caldwell, 1990a, 1990b; French, 1992; Sand, 1990). But whether *effective* international action will be undertaken depends ultimately on what happens within countries. The willingness of governments to conclude international agreements, as well as their record in implementing them, is influenced by the needs, demands, resources (including human), and constraints of the communities that they represent. In the end, it is what occurs at the 'grass-roots' level that makes or breaks policies.

This does not mean that governments are prisoners of their societies, condemned to act only within the confines of societal demands, traditions, or customs. Governments can, and often do, take the lead towards change, even despite significant public opposition (Nordlinger, 1981). It does mean, however, that for their policies to be effective governments need to take into account the needs, feelings, constraints, and opportunities of the people affected by their policies. Policies or leaders are successful only to the extent that they 'take the people with them'.

National governments, then, play a key role in the development of global thinking and local action, as well as in global action and local thinking. In analysing the reasons for ongoing environmental degradation on a national and international level, it is important to focus on what national governments have been doing. Only if we understand why or how governments have failed to halt or reverse environmental decline over the last two decades can we hope to develop more effective ways of dealing with the environmental problematique. Whilst the call for radical or fundamental change is understandable in the light of mounting environmental pressure and a growing feeling that time is running out, we need to keep an open mind as to the type and degree of change that is required.

Since the late 1960s, governments have dealt with the upsurge in environmental demands in different ways, influenced by such matters as the nature and relative strength of those demands, already existing legal and administrative arrangements, the federal or unitary structure of the political system, traditional policy styles, historical patterns of interest group politics and regulation, and the role of science in policy development (Enloe, 1975; Lundqvist, 1980; Vogel, 1986, 1987, 1990; Weale, 1992). Countries differ in the way environmental responsibilities have been (re)allocated, in the stringency of legislation passed, in the kinds of instruments used for implementing policies, and in the degree of openness (availability of information; opportunities for public participation) of the environmental policy process.

Public policy analysis, and in particular environmental policy analysis, which focuses on what governments do and why they do it, is an important tool in trying to unravel why policies are adopted and how they work, and in evaluating their merit or worth. Policy theories, models, or perspectives, which we discuss in Chapter 1, help to make sense of the complexities, contradictions, and often chaotic nature of the phenomena that we associate with the actions of governments. The fact that such theories or perspectives simplify reality is both a limitation and a strength. Although no single theory or model can claim to provide a full explanation, they draw attention to a variety of factors that are possibly important pieces of the big puzzle that the world of public policy presents.

In this book, we will use some of these perspectives in an effort to shed light on four central themes of environmental policy development: the need for anticipatory environmental policy making; the need for changing our ways; the need for institutional reform to enhance environmental policy performance; and the need for more integrated or comprehensive environmental policy development. These themes, like recurrent melodies in music, have time and again surfaced in writings on environmental policy since the concept was advanced in the early 1960s (Caldwell, 1963). Based on an identification of the particular nature and demands of environmental policy, they represent challenges to environmental policy makers that, even though sometimes recognized, have rarely been taken up. It is with respect to these four themes that New Zealand, given the comprehensive and radical nature of the environmental reforms in this country, provides a particularly significant case of environmental policy development.

Anticipatory Environmental Policy

Although it is a tenet of conventional wisdom in all spheres of life that it is better to prevent than to remedy problems, it can be argued that this truth is especially important, even imperative, in the environmental sphere. To the extent that environmental policy deals with choices and activities with big or irreversible consequences, we cannot afford to base policies solely on what 'worked' in the past. Nor is it appropriate to adopt a trial-and-error approach.

Many environmental problems have their origins in activities or technologies that are new, and for which the past provides inadequate guidance as to their potential implications. The invention and introduction of motor cars, nuclear power and nuclear weaponry, synthetic chemicals, and genetically modified organisms—to name just a few—were unprecedented. Decisions on their introduction or promotion could not be based on past experience. Their introduction and spread, without rigorous assessment of the consequences or on a trial-and-error basis, has led to very serious and perhaps irreversible environmental problems, such as the greenhouse effect, depletion of the ozone layer, the nuclear and chemical contamination of the environment, and the possibility of large-scale, even global, destruction of life.

Although governments and policy makers in general often proclaim the wisdom of anticipatory policy making (OECD, 1980a; Williams, 1986), they have not tried very hard in this respect, particularly with regard to environmental problems, nor have they had much success. Anticipatory policy making may be common wisdom, but reactive policy making is common practice.

It can even be argued that most environmental policy, nationally and internationally, has been developed in reaction not just to problems, but to crises. In other words, in order to be addressed by policy makers, environmental problems must often have reached some critical level. In many countries, pollution control policies have been introduced or strengthened only after pollution levels had become unbearable, or when attention to them was triggered by accidents or disasters (Gilg, 1986; Weale, 1992; Weidner, 1986). Natural areas (forests, wetlands) or species have in many cases received protection only once they reached the brink of disappearance or extinction (Postel, 1992; Ryan, 1992; IUCN/WWF/UNEP, 1980; World Resources Institute, 1990). Internationally, the preparedness of governments to undertake action with regard to environmental problems such as ozone depletion and the greenhouse effect also seems to depend on the extent to which scientific uncertainty has been reduced and alarm has reached crisis proportions (Benedick, 1991; Flavin, 1990; Pollock Shea, 1989).

Although it is easy to dismiss the crisis-response nature of much environmental policy as inadequate, it is much more difficult to provide answers to the question of how environmental problems can be prevented. The reasons for the predominance of reactive policy making are many and complex, and, as will become apparent from our discussion of public policy in Chapter 1, the notion of anticipatory policy development is highly problematic. Why issues receive political attention is a question which touches upon the complexities of the processes and structures related to problem definition, agenda setting, and (non-) decision making. Fully anticipating problems also requires a forecasting ability (anticipating effects and risks of activities) that is partly beyond human capabilities. Furthermore, the concept of anticipatory policy making suggests a greater degree of substantive rationality in the policy process than is realistic. Nevertheless, this does not imply that the failure of governments to prevent environmental problems should be accepted as inevitable. It does mean that we need to be more realistic in our expectations of governments than many people, including many environmentalists, have been in the past.

New Zealand, it can be argued, has been in the enviable position of being able to learn from the environmental policy mistakes of other countries. New Zealand is widely perceived to be still a 'clean and green' country, which is not affected—at least not to the same extent as most other countries—by industrial pollution, over-population, and related problems such as traffic congestion, noise, and urban decay. New Zealand is commonly associated with national parks, scenic beauty, wilderness areas, beautiful deserted beaches, green pastures, and a friendly population—an image carefully cultivated in tourism brochures. Arguably, given their density of population and high level of industrialization, it would have been difficult for many countries to prevent their environmental problems from emerging. But inasmuch as New Zealand has had the chance to observe the emergence of such problems elsewhere, its people and government should have been able to use these lessons to put in place anticipatory policies.

Since the 1960s, it has been widely acknowledged that New Zealand is in the fortunate position of being able to learn from the experiences of other countries, and to prevent environmental problems from emerging (Bührs, 1991a, pp. 72, 78, 99, 111). The extent to which this has actually occurred is discussed in Chapter 2. Some policy learning has taken place, but domestic demands and vested interests have often taken precedence over the need to anticipate as yet non-existent problems. Also, New Zealand's image as a 'clean and green' country embodies an element of denial of some already existing environmental problems, an attitude that is carried over into a more recent shift in attention from domestic conservation issues towards global environmental problems. New Zealand's experience contains sobering lessons with regard to the ability of governments to develop anticipatory policies.

The Need to Change Our Ways

A second major theme that has emerged in the environmental literature is the contention that, in order to resolve our environmental predicament, we need to change our ways. Many environmentalists argue that environmental problems are only a manifestation of a more fundamental (political, social, cultural) crisis and that we need to change radically our dominant values and practices if we want to halt or reverse environmental degradation (Ophuls, 1977; Bookchin, 1980; Ehrenfeld, 1981; Kassiola, 1990).

Among environmentalists (as well as in the wider population) there are those who believe that environmental problems and limitations can be overcome by technical means or through modest changes in environmental policies. Such 'technocentrists' or 'cornucopians' (Cotgrove, 1982; O'Riordan, 1981, p. 376) have faith in human resourcefulness and ingenuity, and do not see a need for fundamental changes in values or lifestyles. According to O'Riordan, such attitudes are also likely to be prevalent among resource managers and people working for government agencies (O'Riordan, 1981, pp. 12–14).

On the other hand, there are many environmentalists and analysts who argue that efforts to resolve environmental problems are flawed, and doomed to fail, if they do not involve a radical transformation of society, in political, economic, social, and cultural respects. According to this view, existing political systems or social choice mechanisms, including pluralism (polyarchy), the market, the law, and bureaucracy, have at best displaced environmental problems and are *inherently* incapable of resolving them. These systems fall short because the values on which they are based are at odds with the requirements of ecological rationality or because they are incapable of dealing with the complexity and comprehensiveness of the environmental problematique (Dryzek, 1987; Kassiola, 1990; Milbrath, 1989; Ophuls, 1977).

That fundamental societal change is not only required but also impending is argued by analysts of value change in western societies. Foremost among environmentalists—the 'vanguards of a new society' (Milbrath, 1984)—but also among western publics at large, the growing support for postmaterialist values is seen as an indication of a shift in culture or social paradigm (Inglehart, 1977, 1990). Furthermore, some analysts argue that a shift in values is also bringing about a political realignment, with support growing in many countries for green parties and policies that supersede the traditional left–right political cleavage (Paehlke, 1989). Green parties are not only the political platforms for environmental interests, but are also perceived (particularly by themselves) as the political arm of a broader process of social change (as expressed through 'new social movements'), and as the precursors of a new or green politics, introducing a political style characterized by such principles and things as grass-roots democracy, informal organization, non-violence, sexual liberation, and consensual decision making (Andersen, 1990; Capra and Spretnak, 1984; Parkin, 1989).

The early emergence of a green party in New Zealand (Rainbow, 1987, 1992), as well as its strong revival in the 1990s, raises the question of whether this is a manifestation of a fundamental shift in values, an expression of political realignment on the basis of the emergence of a new societal paradigm, or something else. To what extent is New Zealand's image as a clean and green country matched by a higher level of environmental awareness or 'greenness' than elsewhere? Some analysts have ascribed a deeper philosophical greenness to the environmental movement in New Zealand (as well as in Australia and North America) than to its counterpart in Europe (Hay and Haward, 1988). But is New Zealand society as a whole leading the way towards a cultural paradigm shift, and if so, what implications does this have for environmental policy? These questions lie at the heart of Chapter 3.

Institutional Reform

Whether or not New Zealand leads the way towards the emergence of a new cultural paradigm, it is a country that has recently seen some of the world's most comprehensive and radical reforms of institutions dealing with environmental problems. The nature and extent of change within environmental institutions in New Zealand since 1984 is unparalleled and of great potential significance for other countries. It is also, from a theoretical perspective, of great interest for environmental policy analysts.

The question, 'do institutions matter?', has received some considerable attention in the policy literature. Although the concept of institution is used in a variety of ways, ranging from being synonymous with 'organizations' to much broader denotations such as sets of rules, cultural norms, or political traditions and customs (March and Olsen, 1984, 1989; Ostrom, Feeny, and Picht, 1988), there seems to be a common element in the variety of uses, namely a reference to the contextual elements that guide decision and policy making. Institutional analysis draws attention to factors that supersede the 'will' of actors, that go beyond the process of individual or collective choice lying at the basis of a 'voluntaristic' model of decision-making. From an institutional perspective, a decision or policy is more than meets the eye. Although it may express the preferences of decision makers, it also reflects the influence of things by which a decision is guided, such as cultural preferences (values), symbols and procedures, formal and informal rules (norms; decision-rules), the mandate of decision makers or agencies, the distribution of power and responsibilities, and the role the State is allowed or expected to play.

Obviously, institutional analysis potentially covers a huge range of phenomena. From the point of view of policy analysts interested in enhancing policy performance, however, not all of these are equally interesting. Some things, such as cultural preferences and political traditions, may change over time, but are not easily subject to manipulation by decision makers. Decision-rules and the mandates of government agencies, however, are potentially more open to change, although the ease and extent of such reforms also depends on the institutional framework itself (political systems, for instance, vary in the degree of difficulty with which rules can be introduced or changed).

Institutional reform can be regarded as an indirect ('roundabout') but potentially more effective method of enhancing policy performance compared with efforts directed at improving the substance of policies (Majone, 1989, pp. 95–100). Although often not easily effected, and costly in the short term, institutional reform may be more productive and efficient in the longer term. On the other hand, the consequences of such reform are largely unpredictable. The results of many institutional reforms undertaken by governments have been disappointing, and many reform efforts have failed to achieve their intended outcomes (March and Olsen, 1983, 1989; Scharpf, 1986).

But institutional reform may be significant in respects other than with regard to policy performance. Institutional change, by altering the context in which people think and act, may engage people in a process of value transformation. Changing rules or procedures may require people to give attention to values that they would otherwise not take into consideration. The introduction of environmental impact assessment procedures, for instance, by requiring that attention be paid to the environmental implications of proposals, promotes ecological rationality (Bartlett, 1986b).

In what respects do existing institutional arrangements provide obstacles for the development of more effective environmental policies? To what extent can institutional reform improve environmental policy performance? Can it make environmental policy more anticipatory? How can it contribute to the promotion of environmental values? These questions, placed in the New Zealand context, are the subject of Chapters 4 and 5. In Chapter 4, the focus is on the implications for environmental policy development in New Zealand of the 'revolutionary' change in the role of the State since 1984. Profound institutional reforms of the public service, the management of State enterprises and the economy, and the shift towards a greater role for the market in resource allocation, all have very significant consequences for environmental policy. In Chapter 5, the focus is on the institutional reforms more directly related to environmental management, such as the reorganization of national environmental administration, the introduction of the Resource Management Act, and, given its close association with the latter, the reform of local government.

Comprehensive Environmental Policy

One of the key reasons why environmental policies have not been very successful is that often they recognize only inadequately or not at all the complexity and interrelatedness of the phenomena that constitute the environmental problematique. Inherently, 'the environment' is a broad, potentially all-encompassing concept. Although for analytical and practical reasons it can be treated as having different dimensions, such as an ecological (ecosystems) dimension, an economic (resource management) dimension, and a social (quality of life) dimension (Bührs, 1991a, pp. 11–14), it should be recognized that human activities with regard to one aspect of the environment (such as air pollution) may have repercussions in many other aspects (such as forests, soil fertility, buildings, and human well-being). Such impacts may not always be direct and immediately visible (there may be threshold, sleeper, and synergistic effects[2]), and they may be cumulative, adding to the complexity of environmental phenomena.

There is a growing recognition of the need for integrated or comprehensive environmental policy development to deal with the complexity and interrelatedness of environmental problems. Some analysts argue that the lack of integration in environmental policy has only led to the displacement of

---

2. Threshold effects occur only when an activity or influence reaches a certain level (such as in the case of the eutrophication of lakes because of excessive biological oxygen demand); sleeper effects become apparent only after a considerable lapse of time (for instance, the effect of asbestos or many carcinogenic substances on human health); synergistic effects result from the interaction of different substances or phenomena (for example, acid rain) (Ehrlich, Ehrlich, and Holdren, 1977, p. 727; Ophuls, 1977, pp. 119, 123–27).

problems (Dryzek, 1987), and some governments have taken steps to promote such integration, particularly in the area of pollution control (Haigh and Irwin, 1989; Rabe, 1986).

But from a policy perspective, the concept of integrated or comprehensive environmental policy making, however desirable, is also highly problematic. The difficulties are theoretical, political, and practical in nature, ensuring that it is a concept which has, so far, been the subject of scant theoretical reflection and has been applied only in isolated instances (Bartlett, 1990a). Yet, this does not mean that existing inadequate levels of integration should be taken for granted. Environmental policy, to a large degree, is *unnecessarily ad hoc*, fragmented, and compartmentalized; and there would be significant scope for coping with environmental problems more effectively if policies could be developed and implemented in a more comprehensive and co-ordinated way (Bührs, 1991a, p. 15). Real progress in the development of effective environmental policies is likely to be made only if a higher level of integration or comprehensiveness is achieved.

In Chapter 6 we analyse whether, and if so to what extent, the reforms and developments in New Zealand, described in the preceding chapters, have led or are likely to lead to a more integrated or comprehensive development of environmental policy. In several respects the reforms, notably those related to the introduction of the Resource Management Act and local government reform, seem to indicate that a better basis has been laid for a more integrated approach than in the past. Some other aspects of the reforms, however—notably those related to the shift towards a greater reliance on the market in the allocation and management of resources, as well as aspects of the reform of the public service—appear to be partially counterproductive in this respect.

From Laggard to World Leader?

During much of the 1970s, 1980s, and 1990s, environmental policy development in New Zealand, as in many other countries, has mainly been reactive, pragmatic, fragmented, uneven, and slow (Bührs, 1987). In some areas, such as nature conservation, significant progress was made, but in many other respects, as will be discussed in Chapter 2, environmental policy has been lagging behind developments in other western countries.

A major reason for this can be found in a unique phenomenon at a time when environmental degradation besets most of the world: the 'clean and green syndrome'. During the last two decades, there have been, apart from New Zealand, few if any other western countries where environmental policy has developed on the basis of the notion that environmental problems are still relatively minor. Therefore, it is perhaps the only country where environmental policy has been the result of the 'politics of clean and green'.

More recently, however, the image of New Zealand as a clean and green country has been dented by the 'discovery' of environmental problems similar to those in other western countries. Also, the idea that New Zealand in its position of relative 'splendid' isolation is less affected by processes of environmental degradation than other countries has been eroded by the realization that it is closer than most other countries to the huge, Antarctic hole in the ozone layer.

This change in awareness, combined with a preparedness to take radical steps in institutional reform, has brought New Zealand from the position of 'laggard' to that of innovator in environmental policy. As other countries have done in economic or technological areas, New Zealand can be seen as 'leaping from behind' in the field of environmental policy. Whether it is, or may become, a world leader is a question that, at this stage, cannot yet be answered. In this book, however, we hope to provide a baseline from which future judgements can be made.

1
ANALYSING ENVIRONMENTAL POLICY
Perspectives, Concepts, Tools

Imbedded in the brief overview of New Zealand environmental policy offered in the Introduction are several puzzles and anomalies. Unlike all other developed countries in North America and Europe, New Zealand has an environmental policy agenda that has been dominated by nature protection and international policy initiatives. Support for environmental values emerged early in New Zealand and seems to be very widespread in society, but it has not yet led to fundamental social and economic reordering. Politicians and the tourist industry promote New Zealand's clean and green image, and nature is culturally important to most New Zealanders. Yet this clean and green image is sustained by denial of known problems, challenged by the frequent 'discovery' of previously unknown environmental degradation, and undermined by New Zealand's poor record in anticipating and avoiding future problems. With respect to some of the policy initiatives undertaken in the 1980s and 1990s New Zealand can rightfully claim to be a world leader, but in many respects New Zealand's environmental policy development lags behind that in other western countries.

As we evaluate New Zealand policy in relation to four central themes of environmental policy development (the need for anticipatory policy making, the need for changing our ways, the need for institutional reform, and the need for more integrated or comprehensive policy), we shall also try to make sense of these puzzles and anomalies. However, doing so requires us to have recourse to the concepts, findings, and insights of policy research and, in particular, of environmental policy research.

To provide a foundation for the explanations and analysis to be offered in subsequent chapters, we present in this chapter an overview of the three perspectives which constitute the general approaches to policy analysis. Our aim is to introduce a few essential conceptual tools and theoretical insights necessary for an understanding of environmental policy in New Zealand.

Policy Analysis and the Environment

We can begin by eliminating one avenue of explanation that, while it at first seems to be promising, ultimately goes nowhere. Little understanding is to be gained from simply sifting and rearranging objective facts about New Zealanders and their physical environment. Physical and sociological realities have influenced environmental policy in New Zealand as everywhere else, but policy is not determined primarily by the nature or severity of objective problems. Problems do not just exist. They must be defined, and they cannot define themselves. Moreover, environmental policy does not begin with environmental problems. No amount of scientific study of New Zealand sociology, climate, geology, water resources, or ecology will provide satisfactory answers to the many riddles of New Zealand environmental policy. Nor will it provide much insight into how environmental policy in New Zealand ought to develop.

Rather, making sense out of environmental policy depends firstly on an acknowledgement that policy is political; environmental policy in New Zealand is the politics of clean and green (or, as the case may be, not-so-clean and not-so-green). Understanding environmental policy development requires recourse to concepts and theories from the related fields of environmental politics research and environmental policy research.

Environmental politics is an identifiable, if not precisely definable, subfield within political science. It is concerned with the broad range of political implications arising from the many dimensions of the modern environmental problematique. Environmental politics research might address, among other things, political theory, electoral behaviour, international relations, political culture, and legislative process. Environmental politics may have a substantial policy focus to it, or it may be quite abstract and of little direct significance to policy (policy defined simplistically as what government does to and for citizens (Hofferbert, 1990)).

Environmental policy research is, if anything, even more diverse. People have been conducting policy research for millennia,[1] but policy studies

---

1. To the extent that policy knowledge is a result of systematic analysis of public decisions, it can be said to have emerged with the first civilizations six to seven thousand years ago. Combining skill with enlightenment, professional 'symbol specialists' emerged who achieved a relatively comprehensive view of public policy and made use of their knowledge for policy purposes (Lasswell, 1971, pp. 11–12). Trained classes of expert officials evolved in many parts of the world. In medieval Europe and the great Eastern civilizations, priests provided advice and technical political assistance (Dunn, 1981, pp. 10–11). Later, rulers sought expert advice in law and jurisprudence, finance, and war, making possible the development of modern government (Weber, 1946).

emerged as a field of intellectual enquiry less than fifty years ago. During the modern environmental era, policy analysis has developed an extensive, theoretically rich research literature that offers many helpful conceptual tools for the analysis of environmental policy. Environmental policy studies *per se* date back to a seminal scholarly article by Lynton K. Caldwell (1963) that for the first time used the terms 'environmental policy' and 'environmental administration'. Caldwell proposed a wholly new field of enquiry that would study and offer prescriptive insight into the actions of government in influencing the behaviour of humans towards their environment. Within a decade of the appearance of that article, environmental policy and politics had become established as fields of scholarly research.

Environmental policy itself is essentially political, but policy-relevant research on problems, actions, and possible events may be only tangentially political. Given the breadth of the very concept of 'environment', such research may be done using concepts, theories, and tools from virtually any intellectual discipline or field. But still there is a core to environmental policy research that permits a loosely integrated research community, or set of communities, to find and interact with each other. There is, then, a *de facto* pattern of organization to environmental policy research activities, literature, and knowledge. Four of the recurring themes of environmental policy research, for example, are those around which we have organized this book.

Like Caesar's Gaul, both environmental policy research and modern policy research generally are divisible into three parts: analycentric, policy process, and meta-policy.[2] Of course, these three parts, or approaches, cannot be fully distinguished from each other, as each ultimately influences the others and depends, in turn, on findings and insights produced by the others. But each provides a very different framework for the study of environmental policy. Failure to recognize these different frameworks can lead to confusion among students and to fruitless, antagonizing debates among scholars and analysts.

---

2. We do not necessarily argue that these are the only three approaches to the study of public policy. Many books on public policy begin with a confusing presentation of a much longer list of policy models (Lane, 1990; Dye, 1987). We claim only that these are broad categories that are helpful in understanding the overall policy analysis enterprise as it is relevant to environmental policy. The three categories are based in part on Portney's (1986) typology, which also identified three approaches: the policy-making process approach, the policy cause and consequence approach, and the policy prescription approach. His policy cause and consequence approach and policy prescription approach constitute positive and normative emphases of what we call the analycentric approach. Portney does not recognize or address the meta-policy approach.

In certain respects the analycentric approach is more eclectic and diverse than the policy process approach or meta-policy analysis, but there are, nevertheless, identifiable commonalities underlying virtually every example of it. Certainly the analycentric approach in principle has the least affinity to environmental *politics* research, and unquestionably is the least influenced by it. Partly this is because it is in essence the least environmental of the three approaches, typically reflecting very little of a green standpoint or perspective and being to some degree antithetical in its assumptions to environmentalist ethics, values, and world-view. Environmental policy analyses in an analycentric tradition differ in few respects (other than subject-matter itself) from analyses done in, say, health policy or education policy or any other policy area. It is, however, a venerable approach, generally unquestioned by practitioners or politicians. Moreover, it dominates environmental policy research and much of contemporary policy analysis. Ultimately it provides a fractured, fragmented, almost apolitical picture, which greatly limits its usefulness in understanding environmental policy, in New Zealand or elsewhere. But its dominance as a way of thinking about environmental policy analysis justifies a lengthy description and assessment before we turn to policy process analysis and meta-policy analysis, approaches that will undergird our analysis in subsequent chapters.

The Analycentric Approach to Policy

The heritage of the Enlightenment, with its emphasis on critical examination of accepted truths and institutions, rationalism, and belief in human progress through science and technology, provided the foundation for empirical, quantitative, policy-relevant social research in the nineteenth century, much of it in response to the needs of governments for reliable information. Many social science disciplines emerged in the later decades of the nineteenth century, and in the twentieth century producers of applied social science knowledge became increasingly professionalized. Techniques of large-scale data gathering and analysis were developed and widely adopted, and major theoretical advances were made in all of the social sciences. Economics, in particular, developed applied perspectives and models, often mathematically based, that were increasingly powerful and policy-relevant. Key methodological innovations occurred outside the social sciences in applied mathematics, engineering, systems theory, game theory, and operations research.

World War II provided opportunities for many of these analytical techniques to be further developed and applied in various ways to the war effort, giving a tremendous impetus to the development of policy analysis generally (deLeon, 1988). Wartime applications and successes stimulated the development of a distinctive narrow analycentric perspective—a kind of policy analysis with very limited concern for political, social, and administrative aspects of public policy, which focused on problems and techniques for finding optimizing solutions (Dunn, 1981; Schick, 1977). Techniques were further refined, and found wide application in the 1950s and 1960s in, for example, defence policy, transportation policy, and government budgeting systems.

This analycentric approach was applied to what are now viewed as environmental problems well before the environment became a focus for public policy in New Zealand or elsewhere. For instance, cost-benefit analysis was widely required as a prerequisite to dam building or other environment-altering public works projects. Operations research was used to design and improve operations of sewer systems. Cost-effectiveness analysis was used to evaluate various options for outdoor recreation.

But with the adoption of many new environmental policies by governments in the 1970s came an expansion of policy analysis in the analycentric tradition. Much of it is highly sophisticated quantitative modelling, done by policy analysts within bureaucracies, by interest groups attempting to influence policy making, and by academics and analysts housed in think tanks. Policy models might be simulation or forecasting models of, say, forest or river ecosystems, energy consumption, or atmospheric dispersion. Explicitly normative decision models might be used to determine analytically a best solution and thus specify what ought to be done—by way, for example, of cost-benefit analysis of new regulations, risk assessment of new pollution standards, or cost-effectiveness analysis of different options for a proposed legislative initiative (House and Shull, 1985, 1988). A number of environmental policy journals that have emerged since the 1960s burgeon with reports of research of this type (e.g., *The Environmental Professional, Environmental Management, International Journal of Environmental Studies, Environmental Conservation,* and *Journal of Environmental Management*). And, of course, environmental policy analysis done in the analycentric tradition appears in numerous reports (official and unofficial), books, and general policy journals.

Whether measured in terms of quantity, salience, or energy and attention, most environmental policy analysis is done using an analycentric approach of some kind. Despite presumptions underlying virtually all work in this tradition—that such analysis should be very helpful in public policy making, and that adoption and use of such analysis will result in better policy—the direct utility of such analysis has been modest (House and Shull, 1988, p. 20; Quade, 1982, p. 8). The approach has been especially useful only in addressing 'a narrow, if practically important, range of problems', namely, allocation problems (Majone, 1986, p. 63).

Yet the analycentric approach has become the standard conception of what policy analysis is in the minds of most politicians, citizens, and analysts (Stokey and Zeckhauser, 1978). Majone (1986, p. 61) refers to it as the 'Received View' on policy science, 'a conceptual compound that includes elements from operations research and management science, from microeconomics and decision theory, and a dash of social and behavioral science'. Key assumptions that characterize it are: (1) that politics is about problem solving, particularly with regard to allocation of resources; (2) that policy making is synonymous with decision making; (3) that policy making is instrumentalist, concerned with end results; (4) that rationality is instrumentalist and purely intellectual; (5) that policy makers are unitary decision makers; (6) that policy makers and policy analysts have immense information processing capacity; and (7) that available theoretical and empirical policy knowledge is reliable. But each of these assumptions is problematic and greatly reduces the validity and applicability of policy research based on such a model.

Politics is as much about communication, power, moral action, and the construction of preferences, values, and meaning as it is about problem solving. It embraces much more than the subset of problems involving only the allocation of scarce resources among competing ends. This explains why policy problems are never solved, only at best ameliorated, resolved, or (usually) redefined. Policy making may be less about solutions, outcomes, and end results than about participation and interaction—a process for developing a sense of purpose, identity, and belonging, and for improving cultural values (March and Olsen, 1989, p. 6).

Empirical knowledge is always incomplete, theoretical knowledge is always inadequate, and available information is never wholly reliable or unbiased. Acquiring or improving information is always costly. Even if it were ever politically desirable, purely analytical policy making is severely constrained by the limited capacity of the human mind, augmented though it may be by powerful computers (Simon, 1976a, 1976b, 1978, 1979).

These shortcomings of the analycentric approach—deriving from an assumed model of the policy-making process that is 'characterized by marked reductionist features'—are severe, even if not well recognized by most of its practitioners. It would be an exaggeration, however, to say that policy analysis in the analycentric tradition has no impact on policy making. What it promises is frequently useful, sometimes in addressing highly structured allocation problems and, more often, as another weapon in the struggle of ideas that is politics. Its apparent objectivity and science-like methods, and the credentials of its practitioners, give it a legitimacy in policy discourse—a legitimacy that conveys a political advantage and thus is actively sought.[3]

The larger value of analycentric policy research, however, is independent of the usefulness of individual analyses to individual decisions. Rather, such research contributes to a social process of knowledge cumulation that leads to increased understanding of complex systems. Many highly diverse and varied analycentric studies of environmental policy are shared through professional and political channels. Over time these separate, individual studies accumulate and show consistent policy-relevant results. Established findings are synthesized in new research. Collectively, analycentric studies serve an enlightenment function (Weiss, 1980), contributing invaluably to a social understanding of environmental policy possibilities—among researchers but also among citizens, managers, and politicians. White (1983, p. 11) writes that 'policy analysis is not simply a collection of tools, techniques, or models of analytical nature'; it is, instead, 'the production with those tools of understandings that affect consensus formation and dissolution'. Creation of a cumulative, shared understanding of a system, rather than the recommendations of a single decisive study, is the more likely path of influence of policy analysis on policy making.

But the usefulness of analycentric policy analysis cannot be understood using an analycentric approach. If the full advantages of this approach can be realized only through social processes of sharing and accumulation of diverse and dispersed knowledge and the political uses of knowledge for political ends in political processes, then no comprehensive view of environmental policy can be produced by analycentric policy analysis. Ironically, because of the perceived lack of prescriptive utility of most political science methods of analysis, and because analycentric policy research as traditionally formulated need be only tangentially political, political science has had little to contribute to purely analycentric environmental policy analysis. The substantial policy significance of analycentric policy research can be understood only by use of more politically oriented theories and understandings of the policy process.

Unlike the analycentric approach, the policy process approach and meta-policy analysis provide two other broad frameworks for environmental policy analysis that are thoroughly political in their orientation, draw heavily on

---

3. One of the reasons it is so widely taught and practised is that it has considerable legitimacy in academia as well: it draws upon established theories and methods, it makes possible the standardization of tasks and skills, and it clarifies the aims of professional training and curricular planning (Majone, 1986, p. 63).

political science concepts and theories, and are influenced by broader environmental politics research. Both of these approaches to policy analysis originate partly in critiques of the analycentric approach.

The Policy Process Approach

The policy process approach can be traced back to work of Harold Lasswell in the 1950s. Lasswell, a political scientist by training but by practice an interdisciplinary scholar, first identified a developing policy orientation that cut across existing specializations (Lasswell, 1951). He labelled the kinds of analysis undertaken under this new orientation the 'policy sciences', which he defined to refer to a multidisciplinary orientation concerned with *knowledge of* the policy process and *knowledge in* that process. Subsequently, he advanced the notion of the policy process as featuring basic phases through which policies pass over time—intelligence, promotion, prescription, invocation, application, termination, and appraisal (Lasswell, 1956, 1971). His vision at the time seemed to have little impact on his contemporaries, and little other analysis or theorizing done in the 1950s built on Lasswell's insights. The analycentric approach remained dominant, as systems analysts, economists, and operations researchers came to epitomize policy science and policy analysis while capturing the generally accepted meaning of the terms.

However, a powerful critique of the analycentric perspective was emerging in the work of scholars who questioned the key assumptions of rationality and decisionism (Braybrooke and Lindblom, 1963; Dahl and Lindblom, 1953; Lindblom, 1959, 1965; Simon, 1976a; Wildavsky, 1966, 1974). This critique of the analycentric approach, coupled with forceful and cogent theorizing directed towards the political nature of policy, inspired a great deal of debate and research as, in the late 1960s, political science rediscovered policy. In the 1970s many textbooks, new courses, and new schools of public policy were created, and Lasswell's early work was rediscovered as well.

A standard heuristic widely used in the new teaching and research was the *policy cycle*, a model that characterizes the policy process in terms of several steps or phases through which policies pass over time. Based roughly on Lasswell's seven phases, the policy cycle is variously described by different authors as having five to nine stages (Anderson, 1979; Brewer and deLeon, 1983; Hogwood and Gunn, 1984; Jones, 1970; Ripley, 1987). Basic to all versions are four broad sequential phases: (1) problem definition and agenda setting, (2) policy formulation and selection, (3) implementation, and (4) evaluation.[4] Research on policy formulation and adoption had always been

---

4. Some of these stages are subdivided by different authors. Some add a termination phase, others an estimation or forecasting phase.

seen by political scientists as a central concern of the discipline, although often from an interest more in institutional descriptions and behavioural explanations than in policy *per se*. But thinking about public policy in terms of the policy cycle was enormously influential in directing attention to those phases that had traditionally received less attention from political scientists—agenda setting, implementation, and evaluation—and in inspiring the development of different theoretical insights into policy selection.

Problem Definition and Agenda Setting
The issue of whether a problem even receives attention from the policy process may have little to do with the intrinsic characteristics of the problem itself. What are widely seen as high priority problems for policy action today—e.g., housing, health care, education, environment—may have been, in an objective sense, just as urgent or more so in an earlier period, but ignored in the policy process (Dery, 1984). Indeed, for many issues now thought to be pressing, it may be possible to identify a time when similar or worse conditions prevailed but no one even sought government action (e.g., disposal of hazardous waste, threatened extinction of species, cutting of native timber, wasteful use of energy). The matters to which participants in the policy process pay serious attention at any given time constitute the policy agenda (Kingdon, 1984). Only a small proportion of conceivable problems or issues are ever on the policy agenda, and whether or not an issue achieves agenda status is politically determined.

Moreover, there are many types and levels of agendas in any political system. Cobb and Elder (1972), for example, distinguish between the 'systemic agenda', or the issues seen as meriting discussion by members of the political community, and the 'institutional agenda', the issues getting attention from public officials in political institutions. A subset of the institutional agenda might be the decision agenda, those issues on an institutional agenda that are up for an active decision (Kingdon, 1984, p. 4). A given political system is likely to have national agendas as well as local and perhaps provincial agendas. The agenda of one part of a government institution, such as Parliament, will be broad and eclectic, whereas officials of some bureaucratic agency, like the Department of Conservation, will have a different, more specialized agenda. A policy agenda is not necessarily highly structured or defined (Anderson, 1979, p. 56), but agenda items can be differentiated in various ways—by their prominence, their overall priority, and whether they are old, new, or cyclically recurring.

Whether an issue is even considered in the policy process, then, depends on whether it achieves agenda status. Policy development and policy outcomes are determined as much by whether problems and proposals make it to the forefront of consideration as by any final decision such as legislative passage or executive endorsement. An extraordinarily important question is thus, why and how do some issues get on policy agendas whereas other ostensibly important issues do not?

Of particular concern to environmental policy is the question of how new items get on policy agendas. Institutional agendas favour old or recurring items because of their familiarity, because alternatives for dealing with them may be patterned, and because institutional rules (e.g., necessity of a budget) may force them onto the agenda. Items that deserve attention may never receive it simply because time is limited and agendas are already overloaded (Anderson, 1979; Cobb and Elder, 1972). Those new items that do reach an agenda may do so because powerful interest groups compel government officials to consider them or because of the activities of various other agenda setters, such as elected officials, party leaders, senior officials and advisers, protest groups, and journalists. Or items may be pushed onto the agenda by shifts in public opinion, the perception of a crisis, the occurrence of a dramatic event, election results, or a turnover in institutional personnel. New items may become old or recurring items over time or may, more often, fade and quietly disappear.

Anthony Downs (1972) suggests, with specific reference to the issue of environmental quality, that an 'issue-attention' cycle governs the focus of public attention on any one issue: a problem 'suddenly leaps into prominence, remains there for a short time, and then—though still largely unresolved—gradually fades from the centre of public attention' (p. 39). Issues that go through this cycle are problems that do not cause direct suffering to a majority in society, that require sustained attention and effort and fundamental changes in social institutions and behaviour to be solved, and that are not intrinsically exciting. The issue-attention cycle, according to Downs, has five stages: (1) the pre-problem stage, (2) alarmed discovery and euphoric enthusiasm, (3) realizing the cost of significant progress, (4) gradual decline of intense public interest, and (5) the post-problem stage.

Downs's issue-attention cycle is useful to some extent in understanding how issues become fashionable. The attention given an issue grows as the issue is dramatized by events, disasters, or conflicts and attracts the generous attention of journalists. It is promoted by politicians and other public figures who get publicity from their identification with a new issue. And the issue is followed by a public attracted to emotive or human interest aspects or to novelty of any kind. It fades when it becomes old news and attention begins to turn to new issues. Downs's model, however, does not distinguish trivial issues from the important, or the temporary from the permanent, and is no help in explaining how and why some issues are able to find a place on agendas even as salience varies over time. It undervalues knowledge and ideas (including policy analysis) and it ignores the strategic management of issues as influences on agenda setting. It also provides no insight into how problems are defined, how policy alternatives are generated, or how agenda-setting patterns are altered by fundamental changes in social values or institutional restructuring.

Some of these inadequacies are addressed by more sophisticated theories of agenda setting, such as that offered by Kingdon (1984), based on the garbage-can model of policy making advanced by Cohen, March, and Olsen (1972). Kingdon characterizes the policy system as having three policy 'streams' running through it—streams of problem recognition, generation of policy proposals, and political events. Problems emerge and are defined and redefined, and there is an 'inexorable march of problems pressing in on the system' (Kingdon, 1984, p. 17). A second stream consists of knowledge accumulation and the generation, communication, and diffusion of policy ideas and proposals. Political processes and events constitute the third stream—for example, interest group campaigns, elections, public opinion shifts, changes of administration, and government personnel turnover. These three streams

> are largely independent of one another, and each develops according to its own dynamics and rules. But at some critical junctures the three streams are joined, and the greatest policy changes grow out of that coupling of problems, policy proposals, and politics (Kingdon, 1984, p. 20).

A policy window is an opportunity to make something happen, a momentary opportunity for a policy entrepreneur to couple elements from each of the streams as they momentarily come together.

To understand public policy requires an understanding of agenda setting, untidy as it is. In each of the remaining chapters of this book we examine some aspect of agenda setting for environmental policy in New Zealand. Agenda setting is critical to policy making, and to the study of public policy even from an analycentric perspective. Analycentric policy analysis plays a central role in the accumulation of policy knowledge and the generation of policy ideas, alternatives, and proposals. Over time, analycentric policy research can also importantly influence definition of problems and their recognition. But all three policy streams are in important senses political. Thus policy analysts, however seemingly removed from politics, cannot help but be political.

Policy Selection
The policy process approach directly challenges the analycentric model of how policy is made, in particular its assumptions of decisionism and

rationality (Majone, 1986). The analycentric approach assumes that policy making is merely the making of 'big' decisions (Dery, 1984, p. 56), and that policy is made by unitary policy makers who are external to policy analysis itself. This policy maker is faced with policy decisions, or choices, and has full authority over selection and execution. The logic of choice, then, is the appropriate logic of decision making (policy making). This logic of choice, of course, embodies the ideal of instrumental rationality and implies the possibility of infallibility and omniscience as policy becomes an intellectual exercise.

Even if the concept of 'decision' itself were unambiguous, however, policy making would not simply be decision making:

> Does decision refer both to collective decisions and individual decisions? If decisions can be collective, the issues of structure and process are compounded. Analysts may disagree on the boundaries of a decision: Is a decision a choice occurring in an instant, or is it a process requiring a variable amount of time? Who, exactly, actually 'makes' collective decisions? Are decisions separable and mutually exclusive phenomena? Are the value and factual inputs to a decision part of the decision? If not, when is a decision made? Does decision always, or ever, mean . . . judgment or conclusion? (Bartlett, 1990a, p. 244)

To conceptualize policy making strictly as an intellectual exercise is a hopelessly flawed approach. Policy making is not merely an exercise in cleanly calculating correct solutions to a series of puzzles; it requires much more than an instrumental means-ends rationality, which equates technical or economic efficiency with rationality itself (Stone, 1988). And policy is never made by a single unitary policy maker who establishes the goals and has full authority over choice and action (Majone, 1986). Both the processes and the institutions through which policy is made are complex. Policy making always involves the interaction of multiple participants with different objectives. Arriving at agreement on goals, consequences, and criteria of choice is unusual and difficult; when achieved it is only partial and temporary; and it is accomplished only through cumbersome political processes such as persuasion, negotiation, or bargaining (Gregory, 1989; Lindblom, 1959, 1965, 1979).

In the 1960s Charles Lindblom and others (Wildavsky, 1966, 1974) were particularly influential in suggesting an alternative vision of policy making that emphasized the complex interactive nature of policy selection, the costliness of comprehensive analysis, and the limited problem-solving capacity of humans. Lindblom argued that decision making is not synonymous with public policy making; that policy is necessarily made in a process of political and social interaction to which formal analysis may contribute, but for which it cannot be substituted. He offered a devastating critique of the idea that important public decisions, much less public policy, could ever be technically or economically rational or fully comprehensive, exposing the analycentric fallacy that 'one best way' can be found. In the policy process, a plurality of interests makes it virtually impossible to agree in advance on goals. To strive unnecessarily for clarity, specificity, and agreement is to invite conflict, limit opportunities, and risk policy paralysis. In the real political world, means-ends analysis always gets turned on its head—objectives evolve as agreement is sought on means. Rather than rational, comprehensive, analytical decision making, which is both unattainable and undesirable, Lindblom pointed to incremental analysis as a superior alternative anchored in the inescapably political nature of the policy process.[5] Analysis does not and cannot make policy selection redundant, but it can contribute to and augment policy making through social interaction.

Simple models of rationality do not suffice for analysis of policy selection and choice. Underlying analycentric policy analysis is a commitment to instrumental rationality—the most efficient achievement of a single goal or a plurality of goals. Rational policy making is that which, given the relevant constraints, optimizes achievement of specified goals. Public policy problems are looked upon as puzzles with probable solutions that can be obtained by calculation (Majone, 1986, p. 68). Powerful analytic tools can be brought to bear to facilitate rational policy making so long as efficiency is the only—or at least an appropriate—principle of order (Diesing, 1962). Yet efficiency as a principle of order may be inapplicable to whole realms of policy making. Moreover, such a conception of rationality is applicable only to means and not to ends; ultimate ends cannot be judged in terms of efficiency. Nevertheless, policies about ends are still selected for good reasons. And our most important choices in policy making are about ends, the basic aims of life (Diesing, 1962, p. 1; Lindblom, 1990, p. 10).

Policy process analysis can employ several alternative conceptions of rationality in explaining policies and the processes by which they are selected. For example, social rationality is a rationality of interpersonal relations and social action, legal rationality is a rationality of rules and behaviour appropriate to those rules, and political rationality is a rationality of creating, changing, and defending the boundaries of categories and the definition of ideals (Diesing, 1962). According to Stone, the essence of policy making is the struggle over ideas:

---

5. Lindblom (1979) suggests that there are three types of incremental analysis: simple incremental analysis, disjointed incrementalism, and strategic analysis.

> Reasoned analysis is necessarily political. It always involves choices to include some things and exclude others and to view the world in a particular way when other visions are possible. Policy analysis is political argument, and vice versa (Stone, 1988, p. 306).

All of these forms of rationality might be important in varying degrees both to making policy and to analysing it, depending on the policy and the context. Also of particular importance for environmental policy is ecological rationality, a rationality of living systems, an order of relationships among living systems and their environments (Bartlett, 1986b, 1990b; Diesing, 1962; Dryzek, 1987). Ecological rationality provides criteria applicable to social systems, to individual decisions, or to policy processes—whether systems consistently protect ecological integrity, whether individual actions are ecologically sound, and whether ecological reasoning underlies the processes and procedures by which ecologically important choices are made.

If policy making is not merely a matter of endorsing a choice identified by omniscient and infallible analysis, then the mechanisms by which policy is shaped and selected may determine the quality of policies adopted. Dryzek (1987), for example, identifies and assesses nine mechanisms, or systems, for making social choices: markets, hierarchical command systems, formal rules (law), moral persuasion, bargaining, partisan mutual adjustment, force, conditional co-operation, and discussion. None of these are mutually exclusive; existing societies mix them in a variety of ways to produce distinctive policy systems. None of these mechanisms is in any sense apolitical. There are important differences among and between all of them in the way policy is made and in the kinds of policies that will be produced over time.

In sum, policy process analysis provides invaluable insight into a dimension of policy selection (decision) wholly neglected by the analycentric approach. Many of the analytical concepts applied to understanding policy selection have roots in fundamental criticisms of analycentric policy analysis—namely, that it tends to ignore policy selection processes, or to treat policy choice as though it were done in a black box containing a single unitary, calculating decision maker. Policy process analysis illuminates the rich complexities of selection and the significance of that complexity for the substance of policy. And it also suggests that policy selection cannot be understood apart from other stages of the policy cycle. Particularly in Chapters 4, 5 and 6, we analyze the substance of recent environmental policy making in New Zealand in terms of the context and complexity of selection processes.

Policy Implementation
The development of an explicit focus on the policy process led in the 1970s

to a renewed focus by policy scholars on how policy is carried out, executed, or administered. Analycentric policy analysis, with its roots in management science and operations research, was always explicitly focused on the effectiveness and efficiency of policy execution. But the *political* dimension of implementation had not been subjected to much systematic study. Since World War II, political science had largely exorcized public administration as a subfield; a focus on execution of policies had disappeared by the time the policy process orientation began to emerge. So at first political science was unable to contribute much to explaining the apparent failures of a great many policy initiatives undertaken by activist governments in the 1960s. A surge of interest in implementation as a stage in the policy cycle was based less on fundamental criticisms of the analycentric approach than on a recognition of the more serious inadequacies of political science.

The single most important implementation study, by Pressman and Wildavsky (1973), had an enormous impact in stimulating further research and in focusing inquiry on several key questions. Pressman and Wildavsky noted that policies are seldom if ever executed by a single autonomous organization, or in a static environment, but are implemented by multiple actors in a constantly changing system, actors who are dependent on the assent and active co-operation of each other and various other individuals, interest groups, and bureaus. The complexity of implementation, therefore, was the complexity of joint action in a dynamic context, which required understanding of interorganizational relations and policy networks.

Pressman and Wildavsky also directed attention to the causal theories or policy strategies implicit in policies, examining whether these constituted models of cause and effect adequate for an expectation of policy success. In thus focusing on the relevance of the design of policies (formulation and selection) and on whether policy outcomes have achieved policy objectives (evaluation), Pressman and Wildavsky anchored implementation research firmly in the policy cycle. The viability of clear distinctions between formulation, selection, implementation, and evaluation were further questioned in subsequent research (Browne and Wildavsky, 1983; Majone and Wildavsky, 1979).

One approach to implementation has been a top-down strategy of exploring the extent to which policy objectives are achieved and why, and attempting to diagnose any treatable pathologies besetting implementation (Goggin et al., 1990; Ingram, 1990; Mazmanian and Sabatier, 1983; Sabatier and Mazmanian, 1979). An alternative strategy, critical of the first for its managerial perspective, focuses on the contextual influences on policy and on the actors involved in addressing a policy problem. Implementors in this view are not agents of policy makers but fairly autonomous bureaucrats, professionals, and targets who make policy in the course of implementing it (Barrett and Fudge, 1981; Chisholm, 1989; Hanf, 1982; Ingram and Schneider, 1990; Sabatier, 1986).

In any event, the kinds of issues that implementation research finds critical to effective policy making are quite different from those explained by analycentric research. For example, implementation studies frequently conclude that the most important policy actors are not high-level policy makers but street-level bureaucrats—teachers, inspectors, managers, social workers. Government itself is not assumed to be the sole cause of policy outcomes. The causal models implicit in policies become the subject of analysis, as do numerous other relationships between formulation and implementation, such as a reasonable match between objectives and resources. Conflicts at the formulation and selection stage inevitably extend themselves into implementation. Attention is directed to the time needed for implementation, which may be longer than is popularly assumed. Any policy requiring joint action—between or among governments, bureaucracies, interest groups, or citizens—will be complex and to a considerable degree uncontrollable from above. Finally, political and socioeconomic conditions, and changes in those conditions, can affect the course of implementation.

If policy extends beyond decisions—if policies are not in fact 'made' at some moment of choice—then just as selection is structured by what precedes it, the outcomes of a policy are profoundly influenced by what happens after a policy is selected. Policy is still being made as it is being implemented. The implied sequence of the policy cycle model is consistent with the decisionist model of analycentric policy research in which implementation necessarily follows a policy decision. But actual analysis of the policy process reveals that implementation actors and events also formulate and select policy and, moreover, inevitably play major roles in problem definition and agenda setting, helping drive the selection process from the other end as well. Our analysis of New Zealand's institutional reforms in Chapter 4 focuses particularly on matters of implementation. The full policy significance of some reforms, such as the Resource Management Act, will depend largely on how they are implemented. Thus our analysis in Chapters 5 and 6 is highly contingent on recent and current environmental policy development—development which obviously can still be influenced.

In theory the policy implementation stage can be distinguished from that of policy evaluation. The roles of implementor and evaluator can be similarly differentiated (Browne and Wildavsky, 1983). Yet in practice implementation and evaluation also take place together, and the study and analysis of implementation (as well as agenda setting and selection) entails evaluation.

Policy Evaluation
Evaluation is, of course, an integral part of all policy analysis, and is done even in analycentric research that pretends to be value free. Within a comprehensively rational, decisionist framework, the place of evaluation is wholly prior to the act of determining the best proposal, alternative, plan, or option (decision). But the policy process approach has tended to see evaluation as a stage in the policy cycle that follows a policy decision and its implementation, that is, as an after-the-fact assessment of actual policies—'finding out what happens after a law is passed' (Dye, 1987, p. 349). Similar kinds of activities undertaken prior to selection may be labelled differently, as 'estimation' (Brewer and deLeon, 1983), 'options analysis' (Hogwood and Gunn, 1984), or 'techniques for recommendation' (Dunn, 1981).

But if evaluation is, simply, 'the process of determining the merit, worth and value of things, and evaluations are products of that process' (Scriven, 1991, p. 1), then there is no necessary reason that evaluation must immediately follow implementation in the policy cycle. It may, in fact, precede the achievement of agenda status, or be conducted while a project is under way, or be done long after the fact by policy analysts with historical interests.

But policy evaluation done after the fact does conflict with some of the assumptions of the analycentric approach, at least those assumptions regarding the adequacy and reliability of a priori knowledge, the information capacity of analysts and policy makers, and the final product of policy analysis (a decision). After-the-fact evaluation makes sense only in the context of an ongoing, iterative policy process that embraces trial-and-error learning in policy making.

Nevertheless, the analycentric perspective prevails in much evaluation research, which seeks to focus exclusively on outcomes and to remain wholly apolitical (neutral, scientific, value-free) by using as its only criteria of evaluation the explicitly stated goals of a project, programme, or policy. Such goals-based outcomes evaluation epitomizes policy evaluation for many analysts, and may be viewed as the only possible way to evaluate policies. It is, however, afflicted with serious problems such as 'identifying these goals, handling inconsistencies in them or false assumptions underlying them and changes in them over time, dealing with outcomes that represent shortfall and overrun on the goals, and avoiding the perceptual bias of knowing about them' (Scriven, 1991, p. 179). Policies, programmes, or projects seldom explicitly state clear, consistent, and realistic goals; moreover, those goals that can be identified are frequently vague, contradictory, and idealistic—for good political reasons—and thus may be unachievable (Bartlett, 1993a). Positive and negative unintended consequences are often the most important results of policy making.

The use of multiple values and criteria—of which identifiable goals are only one source—mitigates some of these blind spots and narrowing biases. But the immense difficulties of causally attributing and measuring the tangible consequences of policies means that 'no effect' is sure to be the most common evaluation finding. To equate 'no effect' to 'failure', as is often done, is to bias outcomes evaluation strongly towards finding policy failure and to retard policy progress by arming nay-sayers with apparently rigorous ammunition. One way to address this inherent deficiency of outcomes evaluation, which is imbedded in a problem-solving conception of policy and policy analysis, is to supplement or replace it with evaluation based more on the policy process than on policy outcomes.

The merit of policy processes themselves becomes the subject of process evaluation. This may, in many cases, be information more useful to policy making as citizens and policy officials seek to decide what ought to be done on the basis of how and why things are done, rather than merely on whether certain outcomes are produced. Process evaluation does not presume that policy always, or even usually, begins with a problem. Rather, policy making can be seen as a struggle over ideas (Stone, 1988), a dialectic process of argument and persuasion (Majone, 1989), a process of maintaining and modifying norms and standards over time (Gregory, 1989), or a means for determining values, setting norms, and defining problems (Bartlett, 1993a). Finally, process evaluation easily accommodates moral reasoning—explicit evaluation of the moral elements of policy processes that may be distinguished from the instrumental values they produce (Hofferbert, 1990; Sagoff, 1988).

Much of the evaluation we offer throughout this book is evaluation of environmental policy processes, both long entrenched and newly established or modified. But a key problem of process evaluation, indeed of the whole policy process approach, is how to integrate in it (or with it) a concern for substantive consequences. To say that good policy is whatever is produced by good processes is to trivialize the effect that policy has or can have on the larger world. A second weakness of process evaluation, and the policy process approach generally, is that, like the analycentric approach, they have a limited ability to explain policy change. In the analycentric model change is chosen, or decided upon, as prompted by changes in preferences or externally determined conditions such as drought or economic circumstances. In the policy process approach, change occurs as a by-product of political activity within existing established processes. Within a limited range of variability, the processes themselves are taken as given. Both analycentric and policy process analysis are inadequate for analysing how processes themselves change and are changed, or for understanding how preferences are changed, or to explain shifts in the meaning of external conditions to policy makers.

These are, of course, key issues in environmental policy in New Zealand and elsewhere. Answers to these kinds of questions require an adequate theory of policy development, which must be sought within a third, more encompassing, framework for policy research, that of meta-policy.

Meta-policy Analysis

A meta-policy perspective can be applied not only to policy making but to policy analysis itself. It may involve analysis of those ways by which policy-making systems are modified, created, or evolve, and this may include policy-making policies (Dror, 1983). It might also refer to a critical perspective on and analysis of policy knowledge systems—analysis of the world-views and frameworks within which we do policy research and create policy knowledge. And, finally, a meta-policy approach may seek to explain how policy knowledge contributes to change in policy-making systems.

A meta-policy approach can be quite important in providing consumers of policy research—including citizens, politicians, bureaucrats, and analysts of different persuasions—some means of comparatively assessing the arguments, claims, and conclusions made by policy analysts. Bobrow and Dryzek (1987), for example, offer a meta-policy analysis of five frames of reference that have dominated policy analysis in recent years: welfare economics, public choice, social structure, information processing, and political philosophy. Policy analysis done within each of these frames can be comparatively understood in terms of assumptions, methodologies, practical usefulness, and outlook on the world. Diesing (1982) examines eleven schools of policy science, some of which have now faded and disappeared, in terms of the distinctive standpoint and perspective on public policy inherent in each. Even if such meta-policy analysis is unable to produce a simple algorithm for reasoned selection of an approach to policy analysis, it is invaluable to informed, critical consumption, particularly for environmental policy with the complex interrelationships and encompassing context that must be addressed.

How policy analysis is actually used in policy making becomes a focus for meta-policy as well, as soon as the simplistic vision of the direct policy use of a single definitive analysis is given up, however reluctantly, as being wholly unrealistic. The view that the primary route through which policy analysis ordinarily influences policy is one of cumulative, social enlightenment, rather than the direct adoption of the recommendations of a single study, is a meta-policy perspective. Much of the impetus for meta-policy theorizing since 1970 has come from efforts to reconcile analycentric policy analysis with analysis of the policy process (Wildavsky, 1979). Any such reconciliation requires adoption of some broader, transcendent perspective that can encompass both: 'To understand policy-making one must understand all of political life and activity' (Lindblom, 1980, p. 5).

Dunn (1981) and Stone (1988), for example, integrate analysis into the policy process by emphasizing that both public policy and policy analysis are made of language. Argument and persuasion are thus central to all stages of the policy process; the policy analyst is not a technical, nonpartisan problem solver but a producer of ideas, evidence, and arguments with the aim of persuading. Changes in current policy are an outcome of a dual process of conceptual innovation along with variation and selection from a supply that happens to be available at a given time. The impact of analysis and argument is not limited to policy making within the existing framework: more profound policy development occurs when 'analysis and arguments conceptualize, and thus transform, the institutions and processes of policy-making' (Majone, 1989, p. 166). Likewise, Lindblom (1990) assesses policy analysis as a specialized kind of policy inquiry that differs in degree but not in kind from the more general activity of inquiry that permeates all of political life and is engaged in by ordinary citizens as well as ordinary politicians.

Some theoretical approaches to meta-policy reconcile analycentric analysis with policy process analysis by marginalizing both, that is, by locating the driving force for fundamental policy change outside of, or at least largely independent of, the policy process. For example, if policies are produced by political systems attempting to be responsive to value changes in society, then the explanation for the general direction of policy development is to be found in those patterns of social value changes. Value changes might be variable and cyclical, within the bounds of a basic orientation shared by most members of society that would not itself change often or easily. But a thoroughgoing change in this basic pattern of values could occur, and would constitute a change in the dominant social paradigm, defined as 'a society's dominant belief structure that organizes the way people perceive and interpret the functioning of the world around them' (Milbrath, 1989, p. 116). Such a change would be expected to have wide-ranging repercussions in altering the whole content, direction, and nature of policy making.

Some social analysts and theorists (Catton, 1980; Catton and Dunlap, 1980; Cotgrove, 1982; Dunlap and Van Liere, 1978; Milbrath, 1984) see environmentalism as leading an ongoing shift in the dominant value system of western societies. The previous dominant social paradigm, in this view, is being challenged by an emerging new environmental paradigm. The old, long-dominant social paradigm is one that values nature for its utilitarian value, values economic growth over environmental protection, values the welfare of the present generation of humans with minimal concern for other species or future generations, emphasizes taking risks to generate wealth, disregards possible limits to economic or population growth, and endorses the nature and structure of modern society and the status quo in politics. By contrast, the new environmental paradigm places a high value on nature for its own sake, values environmental protection over economic growth, extends generalized compassion towards other species and future generations, emphasizes avoiding unnecessary risks, believes that policy should recognize limits to growth, and believes that a new society and a new politics should and must be established. The new environmental paradigm is thought to be emerging, but still far from achieving dominance itself (Milbrath, 1989). Milbrath (1984) and colleagues found that about half of the American and Western European publics had not worked out a logically consistent belief structure, simultaneously holding beliefs and values from both paradigms. But there was already a sufficiently widespread acceptance of environmentalist values to influence the course of policy development and change (Dunlap, 1989). In Chapter 3 we will examine available evidence regarding the establishment of a beachhead of the new environmental paradigm in New Zealand.

Simultaneously, we will assess the extent of any shift toward what Inglehart (1977, 1990) calls postmaterial values. Inglehart argues that environmental values are one part of a broader value shift transforming the politics and cultural norms of advanced industrial societies. This broad syndrome of change involves the decline of traditional religious orientations, change in social and sexual norms, emergence of distinctive patterns of economic and political behaviour, and a transition from 'materialist' to 'postmaterialist' values. The materialist emphasis gives top priority to physical sustenance and safety: law and order, a strong national defence, economic growth, and a stable economy. The postmaterialist emphasis gives priority to belonging, self-expression, and the quality of life: more say in the decisions of government, protecting freedom of speech, making cities and the countryside more beautiful, and creating a friendlier, less impersonal society where ideas count more than money. Inglehart's model is one of change by succession of generational value differences. An individual's values and priorities are largely established in pre-adult years and reflect conditions that prevailed at that time, with the greatest subjective value placed on those things in relatively short supply. Majorities of persons in generations that mature in societies enjoying long periods of prosperity and security will adopt postmaterialist values. The proportion of postmaterialists in a society would grow slowly even with decades of prosperity and security, as the change generated by population replacement is slow.

Inglehart's conclusions with respect to Western Europe and the United States are that the economic and physical security of the post-World War II era has led to a value shift. Inglehart found that in 1971 materialists outnumbered postmaterialists four to one. By 1988 the balance had shifted to only a four to three numerical advantage for materialists. Inglehart (1990, p. 103) predicts that by the year 2000 postmaterialists will be as numerous as materialists, but, because postmaterialists are more highly educated, more articulate, and more politically active, their political impact will outweigh that of materialists.

Inglehart's work on culture shift has attracted a great deal of scholarly attention, both confirmatory and critical. From a meta-policy perspective, his theoretical explanations for value change are crude and problematic. His model of value formation is simplistic, unable to account for adult value changes, unable to explain the deep divisions between materialist and postmaterialist values within generational cohorts, and unable to untangle wide variations in value emphases among postmaterialists (some of whom, for example, are deeply committed to certain but not all environmentalist values, whilst others are only superficially supportive of environmentalist priorities generally). Values are determined by a great deal more than extant economic and security conditions; in particular, ideas and institutions, in addition to directly influencing policy, have an indirect influence on policy by their effect on social value change, including any larger coherent paradigmatic value shift that may be occurring.

Eckersley (1989), for example, argues that cognitive development facilitated by education, particularly higher education, is a more important influence on the development of postmaterialist values than is childhood affluence and security. Eckersley also argues that ideas and objective changes in the physical and social environment since 1945 have influenced value change. Environmental quality is more than 'just one among many "post-materialist" issues which suddenly emerged to prominence, unrelated to any change in the environment, through a shift in values among people who had nothing else to worry about' (Lowe and Rudig, 1986, p. 518). To the extent that environmentalism is a rational response to new ideas and a growing understanding of the depth and scale of ecological and social problems facing the modern world (Eckersley, 1989, p. 222), it is part of a new paradigm but also an independent variable driving cultural change (Kassiola, 1990; Milbrath, 1989; Ophuls, 1977; Paehlke, 1989).

Alternatively, values and therefore value change can also be seen as conspicuously influenced by the institutional structure within which politics occurs (March and Olsen, 1989, p. 16). Values are not moulded or altered through some automatic reaction to exogenous conditions or new ideas; rather, institutions define the framework within which ideas and external conditions have meaning and values are constructed. Within political institutions, and in response to other political institutions, individuals come to attribute meaning and value to their pasts and futures. For example, individuals (1) to the extent they are integrated into a political system, see what they like; (2) to the degree they are integrated into a political system, like what they see; (3) to the extent they trust others with whom they have contact, like what the others like; and (4) to the degree they trust others with whom they have contact, see what the others see (p. 44).

Deliberate or inadvertent institutional change, then, can be a powerful influence on social values; certainly any change in social values can be pervasive and permanent, and thus paradigmatic, only if it is woven into the very fabric of the institutions of a society. Analysis of how policy processes work and outcomes are produced, sometimes indirectly, within a larger institutional framework that is *created in part by policies* and within which policies are made and remade (Bartlett, 1993a) is meta-policy analysis. This type of policy analysis assesses 'political architecture' (Anderson, 1977) and posits an independent role for political institutions in policy making and fundamental policy change. The State itself may be analysed as a semi-independent agent in determining the kind of politics, policy processes, and values a society will use in arriving at environmental policies. If the State can be differentiated from the rest of society, then its role in policy development is subject to theoretically based positive inquiry and normative debate (meta-policy analysis).

And institutions are not limited to shaping policy through the construction and elaboration of preferences, values, and interpretation. More obviously, institutions directly shape policies by reducing chaos and bringing order through rules. Much of observable political behaviour, including policy making, is rule-based. Institutional analysis seeks to make sense of policy in terms of rules, and to make sense of policy making in terms of rule change (rather than through utilitarian calculation and anticipatory choice, as in the analycentric approach). Rules are followed even when it is not obviously in the narrow self-interest of the person doing so. Rules are independent of individual actors and are capable of surviving considerable turnover of individuals. Rule-based behaviour is not necessarily trivial or unreasoned: 'intelligent, thoughtful political behaviour, like other behaviour, can be described in terms of duties, obligations, roles, and rules' (March and Olsen, 1989, p. 22).

Meta-policy analysis, then, uses this extended model to assess policy making through institutional change—a 'roundabout' way of policy making (Majone, 1989, pp. 96–7). Instead of securing a single favourable decision and its outcomes, reforms of institutional mechanisms produce 'future streams of valued outcomes'. Institutional change becomes imbedded in a structure of other rules and other values and intentions, in turn forcing further institutional changes as the structure of rules and values is shaped, interpreted, and created during the course of transformation (March and Olsen, 1989, pp. 65–6). Institutional reform can be an extraordinarily powerful way of achieving policy development and change, but its full ramifications can only be imperfectly anticipated and transformation cannot be controlled with precision.

Nevertheless, one response to this catalytic character of institutional reform is to attempt to limit and constrain change, often by establishing additional detailed and demanding rules. Alternatively, strategic use may be made of what Gormley (1987, 1989) calls catalytic controls and McCubbins, Noll, and Weingast (1987) call 'deck stacking': rules that require policy makers to act, directing policy makers toward certain goals but not robbing them of the capacity for flexible, creative policy making. For example, thoroughgoing requirements for doing environmental impact assessment are a catalytic institutional reform (Bartlett, 1990b; Gormley, 1989; Wandesforde-Smith, 1989). They prod, stimulate, and provoke. They permit and require innovation by forcing action. They rely on citizen participation, interest representation, or interorganizational politics, in addition to coercive directives, to promote certain values.

In sum, the meta-policy approach offers considerable insight into policy analysis and policy making, and as such makes possible a degree of understanding and effective action that remains hidden in policy research done entirely within the analycentric and policy process traditions. The kinds of changes that have occurred in New Zealand environmental policy since 1984 are too many, too radical, and too profound to be captured by the kind of analysis made possible by the analycentric and policy process approaches, even together. Only meta-policy analysis attempts to grapple with policy development and system change, recognizing that the same people pursue their goals within a given institutional framework *and* attempt to modify that framework. Yet meta-policy analysis only confronts the rich complexity of the institutional and conceptual frameworks of policy; it does not (and cannot) master them. It does not assume that outcomes can be measured, that causality can be attributed, that knowledge is reliable, or that policy should always be instrumentally rational. But it is nonetheless limited in the explanation and guidance it can offer, given ubiquitous measurement problems, causality confusion, unreliable knowledge, and the limited, complex nature of rationality applied to policy making. Advances in meta-policy analysis depend on indispensable insights and invaluable evidence provided by advances in analycentric and policy process analysis. What a meta-policy perspective provides is not *the* answer but, rather, a level of understanding and appreciation that is more than the sum of separate diverse analyses (Majone, 1989).

The Politics of Clean and Green?

Describing and assessing policy is no simple task then. Because (as the discussion in this chapter should make clear) policy is fundamentally political, in this book we will use both a policy process approach and, where appropriate, a meta-policy approach in our analysis of New Zealand environmental policy. We will look first at the environmental problematique in a New Zealand context, examining how objective conditions and events interact with the policy processes of problem definition and agenda setting (Chapter 2). We shall pay particular attention to how well New Zealand has been able to learn from other countries and thus to develop anticipatory policies. We will examine the values and political culture of New Zealand in relation to environmentalism and environmental policy, asking, among other things, to what extent environmental policy development so far has contributed to—or is driven by—fundamental changes in dominant values and practices (Chapter 3). We will critically analyse and evaluate environmental policy making in New Zealand since 1984 (a watershed year), with particular attention to explaining how and why particular institutional reforms were formulated, selected, and implemented (Chapters 4 and 5). We will assess the merit of new processes and structures created and their likely institutional ramifications, especially with regard to any potential and realized capabilities for more integrated or comprehensive environmental policy (Chapter 6). Throughout, we will evaluate the prospects and likely directions of environmental policy making into the twenty-first century, looking at how study of New Zealand environmental policy can contribute knowledge useful to further policy development in New Zealand as well as other countries.

Not all of the many puzzles and anomalies of New Zealand environmental policy can be easily explained away by application of existing policy concepts and knowledge. But even so, use of those concepts and that knowledge helps structure our thinking about where further research on New Zealand environmental policy is most needed.

2
ENVIRONMENTAL POLICY EVOLUTION
Pressures, Demands, Agendas

New Zealand is widely perceived, both domestically and overseas, as a 'clean and green' country. New Zealand as portrayed in tourism brochures—a country of great scenic beauty, with rolling pastures, majestic mountains, extensive forests, fast-flowing rivers, and deserted beaches—presents an image held close to the heart of most New Zealanders. This picture is cultivated not only by the tourism industry, but also by the mass media and politicians.

As a corollary to this image the claim or assumption is often made that New Zealand's environment is relatively unspoiled. Pollution problems are generally regarded as minor compared with other, more industrialized countries. Given a population of only 3.5 million, the country is seen as sparsely populated, or even under-populated. Large areas of the country are relatively untouched—more than twenty per cent is still under native bush. In general, the quality of life in New Zealand is considered to be very high if not unrivalled by world standards, even though the economic standard of living may not have risen as fast as in other OECD countries during the last two decades.

Being relatively well-off environmentally, New Zealand has been in the enviable position of developing anticipatory policies to prevent the more serious environmental problems that have emerged in more industrialized and densely populated countries. Whereas people in the latter mostly became aware of environmental problems after they emerged, people in New Zealand have been in the fortunate position of being able to learn from overseas experience. New Zealand may therefore have taken the lead—and provided lessons to other countries—in the development of anticipatory environmental policies, the need for which was argued in the introduction.

There are, however, grounds for arguing that New Zealand's clean and green image is, and always has been, an inflated if not false representation of the country's environmental conditions and awareness. Although New Zealand may be environmentally well-off compared to many other countries in the world, it also has its share of environmental problems. Some of these have long been recognized, but others have received much less attention.

As pointed out in the previous chapter, whether a problem receives attention may have little to do with the intrinsic characteristics of the problem itself. Certain conditions may be accepted as normal at some point of time, but be considered a problem at some other point of time. In politics, something is only a problem if it has been put on the political agenda. Whether that happens or not is a political question, and does not necessarily depend on objective conditions.

As discussed in Chapter 1, policy analysts have developed perspectives and insights which help to throw light on why and how certain problems reach the political agenda and others do not. Problems may be identified by the public (public agenda), but not by decision makers (institutional or policy agenda) and vice versa. Given the limited amount of time available to decision makers, only some issues are up for decision (decision agenda) at each point of time (Kingdon, 1984).

Only by taking a longer view as issues come and go on the political agenda is it possible to establish any patterns in the degree of attention given to certain problems, or to develop an overview of relative priorities over time. In this chapter, we will analyse developments in the recognition of environmental problems in New Zealand over a longer period of time than that which encompasses the more recent upsurge in environmental concern. In our analysis we will make an eclectic use of perspectives and insights into agenda setting derived from policy analysis and presented in Chapter 1. Our purpose is to explain why certain environmental issues have received more political attention and others less or very little.

'Environment' is a comprehensive concept, covering potentially everything. Every and any problem could be characterized as having some relevance to environmental policy. Obviously, this makes a study of environmental agenda setting potentially meaningless, as all issues reaching the political agenda could be construed as 'environmental'. To avoid that problem, but at the same time maintain the notion of the environment as a comprehensive concept, we will analyse agenda setting with regard to three dimensions of the environmental problematique. These three dimensions relate to: (1) ecosystems, (2) natural resources, and (3) the quality of life. Environmental policies can be seen as addressing or affecting one or more of these dimensions of the environmental problematique (Bührs, 1991a, pp. 11–14).

The ecological dimension of environmental policy refers to those aspects of government policy that affect ecosystems. Examples are policies intended to protect endangered species and their habitats, and policies to conserve wetlands, forests, and other natural areas. Policies addressing climatic change and ozone depletion are more recent examples in a global context.

The economic dimension of environmental policy refers to the management of natural resources. Natural resources are all those elements found in nature, such as soil, water, air, sunlight, minerals, plants, and animals, which may serve human needs and are used to maintain or improve the human standard of living. This dimension relates to the impact of policies on the availability and quality of these resources, and to the question of the sustainability of a standard of living. Examples are energy policies, policies related to the use of land, air, and water, policies with regard to mining, and more general policies related to economic growth, population growth, science and technology, and the conservation of resources.

The social dimension of environmental policy refers to policies that affect the quality of life or living conditions of people. Although these conditions are affected by material and quantifiable factors, such as the availability and distribution of resources, they are also related to qualitative, relative, and subjective factors, which are often hard to measure. Despite apparent vagueness, this dimension is no less real than the other two. Examples are policies affecting the pleasantness (or ugliness) of the environment in which people live, policies affecting housing conditions or environmental health (for example, pollution, noise, working conditions), and policies affecting the availability of public goods in general (such as parks, recreational facilities, and historical and cultural values).[1]

These dimensions of environmental policy are very much interconnected. Air pollution, for instance, can be a health and quality of life issue (urban smog), an ecological issue (acidification of lakes, forests), and a resource issue (burning cheap but sulphurous coal). Resource use potentially affects ecosystems as well as the quality of life. The destruction of ecosystems, in turn, affects the availability of resources and living conditions. On the other hand, living conditions (both poor and affluent) may be conducive to an unsustainable use of resources. If anything, the identification of these dimensions and their interconnectedness points out the need for a comprehensive approach to environmental policy, taking into account ecological, economic, and social aspects of the environmental problematique (Henning and Mangun, 1989).

But in practice, environmental policies mostly develop in a fragmented way. Some policies may address air pollution problems, whereas other

---

1. A case could be made for the inclusion of the distributional aspects of environmental policy under the economic dimension instead of the social dimension. In fact, this is not a matter of great importance as the distinction between the dimensions is purely analytical (depending on the delineation of boundaries) and is not based on distinctions in reality.

policies affect land use or are directed at the protection of endangered species. Obviously, it is possible for such policies not to be mutually supportive, or even to be in conflict with each other. By using the three dimensions of environmental policy as an analytical device, we may discover gaps or biases in the recognition of environmental problems, as well as inconsistencies or contradictions in the policies addressing them.

In this chapter, we will first provide a sketch, along the lines of these three dimensions of the environmental problematique, of the environmental problems that have become manifest in New Zealand, and we will analyse to what extent these have found political recognition. Then, we will look at the overall picture to assess whether a pattern can be discovered. Finally, we will discuss some of the factors that may help to explain how this pattern has come about.

The Recognition of Environmental Problems

The Threat to Ecosystems

Much of New Zealand's flora and fauna is unique. Given the country's long period of geographic isolation, it developed its own distinct species and ecosystems. Of the 50,000 animal and plant species found in New Zealand, a large proportion are endemic. Among these is the tuatara, the closest living relative to the dinosaurs (Ministry for the Environment and Ministry of External Relations and Trade, 1992, p. 53).

Since human settlement, however, New Zealand's biodiversity has suffered serious losses. For instance, eight species of flowering plants and forty-four species of landbirds have become extinct, and many more endangered (Ministry for the Environment and Ministry of External Relations and Trade, 1992, p. 54; Williams and Given, 1981). Much of this has been the result of the destruction of natural habitats and the introduction of predators and competitors, hunting, overfishing, and pollution.

It is estimated that, prior to human settlement in the tenth century, eighty per cent of New Zealand was covered in forest. This was reduced to fifty-three per cent by 1840 as a result of the activities of Polynesians and early European settlers. After that, the rate of deforestation increased. Large areas of indigenous forests were cleared by burning to be transformed into grassland. In other areas, forests (especially kauri forests) were clearfelled for timber, much of that for export (Fleet, 1984). By 1983, only twenty-three per cent of New Zealand's indigenous forest cover remained (Commission for the Environment, 1985).

Concerns about deforestation go back to the 1860s. Early concerns, however, were more inspired by a fear for the depletion of forests as a timber resource than by ecological considerations. During the nineteenth century, apart from the pleas of individuals, there was 'not much, or indeed any, general support for measures of forest conservation' (Fleet, 1984, p. 97).

Although New Zealand's first national park, comprising the volcanoes on the central North Island, was formally established in 1894, this was not so much due to the efforts of early conservationists as to the fear of Māori that these sacred, ancestral mountains would be taken by white settlers. In 1887, Māori chief Te Heuheu Tukino IV offered the mountains to the Government to be held in trust for the people of New Zealand for all time. The second national park, Egmont National Park, was created in 1900 in response to concerns of farmers in the area about excess runoff if forests on the slopes of the mountain were cut. Although this can be seen as an early recognition of the ecological value of forests, it was more inspired by human interest than by a concern about ecosystems (Department of Statistics, 1989, p. 510).

Until the early 1920s, the advocacy of conservation remained very much a matter of pleas and efforts by individuals. It is only since then that an organized conservation movement in New Zealand started to emerge. The Native Bird Protection Society (now the Royal Forest and Bird Protection Society) was set up in 1923, following concern about widespread devastation among native birds on Kapiti Island which had been declared a sanctuary in 1902 (Dalmer, 1983, pp. 1–3).

In 1928, increased public interest in conservation led to the introduction of the Public Reserves, Domains and National Parks Act. In 1929, New Zealand's third national park, Arthur's Pass National Park, was established. The 1940s saw a successful campaign to save the Waipoua (kauri) forest, which was declared a sanctuary in 1952. In 1950, a Nature Protection Council was established with the purpose of co-ordinating the conservation activities of a wide range of organizations, such as the Federated Mountain Clubs, Forestry League, Geographical Society of New Zealand, the Native Plant Protection Society, the Royal Society of New Zealand, the Waipoua Preservation Society, and others (Dalmer, 1983, p. 22). During the 1950s, another four national parks were established (Department of Statistics, 1989, pp. 512–13).

In the late 1950s concerns and activities of conservationists intensified following the destruction of scenic beauty by State-sponsored development projects, in particular hydro dams. A catalyst in this respect was the proposal to raise the levels of lakes Manapouri and Te Anau to generate electricity for an aluminium smelter. In 1959, the New Zealand Preservation Society was established in reaction to the Manapouri proposal. Calls were made for the establishment of a New Zealand Conservation Authority 'to see that our national parks be preserved in their natural state, for all time, and to advise on the preservation of all our beauty spots' (Dalmer, 1983, p. 81; Wilson, 1982, pp. 9–15).

The logging of native forests and destruction of scenic beauty continued to dominate the concerns of environmentalists in New Zealand during the 1970s and the early 1980s. Battles were fought over government proposals for the utilization of South Island beech forests, over logging of forests at Okarito and Waikukupa (also in the South Island), and over North Island forests at Pureoa and Whirinaki (Wilson, 1982, pp. 107–32). The beech forests proposals provoked the establishment of a new, more radical and action-oriented conservation organization, the Beech Forests Action Council (later named the Native Forests Action Council), and even attracted opposition from overseas (Searle, 1975). Other significant conservation issues centred on the protection of wild and scenic rivers against hydro development (Wilson, 1982, pp. 16–17), and on the protection of natural areas (such as the Coromandel, Aramoana) from mining and other development (Wilson, 1982, pp. 24–33, 88–96).

During the 1980s and early 1990s, the interests of the environmental movement in New Zealand moved increasingly towards conservation issues of an international or global dimension. Issues such as driftnet fishing, the protection of whales and seals, the Antarctic, and tropical rainforests, as well as global climate change and the depletion of the ozone layer, became the focus of attention and action, often in concert with environmental groups overseas. The growing importance of such issues on the government agenda was also reflected in a book written by a former Minister for the Environment who had kept the environment portfolio when he became Prime Minister (Palmer, 1990).

Overall, conservation problems have been on the political agenda in New Zealand for a long time, and have been increasingly prominent during the last three decades. Not only have conservationists been successful in bringing issues to the attention of governments, they have also achieved considerable success in having policies and institutions introduced or changed to meet their demands.

Resource Issues

In one way or another, resource issues—issues related to the availability, quality, use and management of natural resources—have always been on the political agenda of governments. Some natural resources, such as land and minerals, have been the subject of politics and policies since the emergence of human societies and government. As the basis for the satisfaction of material human needs, and as a source of wealth and power, natural resources have been at the root of greed, conflicts, and conquests, as well as of rule-making and government, from the earliest times.[2]

---

2. For an interesting interpretation of history in this light, see Carter and Dale (1974).

In proportion to its population, New Zealand is well endowed with resources. Overall, fresh water is abundant, and seventy-five per cent of electricity is normally generated by hydro-power. The land yields primary products (meat, dairy products, wool, fruit, timber) in quantities far beyond the country's own needs, forming the backbone of its exports. New Zealand's exclusive economic zone (EEZ) is one of the largest in the world. Mineral resources (coal, gas, oil, ironsand, limestone, silver, and gold) are also economically significant (Department of Statistics, 1992, Chapters 15–17, 22; Ministry for the Environment and Ministry of External Relations and Trade, 1992, pp. 29–35). Until the early 1970s, New Zealand was perceived by many people as a country rich in resources. At the Physical Environment Conference in 1970, growing resource use was not yet seen as problematic, and the potential for, and desirability of, economic growth was unquestioned (Bührs, 1991a, pp. 56–89).

Yet the limits of resources in New Zealand have become apparent. Much of the land is steep to very steep. Only six per cent has few limitations for cropping, and forty-four per cent has severe limitations for all types of agricultural or forestry use (Ministry for the Environment and Ministry of External Relations and Trade, 1992, p. 30). Erosion is a severe problem in many areas, both naturally and because of the clearance of vegetation, burning, and overgrazing. The sustainability of agriculture in many high country areas is questionable as a result of mismanagement and pest infestation. The distribution of fresh water resources is very uneven, with the eastern parts of the country prone to droughts. All areas may be affected by extreme weather conditions, such as heavy rain or snowfalls, flooding, and cyclones. Extensive demands on water, particularly for irrigation, have put pressure on water resources, including groundwater. At present rates of use, oil and gas reserves are expected to run out by the year 2010. Environmental impacts, and economics, constrain the development of further hydro-energy resources, as well as the extraction of minerals. Despite New Zealand's huge exclusive economic zone, fisheries resources are not rich by world standards because of the low fertility of the waters of the EEZ. Already, overfishing has occurred, and various fish stocks have seriously declined or even been depleted (Ministry for the Environment and Ministry of External Relations and Trade, 1992; OECD, 1981; *Terra Nova*, November 1991).

Concerns about the effects of use on the availability and quality of natural resources have led governments to introduce laws, rules, and controls. In pre-European New Zealand, the conduct of people towards their natural environment was regulated through such concepts as mauri, kawa, tapu, and rāhui (Marsden, 1988). Since European colonization, and the subsequent large-scale exploitation of natural resources, laws and regulations were gradually introduced addressing the destruction of forests (State Forests Act 1885), the use of Crown land and its preservation for recreational or scenic purposes (Land Act 1892), land erosion and flooding (Soil Conservation and Rivers Control Act 1941), and the allocation and use of water (Water and Soil Conservation Act 1967). Legislation was also introduced to control mineral resources, fisheries, wildlife, and the introduction of foreign species (Commission for the Environment, 1984; Williams, 1980). Over time, many official agencies have been established to deal with these problems. Hardly any problem has not found an institutional home in a government department or advisory body. From this point of view, it would appear that agenda setting for most of these issues has not been problematic.

Despite all these government efforts, resource problems have continued to generate concerns. Even though they may have been addressed, they have not been resolved. An upsurge of public concern about these matters occurred in the early 1970s after the publication of a scenario indicating that the planetary limits of growth would be reached within a hundred years at current rates of resource depletion, pollution, and population growth (Meadows et al., 1972). The most likely outcome of that, according to the report, would be an uncontrollable and sudden decline in population and industrial capacity. The advent of the first 'oil crisis' in 1973 seemed to be a forewarning of the impending problems presaged by the report. Although the fears for a depletion of oil receded during the 1980s, when the oil crisis turned into an oil glut, concerns that the world's 'limits to growth' have already been by-passed have not faded. On the contrary, the thesis has received increased support with the emergence of global environmental issues and the presentation of new evidence of decline of many resources (Brown, 1991; Meadows, Meadows, and Randers, 1992).

Among the concerns about resources, those about energy resources have often taken a central place, given their economic and strategic importance. In New Zealand, energy issues have played an important role on the political agenda since the early 1970s. With the dramatic rise in energy prices since the first 'oil crisis' in 1973, and the resulting deterioration in New Zealand's balance of payments, an increase in the level of the country's energy self-sufficiency became a prime goal of government policy. Although as a result of the 'crisis' governments gave some support to energy conservation, they put the main thrust of their energy policies on the development of new energy projects. An important basis for this was laid by the Labour Government in 1973 with the signing of a 'take or pay' agreement on Maui gas, committing the government to paying for specified quantities of gas each year, whether or not the gas was actually delivered. Under the successive National Governments of Prime Minister Muldoon (1975–84) a 'Think Big' policy was initiated with the purpose of using as much gas as quickly as possible. Apart from using the gas for electricity generation, decisions were made to establish an ammonia-urea plant, a methanol plant, and the world's first commercial synthetic petrol plant, and to promote the conversion of cars to CNG. Many of these projects were criticized by environmentalists as involving wasteful use of gas (Fitzsimons, 1981; Wilson, 1982, pp. 52–5).

That energy policy in New Zealand lagged behind other countries in promoting energy efficiency is also reflected in the increase in energy intensity—measured by the ratio of primary energy supply to GDP—by thirty-six per cent between 1973 and 1989, whereas there has been a decline in average energy intensity of twenty-three per cent during the same period for OECD countries as a whole (Ministry for the Environment and Ministry of External Relations and Trade, 1992, p. 44). Although the increase can to some extent be attributed to the introduction of a few major electricity-intensive industries (such as aluminium and steel manufacturing), and energy conversion losses related to the aforementioned gas-based industries, it is also the result of a general failure by successive New Zealand governments to promote energy efficiency consistently. Campaigns for energy efficiency have been *ad hoc* and have received prominence only at times of 'crises', such as during the 'electricity crisis' in 1992. In recent times, the reluctance to promote efficiency has also been inspired by the belief that leaving energy decisions to 'the market' will bring about their most efficient use, a view which has been criticized on many grounds (Fitzsimons, 1990; McChesney, 1991b; Parliamentary Commissioner for the Environment, 1992a).

During the 1970s, the government's perception of a need to boost energy self-sufficiency also led to the consideration of nuclear energy. But apparently strong anti-nuclear feelings among New Zealanders—fed by French nuclear testing in the Pacific—was reflected in the support of more than 333,000 people for a petition against the introduction of nuclear power in 1976. After a Royal Commission on Nuclear Power had found no immediate need for its introduction, a decision on this issue was shelved (Wilson, 1982, pp. 40–51). In 1987, with the introduction of non-nuclear legislation by the Fourth Labour Government, this option for energy generation has become even less likely, despite the possibility that some future National Government may amend the legislation to allow nuclear-powered ships to visit New Zealand ports.

During the 1980s, the institutional arrangements for the management of resources, and for environmental policy and management generally, received increased attention. This increase in attention was partly due to the frustrations experienced by environmentalists in their attempts to have their concerns recognized by governments, and partly also to dissatisfaction among governments and development interests about the costs and delays involved in getting approval for resource proposals, given the elaborate and fragmented legal and administrative system that had evolved. This led to a comprehensive and radical overhaul of administrative responsibilities and legislation regarding resources. These developments, resulting in the adoption of the Resource Management Act in 1991, will be discussed in Chapters 4 and 5.

Overall, over the last two decades, resource issues have played an important role in the political arena in New Zealand. Among these, energy issues in particular have figured prominently on the political agenda, but other resource management issues (for instance, those related to water and minerals), have also been the subject of controversy. Political attention to resource issues, however, does not necessarily imply that the *environmental* problems associated with such issues have been addressed.

Quality of Life Issues

From a human perspective, quality of life issues comprise both the most and the least tangible of environmental problems. Where people are subject to gross forms of pollution, as in areas with dirty industries and dense traffic, these problems are very apparent, visually and physically. It is often equally obvious that the quality of life of people living in abject poverty and slums is very low. But the notion of quality of life also covers much less tangible phenomena, such as the enjoyment of life, the quality of social relations within society, and the satisfaction of psychological needs.

Although the quality of life is associated with the standard of living, it is not the same thing. A comfortable standard of living may be a good basis for the enjoyment of life, but does not automatically lead to it, for at least two reasons.

First, a high standard of living may be paid for in terms of the physical effects of development on the environment, for instance, in the form of pollution. This, of course, is most notable in highly industrialized countries or areas. To some extent, however, people with a higher standard of living may be able to avoid threats to their quality of life. People on higher incomes often live away from industrial areas and, on a larger scale, the quality of life in rich countries is partly maintained or restored by the exporting of polluting industries to poorer countries, often with less stringent pollution control regimes. But pollution is not always a local phenomenon, and it may make itself felt far away from its source, even threatening the well-being of people in other countries. This is demonstrated by the effects of acid rain, ozone depletion, the greenhouse effect, and the spread of chemicals—such as DDT—all over the world.

Second, the achievement of a higher standard of living does not necessarily generate better social conditions or greater psychological satisfaction. To a large extent this is because the satisfaction derived from a given standard of living is relative to the standard of living enjoyed by others. Rising standards of living cause an expansion in the consumption of (or competition for) the 'good things of life', which may consequently lose some or all of their quality and attractiveness. For example, the pleasure of driving a car is destroyed when more and more people drive cars and collectively cause congestion; having a holiday home in a quiet area to 'get away from it all' loses its attraction if many more people acquire homes in the same area. In other words, apart from the physical limits to growth, there are also social limits to the satisfaction derived from a standard of living if the quality of the products, facilities, or services that can be obtained deteriorates with growing consumption (Hirsch, 1977).

In New Zealand, quality of life issues, including pollution, public health, and human environment problems, did not have a high public profile until the early 1970s. Although some public health issues, in particular sewage disposal and air pollution, had been the subject of some concern in the 1950s, these were primarily of a local nature. Initially considered more as 'nuisances' than real problems, these issues provoked action of only a handful of people.[3]

From 1970, pollution and public health issues started to play a more important role on the public agenda in New Zealand. Pollution issues received a spectacular increase in attention from the media. But this upsurge did not reflect a sudden aggravation of pollution problems in New Zealand; rather, it was associated more with environmental concern about pollution problems in general, inspired by experiences and publications from abroad (Bührs, 1991a, pp. 95–100).

Although during the 1970s and 1980s some environmental health and pollution problems did get on the political agenda, they never aroused the same levels of public concern or activity as conservation or some resource issues, such as nuclear power. One issue that received publicity was the widespread use of 2,4,5-T, but public pressure on this matter was not sufficient to convince the government that the use of the chemical should be banned, as occurred in some other countries. For some time, New Zealand was the only country where 2,4,5-T was still produced, until a decision to cease production was made by the producer, Ivon Watkins-Dow, in 1987 (Commission for the Environment, 1986; Ministry for the Environment, 1989b; Wilson, 1982, pp. 136–43).

---

3. Auckland's sewerage problems had been the subject of vigorous action by only a handful of people, and ultimately one man, Dove-Myer Robinson. See Bush (1980). Air-pollution 'nuisances' in Auckland in the 1950s led to an official investigation, and in Christchurch in the 1960s they led to the establishment of the Christchurch Clean Air Society.

Problems with regard to the high level of pesticides use in New Zealand have received growing attention, but policies in this field—notably the insufficient monitoring of domestic food and environment contamination and the lack of balance between affected interests in the regulatory process—have been found wanting and lagging behind development overseas (MacIntyre, Allison, and Penman, 1989). In 1991, public concerns intensified after surveys of vegetables sold in shops indicated that eighty-five per cent carried excessive levels of spray residues (*The Press*, 7 November 1991).

Other environmental health and pollution issues, such as those related to lead, asbestos, and other hazardous substances, have also been the subject of concern, but they have never developed a high public profile in New Zealand, despite the efforts of concerned experts and some environmental groups. New Zealand was slow in following other western countries in reducing the lead content of petrol. It had, in 1986, one of the highest levels of lead in petrol in the world (at 0.84 g/l) (Commission for the Environment, 1986b; Royal Society of New Zealand, 1986). With regard to asbestos it has been argued that New Zealand is still 'in the very early stages of awareness' (*The Press*, 15 December 1992). Overall, policy development with regard to hazardous substances has been rather lacking, and certainly not anticipatory, despite the production of many reports over the years (Ministry for the Environment, 1987b, 1988c; Parliamentary Commissioner for the Environment, 1992b). That New Zealand is not immune to problems in this area has become apparent in a recent report that identified more than 7000 potentially contaminated sites, 1580 of which involve high risks. Hundreds of these sites have been contaminated with PCPs and PCDDs/PCDFs (polychlorinated dibenzo-p-dioxins and polychlorinated dibenzofurans) used for timber treatment. The problems result from poor management and disposal practices sustained by a permissive approach on the part of responsible agencies. The costs of cleaning up the high risk sites alone has been estimated at more than $600 million, and an additional $1000 million may be required for the remediation of moderate-risk sites (Ministry for the Environment, 1993; Minister for the Environment, Media Statement, 16 December 1992; Stevenson, 1992).

Similarly, problems in the area of human waste/sewage disposal have also been picked up very slowly, with many local authorities (including Wellington and Napier) relying, until recently or even still, on unsatisfactory treatment methods. In many places, sewage is discharged into waterways after only primary treatment—or sometimes even with no treatment at all (Ministry for the Environment and Ministry of External Relations and Trade, 1992, pp. 62–3; Shields, 1991).

Sluggishness in addressing potential problems has also been displayed with regard to waste management in general. Despite early recognition by the

Commission for the Environment of the potential problems in this field and the relatively high public profile of some of these issues (notably with regard to packaging and littering), policy development has been weak and ineffective, based primarily on public education and the delegation of responsibilities towards local government and producers (Bührs, 1991a, pp. 336–49; Ministry for the Environment, 1987c, 1989c, 1991c).

Other quality of life issues, such as those related to urban development and social problems, have not fared much better in receiving political attention. Historically, the responsibility for urban development has been primarily a local matter. During the 1960s, urban development issues were the subject of a few conferences organized by professional groups, such as engineers and architects, but did not generate public concern or action on a broad scale. At these conferences, concern was expressed regarding the quality of urban expansion, and about the effects of the uneven pattern of regional, demographic, and economic growth in New Zealand associated with the 'drift to the North'; but this was not picked up as a serious problem by the central government (Bührs, 1991a, pp. 56–89). On the contrary, this phenomenon has been considered—even more so in the 1980s than in the 1960s—as an essential expression of sound economic ('market') mechanisms with which the central government should not interfere.

Although New Zealand governments since the 1970s have been advised about growing social problems in urban and rural areas (Environmental Council, 1980; Royal Commission on Social Policy, 1988), social policy has become increasingly pragmatic (Easton, 1981), residual (focused on individual minimum income maintenance—Castles, 1985), fragmented, and devolved towards local communities and the 'market' (Koopman-Boyden, 1990). Progressively, the State has been withdrawing from social policy, and has made people more responsible for their own health, housing, education, and welfare in general. Urban public transport has declined under a policy of deregulation, involving significant price increases and a reduction of government subsidies by forty per cent (*Terra Nova*, May 1992). With the tremendous rise in unemployment during the 1980s and early 1990s, and the concurrent increase in impoverishment, social tensions, and crime, the quality of life of many New Zealanders, in particular the poor, elderly, women, and Māori and Pacific Islanders, has been adversely affected (Boston and Dalziel, 1992).

Since the mid-1970s, the plight of Māori has commanded increased attention with the revival of Māori activism, accompanied by stronger claims for resources and reparation of past injustice on the basis of the Treaty of Waitangi. Although successive governments have acknowledged the need to accommodate such demands, they have entered into direct talks and negotiations with Māori on these matters only after the failure of earlier efforts to depoliticize these issues, for instance by referring them to the Waitangi Tribunal and leaving them to the courts (Sharp, 1990a, 1990b). Since then, significant steps have been taken towards settling Māori claims, notably in the area of fisheries (*The Press*, 9 December 1992), but it is unlikely that such agreements, regardless of their historical and political importance, will go very far towards addressing the economic and social deprivation suffered by many Māori—given the very high rate of unemployment among Māori, and the fact that access to resources will still be problematic, particularly for urban Māori.

That economic growth may actually be a cause of quality of life problems, and not a remedy, is a notion that has so far received little political recognition. In New Zealand this view was advanced by the Values Party, one of the first green parties in the world, created in 1972. Inspired by the writings of such people as Erich Fromm, Theodore Roszak, Charles Reich, Barry Commoner, and Paul Ehrlich, and by the *Ecologist*'s 'Blueprint for Survival' and 'The Limits to Growth' report of Meadows et al., Values expressed concern not only about the ecological consequences of unrestrained economic growth, but also about the implications in terms of a deterioration of the quality of life, the loss of community, social decay, and growing alienation. In the Party's 1972 manifesto, a 'Blueprint for New Zealand', it was noted that New Zealand was in the grip of a new depression, 'a depression of human values', which was seen as arising not from a lack of affluence, 'but almost from too much of it. It is the outcome of an obsession with the growth of the economy rather than the growth of the human mind and the non-economic capacities of the population' (New Zealand Values Party, 1972).

Despite the fact that the level of electoral support for Values in 1975 was significant (more than five per cent), it appears that quality of life issues in New Zealand politics have, overall, been secondary to economic 'imperatives' such as restoring economic growth and the country's balance of payments. Since the early 1970s, governments have followed different strategies for restoring economic growth, ranging from heavy State involvement in development projects—such as during the 'Think Big' era under Prime Minister Muldoon—to an extreme emphasis on 'free market' policies since 1984. The priority given by governments to economic growth, coupled with, more recently, a retrenchment of the welfare state, indicates the political dominance of the view that a high quality of life is contingent upon a prosperous economy.

Patterns and Trends

From the necessarily sketchy and incomplete description of environmental issues above, there emerges a particular picture of environmental problem recognition in New Zealand. On the public agenda, conservation issues have figured most prominently. Resource issues (such as forest depletion, mining, and the use of water resources for electricity generation) have drawn most public attention when they had significant impacts on the natural environment and were thus defined more as conservation than resource issues. Other resource issues (such as erosion, and the depletion of energy resources), apart from nuclear power, have generally had a much lower public profile. Such concerns, along with those relating to quality of life issues, were mostly expressed by smaller groups of people, often experts, and have not generated mass arousal or action.[4]

On the government agenda,[5] resource issues have been predominant. Until recently, however, the focus of government attention in this regard has been more on the question of how the use, rather than the conservation, of resources can be promoted in order to stimulate economic growth. Inevitably, this has brought governments into conflict with conservationists, forcing them, given the high level of public support for conservationists' demands, to consider the implications of their policies for the natural environment. It has been much more difficult, however, for quality of life issues to reach either the public or the government agenda. This contrasts with developments in North America and Europe, where quality of life issues, in particular those related to pollution, have very much dominated public and government concern about the environment.

In New Zealand, the relative success of conservation issues in reaching both agendas has also resulted in significant policy developments in this area. Although conservation concerns in New Zealand have not all disappeared, it can be argued that many of the big domestic issues which dominated environmental policy from the 1960s to the early 1980s have at least been partially resolved by governments. In many cases campaigns have been successful (such as in the Manapouri issue, and several indigenous forests campaigns). National parks have been extended, and new ones established. Altogether, more than five million hectares, nearly nineteen per cent of the nation's land area, has come under some form of protection (Department of

---

4. Voluntary electricity savings during the 'electricity crisis' of 1992 are an exception. That such public efforts do not reflect a concern about the long-term availability of electricity is demonstrated by the fact that only a few months later power use soared as the 'crisis' seemed forgotten (*The Press*, 18 November 1992).
5. We use the term government agenda to refer to the range of issues that have been identified by governments as requiring policy making or change (also sometimes referred to as policy or institutional agenda).

Statistics, 1992, p. 262). With proposals in the pipeline for the creation of new national parks and reserves (amongst others, for a Kauri National Park in the North Island and another park in the north-west of the South Island), this proportion is likely to increase even further.

Conservationists have also been able to achieve policy changes and institutional reforms that have significantly strengthened conservation interests. Of the nearly eighty per cent of indigenous forests that are State-owned, the vast majority are now managed by the Department of Conservation as national parks or reserves. The establishment of the Department in 1987 as an advocate for conservation is in itself a major victory for the conservation movement, which has sought such a public advocate since the early 1960s (Salmon, 1960).

This is not meant to imply that the conservation movement in New Zealand has nothing left to fight for on the domestic front. Outstanding issues to date are the logging of indigenous forests on private land, controversy regarding 'sustainable'-yield logging practices on a proportion of public land, the continuing destruction of wetlands from development (ninety per cent of which have already disappeared), the decline of native flora and fauna, and the degradation of marine ecosystems (by overfishing, coastal pollution), to name just a few. From the point of view of conservationists, progress on these issues has been slow or lacking. Government commitment to these matters has been questioned (*The Press*, 4 January 1993) and the funding of the Department of Conservation criticized as inadequate for tackling its many responsibilities, amongst which are the identification and protection of representative ecological areas (*Conservation News*, May 1990).

Nevertheless, the times of mass protests and acrimonious battles between governments and conservationists about development proposals affecting natural areas seem largely over. Remaining issues are now often tackled in a much less adversarial way, with conservationists, local community interests, economic interest groups, and government officials trying to reach agreement ('accords') by negotiation.[6] Although contentious conservation issues remain,

---

6. The first such agreement was reached in 1986 in respect of the West Coast forests that had been designated for sustainable logging (the 'Blakeley Accord'). Another accord, relating to indigenous forests owned by Tasman Forestry Ltd, was concluded in 1989 (the 'Tasman Conservation Accord'). In 1991, a much more extensive agreement (the 'New Zealand Forest Accord') was reached between the New Zealand Forest Owners' Association and a coalition of seventeen environmental organizations (*Bush Telegraph*, February 1987; Ministry for the Environment and Ministry of External Relations and Trade, 1992, pp. 47–8).

conservationists are now often invited by the government to participate on committees to search for solutions.

With regard to the economic (resource) dimension of environmental policy, very significant developments have also taken place in recent years. Since 1984, government policy has shifted from direct involvement in, and support for, resource exploitation, towards relying on a 'market approach' to resource management. Parallel to that, significant institutional changes, separating development and environmental responsibilities, have been introduced. Also, with the introduction of the Resource Management Act in 1991, the sustainable use of resources has become entrenched in law.

Nevertheless, the implications of these changes for the policies on resources are often still unclear (partly because of a devolution of responsibilities towards lower levels of government), and they continue to be the subject of controversy (for instance, regarding the deregulation and privatization of the electricity industry). Given the scope for uncertainty and conflict about the meaning or implementation of sustainable development, and the need to come to terms with the global 'limits to growth', it is likely that many resource issues, and their impact on the environment, will continue to surface on the political agenda.

As both developments will be analysed in Chapters 4 and 5, we will not elaborate on them here, apart from noting that these developments cannot be attributed purely to the demands of environmentalists, and that they are to at least some degree contradictory.

Of the three dimensions of the environmental problematique, quality of life issues have received the least attention in New Zealand, both from governments and the public at large. Policy developments in this area have been slow, *ad hoc*, and reactive. In contrast to North America and Europe, pollution problems in New Zealand have generally not been regarded as serious, and the quality of life in New Zealand is still regarded by many as high.

Increasingly, international and global environmental issues have overshadowed domestic issues on the public and government agendas in New Zealand. Since the late 1980s, driftnet fishing, the Antarctic, the decline of tropical rainforests, the greenhouse effect, and the depletion of the ozone layer have become the focus of attention and action of many environmental groups in New Zealand. These issues have also prompted governments to develop policies within the context of international agreements. Although New Zealand officials have played an important role in the making of various of these agreements (Palmer, 1990), within New Zealand the domestic policies on these issues (notably the greenhouse effect) are still poorly integrated with other policies (such as energy and transport), creating contradictions and sometimes rendering them ineffective (Kennaway, 1991).

In conclusion, the evolution of New Zealand environmental policy shows a reactive, *ad hoc*, fragmented, uneven, and in some ways contradictory pattern in its recognition of environmental problems (Bührs, 1987). This seems to conform to a view of the agenda-setting process, and of the policy process in general, as largely random, chaotic, and unpredictable. Agenda setting and policy development can be seen as resulting from the interaction among relatively autonomous events and developments within three streams—problems, policies, and politics (Kingdon, 1984). Policies by their very nature develop not in a planned, orderly fashion, but in shocks and waves, in reaction to a multitude of uncontrollable factors.

But this view of the agenda-setting process is misleading, even though chance does play a role in the political recognition of problems. In the following section, we will subject the pattern in the agenda-setting process of environmental issues in New Zealand to a closer scrutiny in an effort to uncover some of the structural elements that underlie this seemingly chaotic development.

Agenda Setting: Towards an Explanation

If agenda setting appears to be a random process, this is, to a large extent, deceptive. As Kingdon indicates, there may be patterns to the developments within the streams of problems, policies, and politics. Not all conditions have an equal chance of being defined as problems. Not all alternatives are equally likely to become policy. Nor is all that happens in politics a question of chance or luck. The existence or emergence of policy entrepreneurs is also a matter which is not purely a question of preferences that 'happen to be there'.

Problems have a better chance of being 'discovered' if some form of systematic monitoring of developments is done. In most countries, the identification of economic problems is facilitated by the extensive monitoring of such indicators as inflation, interest rates, imports and exports, etc. Whether or not monitoring systems exist is, however, also a reflection of structural factors, such as the relative political weight behind particular values. Environmental monitoring is a relatively young phenomenon, and many countries, including New Zealand, are still in the process of developing indicators and putting in place monitoring systems (Ministry for the Environment and Department of Statistics, 1990; Ward, 1992). Consequently, the state of the environment in New Zealand is in many respects not known, as exemplified, for instance, in the uncertainty with regard to contamination by hazardous substances referred to above.

Factors that help to explain why certain conditions or problems have a better chance of reaching the political agenda fall into at least five categories.

These can be identified as: socio-cultural factors; the relative seriousness of environmental problems; economic factors; political-institutional interests; and convergence. We will discuss each of these in the context of an attempt to explain the patterns and trends in the environmental agenda-setting process in New Zealand.

Socio-cultural Factors
The perception of problems and their definition is dependent on the socio-cultural context. The assessment of whether a problem or risk exists, and at what level it is acceptable, can vary from culture to culture, and may change over time (Douglas and Wildavsky, 1982; Inglehart, 1977, 1990). Although this factor plays a role in explaining why environmental concerns have undergone a general increase in many western countries, it may also help to account for variations among cultures or countries as to the relative emphasis or bias in environmental policy with regard to the various dimensions of the environmental problematique. In Japan, for instance, conditions posing a threat to human health have a greater chance of being identified as environmental problems than do threats to the natural environment (Nakano, 1986; Pierce, Tsurutani, and Lovrich, 1986).

By contrast, the social and cultural context of New Zealand society has been receptive to nature conservation issues. Many New Zealanders look upon their country's natural environment and scenic beauty as unique, even to the extent of calling it 'God's own country'. Its forests of magnificent native trees, many hundreds of years old, are seen as the equivalent of European cathedrals. Its mountains, rivers, and lakes, and often unique flora and fauna, are not just natural features, but points of identification. Perhaps more so than in many other cultures, national symbols and national identity in New Zealand are associated with the natural environment. Being a New Zealander has as much to do with the country's physical environment as it has with history and culture. Conservation of New Zealand's scenic and natural qualities thus has a cultural as well as ecological significance.

For many New Zealanders, the natural environment is also a source of inspiration and spirituality. This, of course, is particularly true for the country's indigenous population, the Māori. For Māori, everything in the natural world possesses life force or mauri. People are interdependent with the natural world and, as its descendants, are obliged to pay it respect and to protect its integrity. Although these views are not necessarily shared by most New Zealanders of European or other descent, it would be true to say that many feel a strong attachment to the country's natural environment. Consequently, the groups of people identifying with conservationists ('identification group'), and interested in conservation issues ('attention group') have both been very large, providing a good basis for 'issue expansion' (Cobb, Ross, and Ross, 1976).[7]

This significant level of support has allowed the conservation movement in New Zealand to develop professional and politically skilled organizations. With growing numbers of members and increasing financial support, conservation groups have been able to employ staff on a full-time basis, supported by a pool of volunteers. Some of these professional conservationists have proved to be extremely capable lobbyists and 'policy entrepreneurs' (Kingdon, 1984).

According to some authors, the cultural importance of nature in New Zealand manifests itself also in the environmental movement. Hay and Haward argue that the environmental movement in Australasia and North America has a 'deeper' green quality than the environmental movement in European countries. The 'contemporary' experience of wilderness by environmentalists in the former countries is reflected in the fact that they are more inclined to ask 'some very fundamental questions', and to challenge the 'homocentric' assumptions that are at the heart of western value systems, than their European counterparts, who adhere to a more anthropocentric view of the environment (Hay and Haward, 1988).

For the same reasons, however, it can be argued that the preoccupation of environmentalists in New Zealand with the natural environment is a weakness, as they tend to overlook the social, historical, and political aspects of the environmental problematique. Consequently, their approach to developing solutions can be described as narrow, pragmatic, anti-ideological, and failing in terms of addressing the need for change in the social, economic, and political context in which environmental problems exist (Tester, 1987).

Although this assessment may have been valid for much of the environmental movement in New Zealand during the 1970s and 1980s, there has been a marked effort by at least part of that movement, particularly in the Maruia Society in recent years, to incorporate social and economic considerations into its strategies (O'Connor, 1991; Salmon, 1982). The integration of social, economic, and ecological values has also become a key element in the coalition ('the Alliance') formed by the Green Party and three

---

7. In a recent survey of adult New Zealanders seventy-eight per cent expressed the view that conservation was very or most important, and twenty per cent said that it was quite important. Only two per cent said that conservation was not important or less important than other issues. Although a much smaller proportion of people translate these views into personal action or attitudes, they indicate significant support for conservation values on a public level (*The Press*, 1 February 1993).

other minor parties in 1992. Although such efforts are deplored by more purist greens and sometimes depicted as a 'sellout' of green or conservation values, they represent a significant move by environmentalists in New Zealand away from a narrow definition of environmental problems and solutions, and towards an ecological perspective that recognizes the need to address all three dimensions of the environmental problematique.

The Relative Seriousness of Environmental Problems
It can be argued that, although affected by socio-cultural factors, the relative seriousness of environmental conditions also acts, at least to some extent, as a factor in the political recognition of problems. Of course, whether a situation is a problem, let alone a serious problem, is a matter of definition, but when rather drastic things happen to people, the chance that such things will be identified as problems increases. That concerns about the environment have grown is not only or even necessarily a result of changing values or the emergence of a 'new class', but is also a result of deteriorating conditions (Eckersley, 1989; Lowe and Rudig, 1986).

Environmental policies often follow the emergence of particular environmental pressures. In particular, problems are more likely to get on to the political agenda if they lead to more or less spectacular accidents involving considerable damage or casualties. The role of accidents as a catalyst in policy development is well established, and several authors have noted the 'crisis-response' type of environmental policy development, for instance in Britain (Gilg, 1986), Australia (Formby, 1986), and Japan (Weidner, 1986).

Although one should be cautious in depicting New Zealand as a clean and green country—given the fact that pollution and environmental health problems do exist but have not been systematically monitored—there is a plausible basis for arguing that, given the comparatively low levels of industrialization and population, problems in this area have been less serious than in many other countries. As pollution and public health problems in New Zealand have not reached crisis proportions, and few major accidents involving pollution have occurred,[8] there have been few 'focusing events' that put the spotlight on shortcomings in environmental policies. Only in some areas where pollution has reached levels comparable to overseas countries—such as in Auckland's Manukau Harbour—has substantial *ad hoc* action been

---

8. The 'Parnell fumes emergency' in 1973, and the ICI fire in 1984, both involving hazardous chemicals, probably qualify as major accidents in the New Zealand context. In both cases, they led to a review of the management of hazardous substances.

forthcoming (Ministry for the Environment, 1987d; Auckland Regional Water Board, 1988–91, 1990).

The attention to conservation issues, on the other hand, could be attributed to the more visible or dramatic impact of resource exploitation on the natural environment in New Zealand compared to many other (notably European) countries where the most dramatic transformations of the landscape occurred a long time ago. In some of these countries, there is little wilderness to conserve or destroy. In New Zealand, the visual effects of the (potential) destruction of natural areas by resource exploitation have often been highlighted by environmentalists, particularly in the news media. It can therefore be argued that the principal threat to New Zealand's environment has been perceived to be in the area where environmental damage has been most visible, namely that of the natural environment.

Noteworthy by comparison to some other western countries is the New Zealand news media's relatively less prominent role in problem definition and agenda setting. For example, the many all-news stations in the United States, or the many dailies in the United Kingdom, all compete intensely with each other to expose problems. In these countries, a tradition of hard-nosed journalism has developed with a strong appetite for controversy and an interest in reporting problems. New Zealand, by contrast, because of its small size, has only a small number of media channels, especially in television and radio, and no national newspapers—only local newspapers with a monopoly status in almost all cities. Consequently, the media play a much more restricted role in putting problems on the political agenda.

Economic Factors

Economic factors may also help to explain why conservation issues have been more successful than other issues in receiving policy attention in New Zealand. Much of the progress in conservation policy has been achieved because of the economic—and therefore often also political—viability of conservation solutions. Most national parks and other protected areas have been established in less accessible areas where development of resources has been difficult or uneconomic. The halting of logging of native forests on most public land and much private land has been facilitated by a political climate that no longer condones government financial support for uneconomic activities. On the other hand, the significance of national parks as an important source of revenue from tourism has received greater recognition.

As discussed earlier in the chapter, resource exploitation in New Zealand has in many instances been encouraged, and often has only been economically viable, because of financial support from the State. Several (notably 'Think Big') projects involving the use of natural resources have been undertaken at considerable cost to the tax-payer. But with the continuing decline of New Zealand's economy, increasing pressure on the government's financial position, and the shift towards 'free market' and 'user pays' policies, government support for economic activities, including environmentally damaging ones, has dwindled.

On the other hand, however, there has been increased reluctance on the part of governments to put in place environmental policies that would impose a burden on the ailing economy or, more recently, policies that are considered to 'distort' the workings of the market mechanism. Consequently, solutions requiring significant increases in expenditure or prices are politically and economically less viable. As many solutions for problems in the quality of life and resource conservation areas—which are considered by many not to be as serious anyway—often involve price or expenditure increases (for instance to encourage energy conservation, or to introduce more stringent pollution control measures), these problems are also less likely to get on the political agenda, unless cheap alternatives ('educating' people; market mechanisms; devolving responsibility) can be found. In Chapters 4 and 5 we will elaborate further on this shift in policy orientation.

Political-institutional Factors
Whether or not conditions are defined as issues or problems, and the weight they get on the government agenda, depend to a large extent on the institutional framework within which policy development occurs. Problems do not arise in a political or institutional vacuum. Some problems have already found recognition and an institutional home in organizational mandates, laws, rules and regulations. New developments, conflicts, or conditions are 'filtered' through this framework. Vested interests in 'old' problems define the nature of 'new' problems, and determine the way they should be dealt with. 'A conclusive way of checking the rise of conflict is simply to provide no arena for it or to create no public agency with power to do anything about it . . . Organization is the mobilization of bias' (Schattschneider, 1960, p. 71). The relative status and power of agencies within the bureaucratic framework is a reflection of the political weight of the societal values that they represent (Bührs, 1991a).

When new developments or conditions do not fit, and cannot be made to fit, into existing institutional patterns, they tend to 'fall between the cracks'. Problems that require solutions falling outside the range of what is considered normal or acceptable are subject to 'nondecision-making' (Bachrach and Baratz, 1961, 1963). Institutional change (for example, the creation of an advocate for conservation) can be regarded as an avenue for providing a home or arena for new problems, but it is hard to achieve and, given institutional inertia and opposition, is not a way that guarantees improved policy performance with regard to such problems (Scharpf, 1986).

There are two outstanding characteristics of New Zealand's political-institutional system that have had an important influence on the development of environmental policy: the dominant role of central governments in the development of resources, and the high degree of concentration of executive power in government (Palmer, 1987).

From early colonial times until recently, the direct involvement of the New Zealand State in the development of resources has been regarded as essential for improving living standards and social welfare. This factor, which will be further elaborated upon in Chapter 4, gave New Zealand governments and government agencies a high stake in development, often at the cost of environmental neglect.

The second factor, the high degree of concentration of executive power in the government, has meant that there have been practically no balancing power centres to restrain the government in pursuing development, despite environmental opposition and costs. Parliament—controlled by the executive (the Cabinet) through strong caucus discipline—and 'toothless' government agencies with environmental responsibilities, have been largely ineffective in this respect, with occasional exceptions. Although the courts play a role in resolving environmental conflicts, their power has been limited by the absence of a written constitution and by the ability of governments to change the law to suit their needs. The role and function of local and regional government in environmental policy and management has, until recently, also been very limited.

One effect of the State's key role in initiating development proposals was that it put the environmental movement in a primarily reactive role. Environmentalists fought one battle after another in efforts to stop or amend such proposals. The environmental agenda, in other words, was very much dominated by the government. This left environmentalists little room, time, or resources to give attention to issues not immediately connected with development proposals in which the government was involved. Such issues have embraced waste management, the management of hazardous substances (including pesticides), private land use practices (leading to, for instance, erosion), and the inefficient use of many resources.

An important implication of the heavy concentration of power in New Zealand's political system is that few avenues exist for putting environmental concerns—or any other concerns for that matter—on the government agenda, particularly from the 'bottom up'. Using the media—perhaps the most important check on governments in New Zealand—and lobbying the central government are the principal mechanisms for those seeking recognition of concerns. Unlike some other political systems, such as in the United States, where power is more dispersed and environmental concerns have many access points to the political agenda—for instance through a bi-cameral Congress, a separate executive, the courts, independent state and local governments, semi-autonomous agencies, and multiple diverse news media—the New Zealand political system is comparatively closed (Richardson, 1982).

Some environmental groups, notably nature conservation groups with considerable support and resources, have developed excellent skills in both using the media and lobbying, thereby achieving success on a number of occasions (Wilson, 1982). Environmental groups with less public support, fewer resources, and lesser political skills—often those focusing on issues other than nature conservation—have found it much more difficult to get their concerns politically recognized. Lack of success over time has encouraged the creation of fewer such organizations.

In connection with the importance of lobbying in the New Zealand political system it is important to mention the three-year election cycle, as it allows for frequent campaigning on issues. Although it is difficult to assess what weight environmental issues have had in elections, politicians—within both government and opposition—have frequently been lured into making promises and amending election manifestos to accommodate the demands of environmentalists.

Some other interest groups, on the other hand, have been in a more advantageous position than environmentalists for getting concerns on the government agenda. Notably, interest groups representing resource owners or exploiters have acquired powerful positions within the institutional framework. In particular, farmers, mining interests, and energy industry interests have all been given a privileged position in the policy process, often in special advisory bodies (or 'quangos'—quasi autonomous non-governmental organizations), such as producer boards, the Pesticides Board, the Fishing Industry Board, and the Liquid Fuels Trust Board. Moreover, many government departments had the promotion of resource development incorporated into their mandates. Even though some had environmental responsibilities as well ('dual mandates'), these were often allocated lower status and priority, and have been less important in the assessment of their performance.

The entrenchment of development interests within the State machinery, putting them in a position of having 'inside access' to the government (Cobb, Ross, and Ross, 1976), has led to major conflicts between State agencies and the conservation movement, particularly after support for that movement grew significantly. It also led to calls by conservationists for institutional change and the establishment of a strong advocate for conservation within the bureaucratic framework. Although the Nature Conservation Council, set up in 1962, did not fulfil conservationists' expectations, it helped draw attention to conservation problems, and augmented the advocacy for conservation within the bureaucratic framework responsible for the management of national parks and wildlife. With the establishment of the Department of Conservation in 1987 as an advocate for conservation, and other reforms, the institutional basis for getting conservation issues on the government agenda has been further strengthened.

Resource conservation (as distinct from nature conservation) issues—such as energy efficiency, minerals, or water conservation—and quality of life issues, which often had a much lower public profile for reasons mentioned above, have never led to the creation of institutional advocates capable of balancing entrenched development interests. Energy efficiency, for instance, has always received meagre institutional backing (Bührs, 1991a, pp. 323–36). The conservation of ferrous minerals for other than nature conservation purposes has never had institutional representation. Water conservation interests (mainly recreational groups) were outstripped by development interests in the institutions responsible for water management (pp. 297–310).

The Health Department, one of the principal agencies in the area of environmental health and quality of life issues, has generally taken a narrow, medically based, view of environmental issues. Like the Agricultural Chemicals (later Pesticides) Board, the Department has often been perceived by environmentalists as colluding with industry interests—particularly in the area of pesticides. The Commission for the Environment did try to get policies off the ground in the areas of resource conservation and packaging, but was largely unsuccessful because of a lack of co-operation, resources, and 'teeth' (pp. 294–354). Although the Ministry for the Environment is in several respects in a better position than its predecessor, its role as an advocate in these matters is formally limited. It relies primarily on voluntary co-operation strategies to make progress (Bührs, 1991b). As yet, unlike in the United States and Britain, there is no integrated pollution control agency in New Zealand with an advocacy role at central government level.

Overall, institutional arrangements in New Zealand have not facilitated the agenda setting of environmental problems, although conservation interests have been relatively more successful in achieving institutional changes to 'balance' environmental and development interests. More recently, significant institutional changes have occurred with the reform of the public service and the introduction of the Resource Management Act. Whether and to what extent these changes will facilitate environmental policy making in New Zealand will be the subject of Chapters 4, 5, and 6.

Convergence
Despite the institutional differences among countries, policy developments in some areas, notably the management of hazardous substances, are remarkably similar (Hoberg, 1986). This suggests that, even though countries may have quite different ways of making policies, they tend to address the same issues and develop similar policies. Convergence, a process by which outside influences induce countries to adopt similar policies, may explain why problems receive political attention despite the weakness, or even absence, of domestic pressures and demands.

Although the occurrence of convergence is not beyond doubt—evidence is mainly confined to a few policy areas and even there is not conclusive (Hoberg, 1986)—and the concept is still in the early stages of theoretical development (Bennet, 1991), there are very plausible grounds for arguing that external factors do play an increasingly important role in the agenda-setting process, as reflected most clearly in the rise of global environmental issues on the political agendas of individual countries. Some of the factors that can be identified are the rise of common problems, the growing interdependence among nations, and the emergence of international policy communities.

Increasingly, environmental problems have manifested an international and even global dimension (Caldwell, 1990a). The transboundary nature of many pollution phenomena has provoked co-operation among nations on such issues as river pollution, acid rain, the pollution of oceans, the management of hazardous substances, ozone depletion, and the greenhouse effect. Although the intensity and effects of these problems differ among countries, their rise on the political agenda may be promoted by what has been occurring in those countries worst affected. Spill-over effects may be most obvious where the potential threat of conditions or developments has become apparent through major accidents or disasters.

It was pointed out earlier in this chapter that the significant increase in attention for pollution issues in New Zealand in the early 1970s can be attributed to such spill-over effects generated by the recognition of serious pollution problems in the United States and European countries, as there was no apparent increase in pollution problems in New Zealand at that time. Similarly, major oil spills, accidents with hazardous substances (such as in Bhopal in 1985), and the Chernobyl disaster are likely to have promoted the recognition of these (potential) problems in many countries other than those immediately affected. Even in New Zealand, despite its clean and green image and seeming remoteness from major pollution sources, there has been a growing awareness that the country is not immune to these problems and their effects.

Closely connected to this is the factor of growing interdependence among nations. Although probably no nation-state has ever been fully autarkic, there has been a global trend towards increased trade and lower levels of self-sufficiency (Brundtland Commission, 1987, pp. 78–80). With increased international trade and traffic, countries have become more interdependent, even the most powerful and resource-rich nations (Hoffmann, 1982). This has also become obvious with regard to the availability of resources, the global ecosystem, and many other major environmental threats facing countries. Again, those who feel most affected by these problems may stir or even force others into recognizing them and to adopt policies (Bennet, 1991).

Despite New Zealand's high degree of interdependence with the rest of the world (for the import of many industrial products and the export of primary products), the effect of this on the recognition of environmental problems is less apparent. Given its relatively isolated position and relatively small contribution to many of the global environmental problems,[9] New Zealand is not subject to pressures similar to those exerted on many other countries because of their closer proximity to each other or their more significant contribution as a source of pollution.

Yet in some areas, given its dependence on exports and imports (pesticides residues regulations; import of cars that require driving on unleaded petrol), New Zealand is also subject to the forces of harmonization. In some other areas—ozone depletion, the Antarctic, driftnet fishing—on the other hand, New Zealanders may be seen as having a strong incentive to press other countries to recognize problems having potentially greater or more immediate effects on the health, security, and resources of the local population. New Zealand's prominent role in international diplomacy on these matters (Palmer, 1990) may have more to do with self-interest than with a desire to take the moral high ground.

Another factor that may help to explain convergence in the agenda setting

---

9. In global terms, New Zealand's contribution to, for example, the greenhouse effect may seem rather insignificant, with 0.1 per cent of the global total. However, per head of population, New Zealanders contribute more to the problem than the global average. Similar observations can be made with regard to the generation of domestic waste, which is on a *per capita* basis one of the highest in the world (Ministry for the Environment and Ministry of External Relations and Trade, 1992, pp. 41, 69).

of environmental issues is the growing internationalization of the environmental policy community. Although non-governmental organizations have traditionally played an important role in the recognition of environmental issues at the international level (Caldwell, 1990a), the intensity and vigour of action by internationally organized environmental pressure groups has increased during the last two decades (McCormick, 1989). In many instances, environmentalists' demands blend with the knowledge and concerns expressed by experts who form an 'epistemic community' on these matters (Haas, 1990, 1992). As a result, domestic environmental groups, as well as environmental agencies, find themselves more and more supported in their agenda-setting efforts by the voice of the international environmental policy community.

In New Zealand, this factor has been most notable in relation to the Antarctic issue, where the role of the Antarctic and Southern Ocean Coalition (ASOC), consisting of two hundred organizations from thirty-eight countries, has been instrumental in shifting the government's position (Rippingale, 1992, pp. 71–3). Greenpeace, an international environmental organization whose campaigns are subject to central direction, has also been involved in getting other issues, such as driftnet fishing, whaling, and the management of hazardous waste, on to the political agenda. In the ozone depletion and greenhouse effect issues, the international epistemic community has played a key role in promoting the recognition of these problems in New Zealand (Benedick, 1991; Ministry for the Environment, 1990).

Despite these growing international influences on the agenda-setting process, domestic pressures and demands are still the predominant factors in the recognition of environmental problems. If there are no domestic groups that are willing or able to exploit international pressures and demands, governments are in a better position to ignore such demands or pay only lip-service to them. The strength of the domestic environmental movement, as well as its orientation, is of crucial importance in having issues politically recognized and translated into substantive policies. As long as policies are made by governments on a national level, international influences in themselves can only inadequately compensate for the gaps or biases in the recognition of environmental problems in a country.

Conclusion

Although New Zealand is widely perceived, both domestically and overseas, as a clean and green country, it is not free from serious environmental problems. The clean and green image stems largely from the perception of four factors: a low overall density of population, a relatively low level of pollution, the existence of large, protected natural areas of scenic splendour, and the predominance of primary products in the country's economy. Yet, on all four counts, qualifications should be made: with the growing concentration of population, notably in the Auckland region, environmental pressures have emerged; the extent of industrial pollution is largely unknown, but it appears significant in at least some areas; most protected natural areas have been established on land which is unsuitable or too inaccessible for economic use; and the exploitation of natural resources has inflicted large-scale destruction or damage on ecosystems and the quality of resources, notably land. Although calling New Zealand a clean and green country does not necessarily imply that there are no environmental problems at all, there are at least as many grounds for dismissing this claim as a myth as there are for supporting it.

A fifth ground for this claim might lie in New Zealand's record in recognizing or preventing environmental problems. But this ground for the 'clean and green' claim is also very shaky at best. Although environmentalists have made major advances in achieving public and government recognition of the need to protect remaining natural ecosystems, they have been less successful in gaining recognition for problems and needs in the areas of resource conservation and the protection of the quality of life in New Zealand, and much less successful in having anticipatory policies adopted. Whether the major institutional changes that have recently been introduced herald a change towards a greater recognition of these problems and the development of anticipatory policies will be discussed in Chapters 4, 5, and 6.

The principal reasons for the apparent unevenness in New Zealand's record in recognizing environmental problems lie in a socio-cultural framework that has proved to be susceptible to the values of nature preservation and has generated large-scale support for the conservation movement. Related to this are the existence of professional and politically skilful lobbyists or conservation policy 'entrepreneurs', the absence of obvious, large-scale pollution disasters, and the compatibility of conservation demands with politically dominant values, especially in the economic sphere. Also important are political-institutional obstacles for the recognition of relatively 'new' environmental problems—such as those related to hazardous substances—and growing external influences on the agenda-setting process, many of which reinforce and extend the orientation of environmentalists and policy makers towards conservation issues (driftnet fishing; the Antarctic; tropical rainforest protection), although they also assist in the recognition of resource conservation and quality of life issues.

Looking back over the last three decades, it can be concluded that the recognition of environmental problems in New Zealand has been selective, biased, and at least in some respects subject to an element of denial related to the 'clean and green' syndrome. The pattern that can be distinguished in the recognition of environmental problems reflects predominant value structures and vested interests that are also embedded in the institutional framework. Whether the second wave of environmentalism which began in the late 1980s signals a shift in fundamental values, providing a basis for a redefinition of the environmental problematique in New Zealand, is the subject of the following chapter.

3
THE GREENING OF NEW ZEALAND
Towards a New Paradigm?

Since the late 1980s a second wave of environmentalism has swept through the world. The first wave, in the early 1970s, failed to bring about the changes required to deal effectively with, or at least allay, the environmental concerns that were raised. On the contrary, the level of concern seems to have reached new heights, fuelled by such events and phenomena as the Chernobyl disaster, the Exxon Valdez oil spill, the discovery of the ozone hole, and the gradual rise in global temperatures believed to be associated with the greenhouse effect. What governments world-wide have been doing to combat environmental degradation has come to be perceived as too little, too late.

The inadequacy of government performance with regard to environmental problems seems to vindicate those in the green movement who argue that a technocentric approach to the environment is not good enough, and that much more radical change in our societies is required to stem the tide of environmental decay. Instead of relying on 'end of the pipe-line' solutions to contain or reduce the *effects* of environmental problems, we need to address their *causes*, which, according to critics, are to be found in the dominant social paradigm (DSP) of modern societies: in our values, lifestyle, ideas of a 'good life', and in our attitudes and behaviour towards nature and resources. This theme, that we need to 'change our ways' in order to avoid self-inflicted global destruction, is the subject of this chapter.

Is New Zealand, the country that gave birth to the first green party, a vanguard in the change towards a new social paradigm? Does the perception of New Zealand as a 'clean and green' country also reflect the prevalence of a clean and green lifestyle, or the existence of a higher level of support for environmental (or postmaterialist) values than in other countries?

In trying to answer these difficult questions, we will first present and discuss some evidence for the growth in support for 'the environment' in New Zealand. Second, we will consider the question of whether this increase signifies a shift towards a new social paradigm. Finally, the limitations of an exclusive focus on values and behaviour in assessing social paradigm change will be discussed.

The 'Greening' of New Zealand

The growing support for environmental values in New Zealand, and a rise in environmentally conscious behaviour, manifest themselves in a variety of ways. First, there has been considerable growth in the support given to environmental groups. Second, considerable support for environmental issues has been expressed in public opinion surveys. Third, in the economic sphere, the phenomenon of 'green consumerism' is gaining in significance. Also, companies seem to pay more attention to environmental matters, for instance in annual reports and through the introduction of environmental auditing. Fourth, in the political sphere, support for the environment has led to the revival of a Green Party and an environmental 'bandwagon' effect with respect to other political parties.

Support for Environmental Organizations

One of the most readily measurable indicators of the rise in support for environmental values can be found in the degree of public support for environmental organizations. Environmental groups are a manifest expression of commitment to 'the environment', and support for those groups can be measured in membership numbers and income from donations, subscriptions, and sales. Figures for some of the major environmental organizations in New Zealand are summarized in Table 3.1 on page 70.

Support for these organizations grew significantly between the mid 1980s and 1991, with Greenpeace showing the most spectacular increase. Greenpeace's success was undoubtedly influenced by the bombing of the *Rainbow Warrior* in Auckland Harbour in 1985 which sparked off a wave of indignation about the French action and boosted sympathy for Greenpeace and its causes, in particular the halting of French nuclear testing in the Pacific. Other organizations, however, have also seen a rise in public support, as reflected in membership numbers and financial income from subscriptions, donations, and sales.

Increased membership and income enable these organizations to appoint more paid staff. In 1992 Forest and Bird had twenty people on the pay-roll (nine in 1985), Greenpeace seventy-four (two in early 1985), and the Maruia Society six. This was in addition to the number of volunteers who also do considerable amounts of work for these organizations (800 for Forest and Bird, 150 for Greenpeace, twelve for the Maruia Society).

It should be noted, however, that the financial base of these organizations remains vulnerable, dependent as it is on public goodwill and support. That a continuation of financial support on past levels cannot be taken for granted is most clearly demonstrated in Greenpeace's case. A significant drop in income brought the organization into the red in 1991, forcing it to take some painful measures.

Table 3.1: Support for environmental groups in New Zealand

Group	Number of members (000)		Income ($NZ 000)	
	1985	1991	1985	1991
Royal Forest and Bird Protection Society	43.8	62.0	358	1,167a
Greenpeace	4.0b	170.0c	453	1,302d
Maruia Society	9.8e	11.8	238e	336
Totals	57.6	243.8	1,049	2,805

a. The figure includes net income from sales.
b. Before the bombing of the *Rainbow Warrior*; after the bombing numbers went up to 11,000 by the end of 1985.
c. Number of 'supporters' (including those who make donations).
d. Income from donations, subscriptions, fundraising, and sales; this dropped from $NZ 2,227 in 1990.
e. Figures for beginning 1989; the Maruia Society was formed in May 1988, merging the Native Forests Action Council (NFAC) and the Environmental Defence Society (EDS).

Sources: Royal Forest and Bird Protection Society of NZ Inc., Annual Reports 1985, 1991; Greenpeace, Annual Reports 1985, 1990, 1991; Belinda Davies, Maruia Society.

Overall, support for environmental groups has significantly increased between 1985 and 1991, and this can be interpreted as a sign of growing environmental awareness. With respect to numbers of members or supporters, these environmental groups are now among the largest interest groups in New Zealand, outstripping various traditionally strong sectoral interest groups such as Federated Farmers (approximately 25,000 members) and trade unions.

Significant growth in membership or support for environmental groups is not purely a New Zealand phenomenon, but has also occurred in other countries. For instance, between 1980 and 1989 membership of—selected—environmental groups more than doubled in Britain (McCormick, 1991,

p. 152), and tripled in the US (Mitchell, 1990, p. 92). Measured between 1985 and 1991, membership growth in New Zealand has been bigger—more than fourfold with regard to the three organizations mentioned in Table 3.1. Even more than in Britain and the United States, much of that growth was concentrated in just one organization, Greenpeace. Between 1989 and 1991, membership of Greenpeace New Zealand saw a spectacular increase from 48,500 to 170,000, which makes it one of the biggest national branches of the organization in the world, and probably the biggest in proportion to population (UNEP, 1991, p. 399).

Comparing environmental membership between countries—and even organizations—is, however, a tricky procedure. Apart from the difficulty, in this case, of different years having been used to measure growth in membership, there may also be a significant element of multiple counting, as individuals may be members of more than one organization. There is also the problem that organizations use different criteria in defining membership—from formal membership registration and subscriptions to the organization's journal to the donation of money. And counting membership of selected, national organizations does not necessarily indicate the strength of support for grass-roots organizations.

Given these problems, and the probability that direct membership of environmental groups is confined to a particular section of the public, it is necessary to rely on other indicators as well to gauge the level of public support for environmental values in society.

Public Opinion on Environmental Issues
There have not been many studies of the degree of concern or support for environmental matters in New Zealand. Only a few opinion surveys have been conducted addressing these matters, and their results are summarized below.

In 1980, a survey found that 59% of New Zealanders expressed a preference for a moderate emphasis on growth in economic living standards and limited emphasis on growth in social-environmental living standards. Although only 7% put a strong emphasis on growth in economic living standards, and no emphasis on social-environmental living standards, there was also not much support—only 13%—for the 'green' option, i.e., no emphasis on growth in economic living standards and strong emphasis on growth in social-environmental living standards (Murphy, 1980, pp. 1–10).

The 1989 New Zealand Study of Values (Gold and Webster, 1990) included questions on attitudes towards the environment and found that protection for the environment came third in the ranking of priorities among social goals for New Zealand. Environmental protection was considered to be 'most important' by 11% of the respondents, after reducing unemployment (45%), and maintaining law and order (15%), but before living standards (9%). When first and second priorities were combined, environmental protection came in fourth position with 24%, after lower unemployment (68%), law and order (36%), and fighting crime (30%), but again before living standards (22%). Environmental protection was also seen as an urgent problem requiring immediate attention by 85% of the respondents. This was backed up by 64% who also expressed the view that an increase in government spending was needed in this area.

Support for environmental protection in this survey is more controversial, however, than for other top priorities, in the sense that there is more disagreement along political party lines (more support from Labour voters and non-voters than from National voters), by age groups (more support from the young and middle-aged than from older people), and by educational level (more support from the higher educated). These findings concur with overseas findings in identifying political orientation, age, and education as the most important discriminatory factors with regard to environmental support (Dunlap and Van Liere, 1978).

A third survey, undertaken in 1989, covered behaviour, especially consumer behaviour, as well as opinions regarding the environment (Colmar and Brunton Research, 1989). On the basis of the responses, the researchers identified four consumer segments. The first group, 28% of the respondents, were labelled the 'Deep Greens', comprising those people who hold strong environmental attitudes, even to the extent that they find the environment 'the most important issue'. These people make big personal efforts to translate this view into their behaviour (recycling, buying organic food, avoiding products sold in plastic packaging). They are prepared to pay more for environmentally friendly products, and try to learn more about environmental issues. They watch little TV, but read books and information magazines, are socially and culturally active, and go for walks or tramps. Most of these people are female (72%), well-educated, and on high incomes.

The second segment, 22% of the respondents, were characterized as 'Green Pragmatists'. This group comprises those who are concerned about environmental issues, particularly those that affect themselves, but who do not go to the same length as the first group to translate their views into behaviour. People in this category are inclined to regard environmental issues as transient, and less important than unemployment. These people tend to be older, poorly educated by today's standards, and belong to the lower socio-economic class. They are often retired people, who have grown up in a world where thrift and avoiding waste were important.

The third segment, 25% of the respondents, were called 'Green Faddists'.

They consist of people who are not really interested in green issues, but who conform to environmental behaviour not requiring much effort, such as using ozone friendly sprays, and buying other products labelled as environmentally friendly. These people are fashion conscious, run electronic appliances, and use plastic cards. They rely on TV as their main information source, watch videos, eat takeaways, and are socially active. They tend to be younger (under forty), have middle to high incomes, and live in households with school-age children.

The fourth segment identified in the Colmar and Brunton survey are the 'Green Indifferents', 25% of the respondents. They have the least knowledge of green or social issues and the least interest in knowing about them. They belong to the lower socio-economic class, are generally poorly educated, punch the timeclock, and live from pay packet to pay packet. Two thirds of this group are males.

Another result coming from the poll was that most respondents laid the responsibility for solving environmental problems with governments, whereas only 8% felt an individual responsibility to address these issues. An even smaller segment, 5%, indicated a preparedness to participate in various forms of protest action to support environmental issues.

A fourth poll, conducted by NBR–Mattingly in October 1991, asked four questions: (1) 'Is New Zealand currently protected adequately in terms of environmental issues?'; (2) 'Do environmental groups receive too much publicity?'; (3) 'Do you think that concern for the environment is costing New Zealand jobs?'; and (4) 'Do you think that environmentalists are going too far in their demands?'

Of those interviewed in the NBR poll, 55% thought that New Zealand is currently not adequately protected in terms of environmental issues, against 34% who found that it was. With regard to the second and fourth questions, more than 60% did not think that environmental groups receive too much publicity, or that environmentalists are excessive in their demands. More divided were the answers to the question on employment, with 47% thinking that concern for the environment costs jobs, and 40% believing that it did not.

Dissatisfaction among NBR respondents with the degree of protection was greater among females than males (59% as against 50%), and greatest in the 35–39 age group (67% compared to 61% of 18–24 year olds and 43% in the 55 plus age group). Satisfaction was lower among higher income groups (47% of those earning $45,000 as against 57% with an income less than that) and among Labour voters (59% dissatisfied compared to 45% of National voters). Again, political orientation, age, and sex come forward as discriminatory factors, but income also emerges as an explanatory factor.

Although these data hardly warrant the making of strong generalizations about the degree of concern or support for environmental matters in New Zealand, they indicate that concern and support are not confined to those directly supporting environmental groups. Many people apparently agree with environmental groups that current policies do not go far enough, and that something 'more' or 'else' is needed. The data, however, provide no insight into how much 'more' or what 'else' New Zealanders are in favour of, but seem to confirm overseas findings that environmental issues are not as salient as other (e.g. economic or security) issues and that environmental opinions are not as intensely held as other opinions. This is reflected in the relative ranking of environmental issues in the polls and in the preparedness of few people to join in protest action (Dunlap, 1989; Mitchell, 1990). Also, most people think that this is an area in which governments and other agencies rather than they themselves carry prime responsibility.

Because there are no comparative studies or polls which include New Zealand, it is difficult to say whether public opinion regarding environmental issues in New Zealand differs greatly from that in other countries. International surveys indicate that in many countries the level of public concern about the environment is high, and has significantly increased during the 1980s (Dunlap, Gallup and Gallup, 1992; OECD, 1985; UNEP, 1991). In many OECD countries around fifty per cent or more of the public indicate that they are 'very concerned' about national and international environmental problems (OECD, 1991, pp. 270–1). In 1985, a majority of the public in nine out of ten selected western countries gave priority to environmental protection above economic growth, even at a time of adverse economic conditions (OECD, 1985, p. 265). In 1992, a Gallup poll covering 22,000 people in twenty-two countries found that a majority of people in twenty countries favoured putting the environment ahead of economic growth (*The Press*, 7 May 1992; Dunlap, Gallup, and Gallup, 1992). Whether people in New Zealand share that view is not known. Although a slightly larger proportion of people in New Zealand assign the 'most importance' category to environmental protection than to living standards—24% as against 22% if first and second priorities are combined—this is no conclusive evidence that a majority will hold this view if a choice between only these two values must be made. As the New Zealand Values Survey indicates, the highest priority for most New Zealanders is lowering unemployment, something which is commonly associated with economic growth.[1] Yet, perhaps economic growth

---

1. In 1992 this was confirmed by a Morgan poll that found that nearly half of New Zealand voters regarded reducing unemployment as the most important political issue facing them in an election, followed by improving education and hospitals (both mentioned by 33%), promoting industry and business growth (20%),

and environmental protection are seen as becoming more compatible with the greening of the economy?

A Greening of the Economy?
Other indicators of increased support for environmental values can be found in the economy. One such indicator is the phenomenon of 'green consumerism', the sale of products or services that are considered to be 'environmentally friendly'. More and more products are advertised as being 'green' and 'good for the environment', ranging from spray cans containing no fluorocarbons as accelerants, to unleaded petrol, unbleached products, organically grown fruit and vegetables, fuel-economic cars, and less noisy aeroplanes.

As an indicator for measuring commitment to environmental values 'green consumerism' is attractive, particularly because it connects commitment with *behaviour* as well as values. It provides people with an opportunity to *do* something about environmental protection on a day-to-day basis, and there is no doubt that changing consumer behaviour can be a potent force inducing producers to change their practices.

Whether products or services praised by producers as 'green' or 'environmentally friendly' deserve to carry that label is, of course, subject to debate. It is a complex and contentious issue, with uneasy cut-off points between genuine commitment and commercial exploitation. 'Green consumer guides' try to provide guidance, and the New Zealand Government, following the example of various other countries, recently introduced an environmental labelling scheme, 'environmental choice' (Minister for the Environment, 1992). Of course, for the sake of measuring environmental *support*, it does not matter whether a product or service is 'really' green or not. It is the fact that people buy products which are *perceived* to be 'green', partly because of marketing activities, that counts.

The Colmar and Brunton study referred to above found that, in the twelve months prior to the survey, 60% of the New Zealand population had used ozone friendly spray, 49% had returned bottles to bottle banks, and 41% had used products with environmentally friendly labels. Also, 31% had refused to use products harmful to the environment, 26% had eaten organically grown food, and 25% had made a big effort to buy green products. Such figures suggest that a sizeable proportion of people in New Zealand already engage in various forms of 'green' behaviour and 'green consumerism'.

---

increasing overseas trade and exports (14%), and managing the environment and more social spending (both 12%). Reducing the size and cost of government trailed with 11%. (*The Press*, 31 July 1992).

Even more problematic is measuring the degree of 'green producerism'. Although more and more products are advertised as 'environmentally friendly', data on the sales of such products are hard to obtain. Many companies are secretive about the commercial record of these products. In an effort to obtain some data in this area, we asked twenty-five companies in New Zealand to provide gross sales figures of products that they considered to be 'green'. Most companies did not respond. Only two companies were prepared to release some figures, six responded that data on these matters were confidential, and one said that no figures on 'green' products in particular could be given because all its products were 'green'.

In New Zealand's National Report to the United Nations Conference on Environment and Development (Ministry for the Environment and Ministry of External Relations and Trade, 1992, p. 92), reference is made to an increasing receptivity in private enterprise to community desires for environmental responsibility. Support for that statement is provided in the form of examples, ranging from the elimination of CFCs and the introduction of equipment for controlling water and air pollution to the contribution of financial support for wildlife conservation (the kakapo and the kiwi). But apart from the fact that various of these examples are likely to have been inspired by existing or anticipated legal requirements, or by a desire to polish a company's image, they are no indication of a more structural change in corporate behaviour.

Goodwin and Hille (1992) undertook a more systematic effort to measure corporate support for environmental values through a study of the annual reports of corporations. Environmental constraints and opportunities affect corporate performance, and the treatment of such matters in annual reports can be interpreted as an indication of a company's environmental awareness. Scrutiny of the annual reports of thirty-nine of the top forty companies in New Zealand found that only fourteen companies made reference to environmental issues, whereas twenty-five did not mention the environment at all. Six companies referred to environmental issues in passing ('minimal coverage') and another three included a statement implying some commitment to the environment, whereas four reports encompassed a more detailed discussion of environmental matters. Only one company, however, gave a comprehensive coverage of environmental issues, and expressed a commitment to the principle of sustainability. The study noted that the level of environmental reporting by companies in New Zealand compared unfavourably with that of some other countries, notably the United Kingdom and the United States.

These findings are confirmed in a comparative study of the priority given by chief executives in New Zealand and Canada to research topics, which showed that the environment ranked only twentieth on the New Zealand chief executives' list, compared to fourth on the Canadian list (Cartner, 1991).

The relatively low priority of environmental values in the corporate sector in New Zealand is also reflected in the practice of environmental auditing in New Zealand. Corporate environmental auditing refers to the assessment of environmental aspects of a company's activities. It can take place on various levels, ranging from assessing the extent of compliance with regulatory standards ('first stage'), and assessing compliance with a company's own environmental policy ('second stage'), to assessing company activities on the basis of the principle of sustainability ('third stage' or 'cradle to grave' auditing).

According to a survey of environmental auditing practices in New Zealand, only 35% of the companies responding appeared to have well-developed auditing programmes. The main reasons why companies engage in environmental auditing are to verify compliance with regulations (40%) or to avoid costs by identifying risks (35%). Only 10% see it as a means of minimizing environmental impacts or assessing environmental sustainability of company practices—and most of the companies in this minority category are foreign owned. The study concludes that New Zealand owned companies lag behind in the development of environmental auditing compared to overseas owned companies (Lambert, 1991b).

Overall, the level of support for environmental values amongst New Zealand companies is not very high. Many companies apparently still need to discover that being environmentally aware can also mean good business. Very few have made a commitment to putting their operations on an environmentally sustainable footing.

The Greening of Politics
New Zealand was one of the first countries to give birth to a green party, the Values Party, established in 1972. Despite a good showing in the elections of 1972 and, particularly, 1975, the party, obstructed by the electoral 'first past the post' system, never gained a seat in Parliament and gradually withered away, plagued by internal divisions and declining public support.

But amid the second wave of global environmentalism a new Green Party arose from the ashes of the Values Party in 1990. Six months after it came into being, the party gained 6.9% of the votes in the national elections, an impressive result considering that it had fielded candidates in only seventy-one of ninety-seven electorates and that it had hardly produced an election programme.

In February 1992 the Greens joined forces with other small parties in an 'Alliance' to contest the Tamaki by-election. The Alliance candidate, a

Democrat, came close to defeating the National Party candidate in this traditional National stronghold. Given the success of the Alliance, also reflected in the election of some of its candidates in regional council by-elections, this coalition of smaller parties may become a permanent feature on the political landscape, and a serious contender for the 1993 elections. Given the presence of the Greens in the formation of the Alliance and the strong environmental programme adopted along with an egalitarian philosophy by the NewLabour Party, the Alliance may evolve into a strong green/red force in New Zealand politics.

The greening of politics in New Zealand is also reflected in the fact that both National and Labour now assign considerable space in their manifestos to environmental issues, trying to outdo each other in presenting a green image. In government between 1984 and 1990, Labour initiated a large-scale reform of environmental legislation and administration, leading to, among other things, the establishment of three new environmental agencies and the introduction of the Resource Management Act.[2] In 1990 National, trying to outbid Labour, promised, among other things, to reduce carbon dioxide emissions faster than Labour (20% by the year 2000 instead of 2005), and to generate thousands of jobs on the basis of a 'Task Force Green' programme, involving wage subsidies for projects benefiting the environment.

However genuine the commitment of politicians to environmental goals and values, green demands and interests have become a force to be reckoned with. People expect governments to take these problems seriously. More than ever, environmental concerns have created a bandwagon effect, even in a time of economic recession and mass unemployment. Indeed, it would appear that the rise of environmental values on the political priority list of the public and politicians represents a significant shift away from traditional dominant values towards a new social paradigm.

A Shift towards a New Social Paradigm?

As briefly discussed earlier in Chapter 1, the contention that the rise in support for environmental values is part of, or contributes to, a shift towards a new social paradigm has become a familiar claim in the literature (Cotgrove, 1982; Dunlap and Van Liere, 1978; Inglehart, 1977, 1990; Milbrath, 1984). The argument can be approached from two sides. On the one hand, the growing

---

2. Although the Act was passed by the National Government in 1991, the bulk of its substance was produced under the previous Labour Government. The new agencies were a Ministry for the Environment (replacing a Commission for the Environment), a Parliamentary Commissioner for the Environment, and a Department of Conservation (see Chapter 5).

support for environmental values can be seen as part of a broader development towards 'postmaterialist' values and towards a culture change caused by an increase in physical and material security. On the other hand, it can be argued that environmentalism itself is a driving force behind the development of a new social paradigm.

Inglehart, a leading analyst of the first line of argument, argues that there is a demonstrable change in culture in societies which enjoy a high level of physical and material security. Materialist values such as economic growth, higher incomes, and strong defence have diminishing marginal appeal, and other values such as participation, freedom of speech, and protection of the environment, become more important. A generation that has grown up in prosperity and security will continue to embrace postmaterialist values, despite temporary set-backs in material living conditions. Cultural change occurs slowly as postmaterialist generations move through the life cycle (Inglehart, 1977, 1981, 1990).

The second line of argument is not incompatible with the first, but puts greater emphasis on environmentalism as an independent variable in the shift towards a new paradigm. Environmentalism—embodying a growing recognition that people need fundamentally to change their values and lifestyles if continuing environmental degradation, or even environmental catastrophe, is to be avoided—is a driving force behind cultural change. In this view, a shift towards postmaterialist values, although perhaps partly resulting from conditions of physical and economic security, springs also from a genuine concern about environmental degradation and from a recognition that existing lifestyles are unsustainable (Eckersley, 1989; Milbrath, 1984; Ophuls, 1977; Paehlke, 1989).

One major difficulty with the paradigm shift thesis is that of defining and measuring what 'old' and 'new' paradigms are. The terms materialist and postmaterialist are open to different interpretations. Flanagan, for instance, argues that Inglehart's classification mixes three distinctive types of item, namely libertarian/postmaterialist (e.g. participation, freedom of speech, tolerance of minorities, environmental protection), materialist (e.g. economic growth, high income, comfortable life), and authoritarian (e.g. strong defence, law and order, patriotism, and discipline). Given that the questions which Inglehart uses to measure materialism comprise materialist and authoritarian items, his findings confuse a trend towards non-materialism (defined in terms of the relative priority attached to economic issues), with a shift from authoritarian towards libertarian values (Flanagan, 1987).

The difficulty of defining social paradigms also becomes apparent when environmentalists who advocate a shift towards a new paradigm try to identify the core values that should underlie such a paradigm. Although many authors have identified the central values associated with old and new paradigms (see e.g. Colby, 1990; Cotgrove, 1982; Milbrath, 1984; Ophuls, 1977; O'Riordan, 1981; Paehlke, 1989), Cotgrove's assessment—that, apart from the agreement that fundamental changes are needed in contemporary societies, the consensus among environmentalists evaporates—seems to a large extent valid (Cotgrove, 1982, p. 102). In particular, environmentalists disagree about the degree of control over individual liberties that is required, and there are divisions between 'deep' and 'shallow' environmentalists with regard to the place to be allocated to humans in the natural and societal order (Devall, 1980; Ophuls, 1977). As an ideology, environmentalism is influenced by, and compatible with, the three classical ideologies of liberalism, conservatism, and socialism, none of which has 'an exclusive claim on environmental wisdom' (Paehlke, 1989, p. 103). Environmentalists struggle with the problem of how to organize the economy (what place to give to the free market?), and with issues such as economic growth (in particular with regard to developing countries), the distribution of resources and income (property rights, equity), and decentralization (enhancing community control in the face of a concentration of power, also on a global scale). There is, therefore, no clear yardstick for measuring a shift in the direction of a new paradigm.

Another problem with regard to measuring paradigm shift is that there may be discrepancies between expressed values (e.g. through a questionnaire), and behaviour. As noted by Dunlap and Van Liere (1978), 'the link between attitudes and behaviour is often rather tenuous, especially when dealing with very general attitudes such as those embodied in the NEP (New Environmental Paradigm)'. The problem, although acknowledged by analysts, has received little attention in the form of work on the development of alternative indicators for paradigm change. Analysts of paradigm change continue to rely primarily on survey techniques measuring value change, apparently assuming, with Milbrath, that expressed values rather than behaviour are more likely to reflect what people 'really' believe (Milbrath, 1984, pp. 17–18). But the relation between values and behaviour is not unidirectional. Behaviour is also subject to institutional constraints, and it seems to make little sense to discuss whether paradigm shift occurs without assessing the extent to which institutions also change. We will return to this issue in the next section.

What then, is the significance of the rise in support for environmental values in New Zealand indicated in the previous section?

With regard to values or attitudes, it should be noted that none of the surveys referred to above was based on Inglehart's model; and this makes comparison in terms of the degree of support for postmaterialism in New Zealand problematic. Nevertheless, the New Zealand Study of Values provides a basis for some useful comparisons with surveys analysed by Inglehart (1990).

A question about priorities among social goals in the New Zealand Study of Values contained authoritarian (law and order, fight crime), materialist (lower unemployment, living standards), and postmaterialist items (environmental protection, more say in government, and civil freedoms and liberties). The highest priority was given to lower unemployment (45%), but raising living standards received only a 9% score. If the scores for *first and second* priorities are combined, materialist values score 90%, authoritarian values 66%, and postmaterialist values 46% (Gold and Webster, 1990, Table 1.2).

Compared with the weighted results of surveys in nine West European countries in 1988, New Zealand scores higher on support for materialist items (90% compared to 66%), higher on authoritarian items (66% compared to 53%), but considerably lower on postmaterialist items (46% compared to 80%). The total score for materialist support in Inglehart's definition (comprising materialist and authoritarian items) is 156 for New Zealand, and 119 for the European countries. These figures suggest that the support for postmaterialist values in New Zealand is considerably lagging behind that in some West European countries (Gold and Webster, 1990, Table 1.2; Inglehart, 1990, p. 98).

Table 3.2: Degree of support for postmaterialist values in New Zealand

Scale	Degree of support	Percentage of respondents
0	Only 'materialist' choices	12.5
1	Only one postmaterialist goal in top four, rated fourth priority	23.8
2	Only one postmaterialist goal among top three choices	49.6
3	Two postmaterialist goals among top three choices, but neither as first	4.4
4	Two postmaterialist goals among top three choices, one of which first	8.1
5	Only postmaterialist goals in top three choices	1.5
Total		99.9

Although the NZSV survey does not provide the data to allow the calculation of the exact proportion of materialists and postmaterialists in New Zealand according to Inglehart's criteria (those whose first two priorities are either materialist or postmaterialist), a modified postmaterialism index (*vis-à-vis* the index used by Inglehart) can be constructed. Using three choices—creating individual freedoms and civil liberties, protecting the environment, and giving people more say in government decisions—as an indication of postmaterialist support, six classes of support (on a scale from 0 to 5) for postmaterialist values can be identified.[3] The results are summarized in Table 3.2.

Only those who score 4 and 5 on this scale can with reason be labelled as postmaterialists,[4] which implies that at most just under 10% (9.6%) of New Zealand's population would fall into that category. According to Inglehart's 1986–87 data, the Netherlands, with 25%, has the highest proportion of postmaterialists in the total population, followed by West Germany with 24%, Denmark with 18%, and the United States with 16%. Compared with the twelve countries surveyed by Inglehart, New Zealand is at the tail end together with Ireland (9%), Greece (8%) and Portugal (6%) (Inglehart, 1990, p. 93).

On the other hand, however, it appears that New Zealanders share the views of many people in other countries with regard to the need for social change. Fully 64% of New Zealanders agree with the statement that our society must be improved through gradual reforms (compared to 73% in Britain, the U.S., Belgium, France, and Italy, 69% in Denmark and Luxembourg, 59% in West Germany, and 50% in Norway). There is even a rather large proportion in New Zealand in favour of radical change (14%), compared to less than 10% in eighteen out of twenty-two surveyed countries in Inglehart's study, putting New Zealand in line with countries like Mexico, Argentina, and Portugal (12, 13, and 14% respectively) (Inglehart, 1990, p. 39). At the other end of the spectrum, 22% of the New Zealand public wants to preserve the status quo or return to the traditional ways of the past (9 and 13% respectively) (Gold and Webster, 1990, Table 1.1). It appears, however, that the desire for reform in New Zealand refers more to political and economic change (the macro dimension) than to a change of morals or values (the micro dimension). On

---

3. We are very grateful to Hyam Gold of the Department of Politics of Monash University for providing us with this information.
4. As Inglehart labels only those whose two top choices are postmaterialist as postmaterialists, it is appropriate to exclude those whose first choice is not postmaterialist from this category. Those scoring 3 on this scale are more appropriately included in the 'mixed' category of Inglehart's classification. Probably even some of those scoring 4 on this scale would need to be classified in the 'mixed' category. But as the top score of 5 is more restrictive than Inglehart's postmaterialist criteria (three postmaterialist goals amongst first three choices versus two such goals in the first two choices), the proportion of postmaterialists according Inglehart's criteria is likely to be somewhere between 1.5 and 9.6%.

the basis of questions regarding morality issues, the authors of the NZSV report conclude that there is 'a strong strain of moral conservatism in New Zealand concerning matters of personal lifestyle' (Gold and Webster, 1990, pp. 25–6).

One area in which change on the micro level has been studied in New Zealand is that of consumer behaviour. The Colmar and Brunton survey identified 28% of the respondents as 'deep green', indicating a preparedness to go to considerable lengths to purchase environmentally friendly goods and services. Such behaviour, however, does not necessarily imply or coincide with a significant change in lifestyle. Green consumerism is not incompatible with materialist values, and may even contribute to a rise in consumption (e.g. by the sale of pollution control devices added to cars). It also occurs among the 'pragmatists' and 'faddists' in the survey. Although green consumerism is an expression of growing concern about the environment, it is not necessarily an indication of a change in behaviour on the basis of postmaterialist values. The proportion of 'deep greens' identified in the Colmar and Brunton survey does not tell us the proportion of postmaterialists in the New Zealand population.

Also the NBR–Mattingly survey does not provide data to support claims about a paradigm shift. Although the data could be interpreted as a sign that there is significant support in New Zealand for the introduction of tougher environmental policies (with 55% saying that New Zealand is not adequately protected in terms of environmental issues, and more than 60% indicating that environmental groups do not go too far in their demands), we do not learn what, or how much, change New Zealanders want, or whether people are prepared to accept changes that would require a change in lifestyle or behaviour based on environmental or postmaterialist values. The question as to whether people think that concern for the environment is costing jobs (40%, yes; 47%, no) is not necessarily an indication of whether they are prepared to make trade-offs in this respect.

With regard to the upsurge in support for the environment in the political arena, one should be cautious not to equate the support for a Green Party with support for environmental issues, let alone for a shift in social paradigm. Given the nature of the electoral system in New Zealand, it is likely that at least part of that support is inspired more by dissatisfaction with the Government of the day than with a commitment to green issues. For instance, an NBR poll found that, despite the enormous upsurge in support for the Alliance in the Tamaki by-election, 63% of that support came from protest voters (*National Business Review*, 14 February 1992). The move in voting behaviour away from the two main parties is also a reflection of growing disillusion with politics and the political system in New Zealand.

More direct support for the postmaterialist thesis can be found in a poll among Green Party activists. The survey, conducted by Vowles and Miller, revealed that the value commitment of Green Party activists fits the postmaterialist model, although imperfectly. Green Party activists, apart from being advocates for stronger environmental protection and proponents of reduced government spending on defence, are also overwhelmingly liberal, supporting social change that favours minority groups. But they are suspicious of trade unions and ambivalent about the welfare state. In this respect they distinguish themselves from activists of the NewLabour Party, also a party with a strong pro-environmental profile. The Greens, however, eminently fit the social profile of postmaterialists: predominantly of the post-war generation, tertiary educated, relatively affluent, and belonging to the 'new' middle class (Miller, 1991).[5]

Apart from this, very little is known about the environmental attitudes of particular groups such as industrialists, government officials, trade unionists, and politicians in New Zealand. The data available on environmental attitudes in the corporate sector, discussed in the previous section, indicate that environmental commitment in this sector is shallow, and that environmental values do not have a high priority. If considered, environmental aspects primarily serve commercial interests (enhancing image, avoiding costs).

Overall, available data indicate that most New Zealanders do not (yet) give a higher priority to environmental or postmaterialist values than to materialist values. Despite a high level of concern about environmental issues (particularly global ones), environmental problems do not receive a greater priority than reducing unemployment, maintaining law and order, and fighting crime, and are seen as only slightly more important than raising living standards. Postmaterialist values other than environmental protection, such as 'more say in Government' and 'civil freedoms and liberties', receive very little support (Gold and Webster, 1990, pp. 3–4).

The data seem to confirm Dunlap's assessment (1989) that environmental values, although considered important by many people, are not held intensely enough to have significant electoral impact. Most people continue to vote on the basis of other, more intensely held, values (economic, security-related). Consequently, governments may well enjoy more flexibility ('permissive consensus') in this area than in more prominent policy areas, and will be

---

5. In part, the 'imperfect fit' may be due to the fact that values other than those used by Inglehart were used as proxy for postmaterialism. This raises the broader question of what values are appropriate for measuring 'postmaterialism', and to what extent these are inter-culturally comparable.

electorally punished only if they are perceived as explicitly trampling environmental values (Dunlap, 1989).

A question emerging from this assessment of the greening phenomenon in New Zealand is, what does the rise in support for environmental values actually signify? If not a shift in paradigm, is it a temporary phenomenon that is bound to fade if environmental concerns are given more serious attention by governments? (Dunlap, 1989) Will concerns about policy failure in this area be accommodated by a continuation of the pragmatist or technocentric approach to environmental problems that has been predominant so far? Or will the growth in support for environmental values continue and deepen, possibly leading to a shift in social paradigm in the longer term?

The Prospects for Paradigm Change

Following Inglehart's theory, the discrepancy between New Zealand and other western countries in the degree of support for postmaterialist values could be explained on the basis of economic factors. Although most western countries have experienced economic set-backs since the 1960s, New Zealand has seen a dramatic relative decline in its economic status amongst OECD countries from second (in GNP per capita) in the 1960s to nineteenth in 1992 (OECD, 1992). Whereas in other western countries postmaterialist support may have grown because of a continuation of prosperity and security for most of the younger generation, support for postmaterialist values among the generation growing up in New Zealand during the same period would not have kept pace, due to that generation's experience of a decline in prosperity and economic security.

Given the fact that New Zealand's economic plight has, despite radical policy changes, continued to deteriorate (certainly in terms of employment, a vital element in experiencing economic security), and because of the hugely unsettling effects of social policies introduced by both Labour and National Governments since 1984, one would even expect a decline in support for postmaterialist values and a further strengthening of materialist values. Although a proportion of the generation that has grown up in relative prosperity and security may continue to adhere to postmaterialist values, there is little basis, if we rely on Inglehart's theory, for expecting much support for such values among the generation that passes through its formative years in the present social and economic climate.

Economic conditions, however, seem to explain only part of the shift towards postmaterialism. Although some countries, such as Germany, have experienced economic conditions much more favourable than those in New Zealand, support for postmaterialist values in those countries has still not exceeded a minority, even among those age groups that have enjoyed high levels of security. The highest proportion of postmaterialists among age groups in the surveys discussed by Inglehart is found among the fifteen to twenty-four year olds in Germany (in 1986–87), but is not higher than 35% (Inglehart, 1990, p. 93). Among occupational groups, the highest proportion of postmaterialists is expected to be found in the more secure professional and executive occupations, but here also, in the surveys covered by Inglehart, the proportion of postmaterialists does not exceed 50%; rather, it varies between 20 and 30% in the countries with a higher economic standing than New Zealand, including Germany, the Netherlands, and Canada (p. 164). In other words, a high level of economic prosperity or security is not a sufficient condition for inducing a shift towards postmaterialist values.[6] Clearly, other factors play a role, and prevent *most* people from adopting such values.

In order to explain this phenomenon it is useful to return to the question, first raised in Chapter 1, of the relationship between values and behaviour and their relation to institutions. Although it is true that people may be led to change their attitudes because of a change in conditions, such as prosperity and security, their values and behaviour are influenced by other factors as well. Notable among such factors are *social institutions*, culturally ingrained rules, norms, conventions, procedures, and practices that allow, facilitate, prescribe, discourage, or prohibit behaviour. Institutions are socializing agents that tend to have a life of their own. They are enduring and, given their collective or social nature, not easily changed. They crystallize in symbols and organizations, and, because of the emotional appeal and vested interests they engender, they often survive dramatic changes in conditions (March and Olsen, 1984).

Although a focus on institutions is nothing new (sociology derives much of its existence from their recognition), it can be argued that their importance has only recently been rediscovered in the study of politics and policy (March and Olsen, 1989). That rediscovery is partly due to the perceived shortcomings of approaches which have for a long time prevailed in the study of politics and policy, notably pluralism. Pluralism, with its emphasis on the demand side of the political process, has paid little attention to institutions (Nordlinger, 1981, 1988). Furthermore, explanations of political behaviour based on assumptions of individual egoism, such as those found, for example, in public choice theory, have tended to present a distorted view of institutions, regarding

---

6. An even stronger rejection of Inglehart's thesis can be found in a recent study based on surveys in the United States and West Germany which found no strong correlation between economic conditions and materialist or postmaterialist values. See Trump (1991).

them as rather malleable, subject to manipulation or reform for the purpose of achieving desired goals (March and Olsen, 1989). Although it may be true that many efforts of institutional, and particularly organizational, change have been undertaken by governments, it is also true that many of these efforts have proved to be failures in terms of the goals that they set out to achieve (March and Olsen, 1983, 1984, 1989; Scharpf, 1986). Conventions, practices, informal rules, and vested interests may continue to exert important influence despite organizational change.

In all spheres of life institutions impose constraints on changing values and behaviour, from the spheres of leisure and fashion to the realms of work and politics. Although people may indicate their support for particular values, this does not necessarily mean that they behave in conformance with those values. People may, for example, support the view that it is environmentally preferable to use public transport instead of private cars, yet never or seldom do it. Some consumer behaviour is subject to deeply ingrained cultural habits and conventions, e.g. with regard to what should be on the menu, or to what are considered to be the ingredients of a 'good life'.

On the other hand, people may engage in forms of 'green' activity without a commitment to fundamental value change. For instance, recycling may be inspired by economic motives (fundraising for school or club-activities), and may have little to do with the idea that we need to change our lifestyles. Similarly, those who cannot afford a car and use public transport may very well prefer to go by private car. It is plausible that surveys are more likely to reveal what people 'really' want or value; however, we need to look beyond these preferences and examine behaviour in its institutional context in order to assess what people can or cannot do, are induced to do, or are prevented from doing.

Likewise, producer behaviour, under capitalist conditions, operates from the bottom line that profit must be made in order to survive, with consequences for the choice of materials, technology, and durability (from shelf-life to built-in obsolescence). Ultimately, where environmentally desirable behaviour clashes with the need to minimize costs and maximize revenue and profit, the environment will lose out. As a system, capitalism needs continued growth, even though such growth may increasingly be in the form of goods and services that require fewer physical resources ('angelization'). Under capitalism, people's lifestyles will continue to evolve on the basis of the need to sell 'more'.

If green consumerism and producerism are subject to institutional constraints, so is political behaviour. Despite the considerable support for the Green Party in New Zealand, it is unlikely that, without a reform of the electoral system, the Party (or the Alliance) will obtain a significant number of seats in Parliament, let alone participate in a government. Under the 'first past the post' system it is very difficult to overcome the 'wasted vote' syndrome, except in special circumstances. Not surprisingly, small parties in New Zealand see the introduction of a form of proportional representation as essential for their long-term survival.

Given the key role played by institutions in guiding people's values and behaviour, the question of whether paradigmatic change occurs cannot be answered by counting only the numbers of individuals who express support for new values. Real social change takes place only when the criteria for 'normal' or desirable behaviour, as defined by institutions, change. An assessment of paradigm change, therefore, must also encompass institutional analysis to find out how institutions and institutional changes facilitate or obstruct a change of values and behaviour, or how they accommodate new demands arising from new conditions.

Moreover, the use of the concept of paradigmatic change to identify a gradual process of culture shift such as that envisaged by Inglehart—a process whereby postmaterialist values slowly become those of the majority in society because of a succession of generations grown up in conditions of physical and economic security—may not be appropriate. Paradigmatic change, as described by Kuhn and others, may be revolutionary in the sense that it is swift and radical, even though it is preceded by a cumulation of 'misfits' under the old paradigm (Cotgrove, 1982; Kuhn, 1962). If paradigmatic change also involves institutional change, as we suggest, it may well be much less gradual than Inglehart foresees, but be more like a process of 'punctuated equilibrium', in which long periods of stability are interrupted by short bursts of radical change (Krasner, 1984).

Whether paradigmatic change occurs, however, is ultimately dependent on the eyes of the observer. To what extent a change in values, behaviour, or institutions is paradigmatic depends on one's assessment of whether the changes are 'fundamental' or not.

Since 1984, New Zealand has passed through a period of institutional change that may well be called radical, if not revolutionary. In particular, changes have been introduced that have redefined the role of the State. These changes have important consequences not only for economic policy and behaviour but also for environmental policy and behaviour. It is therefore theoretically possible that, despite the relatively low level of support for postmaterialist values in New Zealand compared to other western countries, these institutional reforms are facilitating and encouraging postmaterialist *behaviour* and value change. Whether this is the case or not is considered in Chapters 4 and 5.

Conclusion

Since the late 1980s, New Zealand, along with many other countries in the world, has experienced a new wave of environmentalism. Growing support for environmental issues has manifested itself in an increase in support for environmental groups, in responses to opinion polls, in the phenomenon of green consumerism, in a display of interest in environmental matters by companies, in the revival of a Green Party, and in a green political bandwagon effect.

The rise in support for environmental issues and values could be seen as endorsement for the thesis that a shift towards a new social paradigm is needed and under way. The upsurge can be interpreted as a recognition that governments have failed to address environmental problems adequately and that more fundamental changes, in policies and lifestyles, are required.

Yet a closer look at the various manifestations of the rise of environmental support in New Zealand does not seem to support this thesis. Overwhelmingly, New Zealanders continue to adhere to materialist (including authoritarian) values and do not appear to be ready for a radical change in their lifestyles and values. In part, this can be explained on the basis of Inglehart's thesis, which posits a relation between economic prosperity and security on the one hand, and support for postmaterialist values on the other.

But an explanation of paradigmatic change on the basis of a quantitative analysis of support for postmaterialist values related to economic prosperity and security is incomplete. Paradigmatic change involves not only a change of values, but also of behaviour and institutions. Institutions impose important constraints on values and behaviour, and may explain why a shift towards environmental values and behaviour has not been more widespread. On the other hand, it would appear that radical institutional change, as experienced in New Zealand from 1984 to 1992, may offer new prospects for a further dissemination of environmental values and behaviour.

4
THE ROLE OF THE STATE
From 'State Vandalism' Towards a 'Market-led' Environment?

Prior to 1984, the New Zealand State, according to many environmentalists, had a dismal record in managing the environment and was directly responsible for much environmental degradation ('State vandalism'). The principal reason for that record was seen by many as lying in the promotion of economic development by the State through direct involvement in the ownership, allocation, and management of resources. Since 1984, the role of the State in the management of resources has been redefined dramatically, largely under the influence of 'New Right' philosophies embraced by successive governments. In this chapter the principal features of the change in environmental policy will be analysed in the context of the broader State sector reforms—in particular, the shift towards market-led resource management, the drive towards greater efficiency, and the development of new frameworks for social choice. The implications of these changes are assessed in terms of environmental policy direction, the integration of economic and environmental policy making, and implementation problems. Conclusions are drawn about the difficulties and limitations of the drive towards a market-led environmental policy in New Zealand.

Reshaping and Rolling Back the State

When the Fourth Labour Government came into power in 1984, no one expected the kind of radical transformation of the State that was to follow. Although Labour's election manifesto contained many promises for change, including proposals for change in the area of environmental administration, it in no way foreshadowed the comprehensiveness, incisiveness, and speed of the ensuing reform programme. Even less expected was the wholeheartedness with which the new Labour Government embraced New Right principles as a basis for the reforms.

Although this chapter will not venture into explaining why the Fourth Labour Government took this route, the reasons for the environmental reforms cannot be traced exclusively to the efforts of environmental groups, nor to government commitment towards the environment. Instead, the reform process should be seen in a broader context which encompasses New

Zealand's declining position in the global economy, the failure of Keynesianism to cope with economic stagnation, the influence of New Right ideas on people within Treasury and key members of the Government, the strategic position of Treasury within the policy process, and changes within and among social classes (composition of the working class; shift in balance of power from labour to capital; growing power of the financial fraction within capital) (Easton, 1990; Jesson, 1987, 1989; Roper, 1991).

Although Treasury played a key role in the reform of the State sector, it would be simplistic to attribute all the credit or blame to that agency. For the reform to be able to take place, political support was vital. Whereas Treasury was very much the 'think tank' behind the push for reform, it was given political clout by a core group of ministers within Cabinet who shared the New Right views of Treasury. In particular, a cohesive group of half a dozen 'free marketeers' within Cabinet, with a 'troika' of ministers responsible for the finance portfolio (Roger Douglas, David Caygill, and Richard Prebble) at its centre, played a crucial role in setting the agenda for reform within Cabinet. Despite significant opposition from within the Labour Party that saw much of the reform as a betrayal of traditional Labour Party principles and as an undoing of the policies and achievements of previous Labour Governments, this coalition of Treasury and Cabinet forces was able to dominate the policy process (Jesson, 1989).

Ideologically, these developments converged in the New Right view that the State was part of the problem, rather than the solution. Theories of government failure were, of course, not endogenous to New Zealand, but had already been developed overseas, notably in Great Britain and the United States (Brittan, 1983; Hayek, 1982; King, 1975; LeGrand, 1991; Rose, 1984; Self, 1985; Wolf, 1979). In New Zealand, some of these theories—notably from the Chicago school of economics as well as public choice theory, agency theory and transaction-cost analysis—were embraced by Treasury as underpinnings for the reforms that it advocated (Boston, 1991a; Boston and Cooper, 1989; Easton, 1990).

Put simply, the prevailing approach of Treasury and New Zealand governments since 1984 can be characterized by the slogan that was adopted by the National Party in the 1949 election: 'less government in business, more business in government' (Mascarenhas, 1982, p. 42).

Six areas of reform embarked upon since 1984 can be identified as having particular relevance for environmental policy and management. These are:
(1) The corporatization, and in a number of cases subsequent privatization, of the commercial operations of government;
(2) The reform of the public service generally;
(3) A move towards the consideration of economic incentives and 'market

instruments' in policy implementation;
(4) The reorganization of national environmental administration;
(5) The reform of local government;
(6) A comprehensive reform of environmental statutes, notably through the enactment of the Resource Management Act.

Although these reforms had their starting point under the Fourth Labour Government, they were in several respects not completed by the end of its second term in 1990, and found continuation under the National Government elected that year. Given the scale and depth of these reforms, many of their implications have not yet crystallized.

In this chapter, only the first three areas of reform will be discussed. The other three reforms are the subject of Chapter 5. The focus in this chapter is on the extent to which the reforms signify a shift towards a reliance on 'the market' in the management of environmental resources and problems, and on the environmental policy implications of that shift.

Getting the Government out of Business

Although State involvement in economic development is not peculiar to New Zealand, the reasons for it were different from those for State intervention in European countries. Historically, State intervention in New Zealand was inspired more by pragmatic than ideological grounds ('socialism without doctrine')[1], and resulted from the need to create an infrastructure for the development by white settlers of a resource-rich but undercapitalized and underpopulated colony. Since its early colonial beginnings, the New Zealand State facilitated the development of resources by, for example, the construction of railways and roads, the development of telecommunications and electricity, and the establishment of a legal and administrative order within which property rights could be allocated, transferred, and protected, resources could be exploited, and markets could operate. The State also played a key role in the acquisition and distribution of land for settlers, the raising of (overseas) capital to finance development, the provision of insurance, and in assisting exports (Condliffe, 1959; Hawke, 1985; Mascarenhas, 1982).

On the basis of this pragmatic approach, however, the State in New Zealand also got involved in many activities that went beyond building an infrastructure, such as the provision of state houses, the establishment of industries, the promotion of tourism, and the development of a welfare state. Services were provided and industries set up where the private sector was reluctant to enter (avoiding risks), or to compete with private sector enterprise

---

1. A book with this title was written by the French socialist Albert Metin (Castles, 1982, p. 12).

in order to protect the public from exploitation (the 'yardstick theory of public enterprise', Mascarenhas, 1982). In 1898, at a time when British governments still relied on the 'invisible hand' of the market, the New Zealand Government introduced the world's first pension scheme. New Zealand's leading role in this area was confirmed by the introduction of Labour's comprehensive social security legislation in 1938, and was also reflected in the doctrine of a 'living wage'.[2] Despite the ideological differences between them, both Labour and National governments took, up to 1984, a 'hands on' approach to the role of the State in promoting and directing development.

But the expansion of the role of the government in New Zealand, as elsewhere, also led to difficulties. Since the early 1970s big government had become problematic in terms of expenditure ('burden on the economy'), but also with regard to such issues as effectiveness, efficiency, and accountability. The growth of government came under scrutiny, and led to the development of theories about 'government failure' as referred to above. In New Zealand, Treasury played a key role in disseminating such theories, and in advocating fundamental reforms of the State sector (Treasury, 1984, 1987).

One major plank of the reforms advocated by Treasury, and adopted by the Fourth Labour Government, was the corporatization of the commercial operations of the State. In 1986, with the introduction of the State Enterprises Act, nine State owned enterprises (SOEs) were established for the purpose of running State trading activities on a commercial footing, with minimal political interference.[3] Political meddling in these activities in the past was regarded as an important reason for poor decision making and performance from a commercial point of view. The mission of the new SOEs was to operate primarily as commercial businesses. Although the government retained ownership and ultimate control of these companies by being formally entitled to modify their statements of corporate intent and by setting expected rates of return on invested capital, the managers were given full freedom with

---

2. This doctrine implied that wages had to be high enough to allow workers to enjoy a 'decent living according to the colonial standard, which is higher than the British standard, considerably higher than that of continental Europe, and immeasurably higher than that of the Chinese or Indian coolie'. This level was sustained by the protection of domestic industry, which was thereby enabled to pay higher wages. (See Castles, 1985.)
3. The nine new SOEs were: the Airways Corporation, Coal Corporation, Electricity Corporation, Forestry Corporation, Land Corporation, Telecom Corporation, New Zealand Post, Postbank, and the Government Property Services. The legislation also covered five already existing State owned enterprises, namely Air New Zealand, the Petroleum Corporation (Petrocorp), Railways Corporation, Shipping Corporation, and the Tourist Hotel Corporation.

regard to decisions on inputs, pricing, and marketing (McKinlay, 1987; Mascarenhas, 1991).

Although it may not have been the original intention of the Fourth Labour Government, corporatization was a stepping stone towards privatization.[4] After corporatization, a process of deregulation followed to put SOEs in a 'competitively neutral' environment (so that they no longer enjoyed special government support or advantages), before a number of them were sold. This step took the principle of getting the government out of business to its logical conclusion.[5]

To some extent, the move towards corporatization was supported by the environmental movement. In the eyes of many environmentalists, the New Zealand State has been directly responsible for much environmental degradation as a result of its involvement in resource allocation and development. Land development policies caused large-scale deforestation, often on land vulnerable to erosion. Government subsidies contributed to the drainage of wetlands, to an intensive use of pesticides and inorganic fertilizers, and also to farming on land considered to be marginal or uneconomic in terms of productive potential. The State's involvement in energy projects led to the despoliation of natural and scenic values, for instance of lakes and rivers, as a result of the construction of hydro dams ('State sponsored vandalism', Salmon, 1960). More recently, the State has been held responsible for the highly inefficient use of energy resources in New Zealand (Fitzsimons, 1981; McChesney, 1991b). For many environmentalists, the State has been the main culprit of environmental degradation. Government departments were perceived to be 'tuned entirely towards complete economic exploitation of every available natural resource, as rapidly as possible' (Salmon, 1960, pp. 15–16).

One of the criticisms made by environmentalists of the way environmental decisions were made relates to the 'dual mandates' held by government agencies. Government departments such as the New Zealand Forest Service, the Department of Lands and Survey, and the Ministry of Works combined a

---

4. It has been argued that Treasury had privatization in mind from the very outset of the corporatization process, but that this was not initially on the government's agenda. It was only later adopted by the Labour Government for the purpose of reducing government debt (McKinlay, 1987; Mascarenhas, 1991).
5. By the end of 1990, more than twenty State owned enterprises had been sold, for a total value of $NZ 9.8 billion. Amongst these were: the Telecom Corporation, New Zealand Steel, the Petroleum Corporation (Petrocorp), Post Office Bank, the Rural Bank, and Air New Zealand. The State also sold forestry cutting rights for more than $NZ 1 billion, and its stake in Maui gas (Department of Statistics, 1992, p. 443).

development role with environmental responsibilities. The New Zealand Forest Service, for instance, was responsible for the protection of indigenous forests, but was also involved in converting native forests into exotic plantation forests for commercial purposes. The Department of Lands and Survey carried responsibility for national parks and the management of other Crown land of environmental significance, while at the same time promoting the development of Crown land. The Ministry of Works was, among other things, responsible for the protection of wild and scenic rivers, but at the same time had responsibility for building dams and issuing rights for using water. The rationale advanced by governments for combining apparently conflicting responsibilities into one agency was that in this way the integration of development and conservation interests in the making of policies and management of resources was guaranteed.

Environmentalists, however, saw this as a case of 'goats minding the cabbages'. Conflicts between these two types of responsibility were resolved within the agencies, in the absence of clear criteria for the relative weight given to competing values, by allowing a high degree of discretion in the decision-making process. According to environmentalists, environmental considerations lost out consistently, as performance was measured primarily in terms of development values and was affected by professional bias in the same direction (Royal Forest and Bird Protection Society of New Zealand et al., 1982; Salmon, 1984).

Environmentalists sought a solution to the problem of 'State sponsored vandalism' and dual mandates in a reform of environmental institutions. In particular, they sought the establishment of a strong Ministry for the Environment that would combine many of the regulatory and conservation functions dispersed over a wide range of government agencies, and through an institutional separation of conservation and development responsibilities. Overall, environmentalists did not seek to *reduce* the role of the State in the management of resources, but sought rather to separate development and environmental responsibilities among agencies and to alter the balance of forces within the machinery of government by strengthening those agencies with an environmental advocacy role (Royal Forest and Bird Protection Society of NZ et al., 1982, 1985).

Although the changes advocated by environmentalists were not inspired by a desire to reduce government intervention, their solutions proved to be to a large extent congruent with, and even a catalyst for, the reforms advocated by the New Right. Treasury was very receptive to the argument put forward by the Native Forest Action Council that many of the practices of the New Zealand Forest Service did not make any economic sense. Treasury was also a strong advocate of allocating conflicting tasks (such as development and protection of resources) to separate agencies, an idea supported by environmentalists. Some environmentalists entered into an 'unholy alliance' with Treasury for the purpose of overcoming bureaucratic opposition to a reform that various departments rightly saw as a threat to their very existence.

The principles of reform advocated by Treasury and adopted by the Government were pioneered in the area of environmental administration. The conservation functions of the New Zealand Forest Service, the Department of Lands and Survey, and various other government agencies were brought together into a new Department of Conservation (see Chapter 5), whereas the commercial operations of these departments were vested in new State owned enterprises, the Forestry Corporation of New Zealand Ltd and the Land Corporation Ltd.

Although the establishment of the Department of Conservation has been interpreted as a major victory for environmentalists, the environmental implications of the corporatization or privatization of State trading activities are far from clear-cut. The rationale for the setting up of SOEs was that their activities are primarily commercial, and that political interference in these areas had led to poor decisions and inefficiency in the allocation and management of resources (Treasury, 1984, 1987). It can indeed be argued that, if this approach had been adopted earlier, it would have been highly unlikely that the 'Think Big' energy projects adopted by the National Government—widely denounced as disasters by environmentalists and economists—would ever have got off the ground. The fact that the government has got out of business in these areas has, so runs the argument, avoided the continuation of poor decision making in the allocation and management of resources.

Implicit in this argument are at least three assumptions. One is the assumption that resource management purely on the basis of market principles leads to superior decision making in all areas including those with environmental implications. A second assumption underlying the separation between commercial and non-commercial operations is that resources can be conveniently split into private and public goods, or into environmentally sensitive and insensitive categories. A third, somewhat contradictory, assumption could be added to these, namely that if both of the first two assumptions do not hold, the government can still always jump to the rescue if things do not work out.

From an environmental point of view there is, of course, no logic to the argument that, if the State happens to be a poor decision maker with regard to resources, then the market must necessarily be a better one. Environmental degradation and resource mismanagement are as much outcomes of market failure as they are of government failure (Dryzek, 1987, pp. 67–87). In many cases, government intervention (such as in pollution control) is the very result of the failure of the market to control 'externalities' of resource use, and of failure to generate prices to reflect the real costs of producing goods and services (in social, environmental, short- and long-term respects). Shifting decision making on resource use and allocation from the State to agencies operating on commercial principles does not eliminate the need to address the social and environmental implications of such decisions (Rees, 1990).

The most obvious illustration of this in the New Zealand context can be found in the energy policy area. With the corporatization and part privatization of the government's assets in this sector (Electricity Corporation, Petroleum Corporation, Coal Corporation), resource policy has become almost exclusively subject to commercial considerations. Although this has resulted in a boost in the financial returns of the companies involved, it has not led to the introduction of policies and practices directed at increasing energy efficiency and conservation, to a reduction of greenhouse gas emissions, or to a greater reliance on renewable energy resources—all elements of any policy of sustainable energy management. The market in energy resources is in itself incapable of overcoming the many barriers (such as: lack of information, lack of affordable technology and expertise, long pay-back periods, weakness of supportive attitudes) to the introduction and implementation of sustainable energy policy. Without sustained government commitment and efforts to develop and implement a policy of sustainable energy management very little, if any, progress in that area will be made (Fitzsimons, 1990; McChesney, 1991b; Parliamentary Commissioner for the Environment, 1992a).

That the failure of the market to deliver in this respect may have serious consequences, even in the short term, was illustrated by the 'power crisis' in New Zealand in the first half of 1992. Strong suspicions were raised that the crisis was as much a result of commercial decisions made by the Electricity Corporation as of weather (drought) conditions—suspicions which led to the establishment by the Government of a committee to conduct an inquiry into the issue. Although questions have also been raised about the responsibilities of SOEs with regard to social and environmental needs and objectives, and about their accountability to the government, no steps have as yet been taken to review the SOE model as such.

The second assumption underlying the corporatization and privatization of resource management, also affecting the social and environmental performance of SOEs, is that goals and goods can be conveniently split into predominantly private and public categories. SOEs, like companies in the private sector, concentrate almost exclusively on producing those goods and services with excludable benefits (benefits which can be denied to those who do not pay), whereas the use of resources for goods or services that are non-excludable (such as clean air, the benefits of which cannot be confined to those who pay for it) are mostly seen as the responsibility of the government. Because of their public nature, goods of the second type are often also considered to be environmentally and socially more sensitive, whereas private goods are usually regarded as primarily important for the welfare of individuals. The shift towards corporatization and privatization has also been justified on these grounds: why should the government be involved in providing goods and services that are predominantly private in character and which can be left to the market?

In the New Zealand context, the views of the Treasury and government on energy can again be referred to as an illustration of this point. Treasury takes the view that there is nothing about energy to warrant it being treated as a public good, and believes that the allocation and management of energy resources by the market not only results in the most efficient use of resources, but also provides optimal incentives for the conservation of energy (through the price mechanism). This line has been adopted by New Zealand governments since 1984, and was most vividly expressed by an energy minister who compared the provision of energy with that of bananas (McChesney, 1991b, p. 28; Welch, 1992).

A flaw in this line of thinking is, of course, that the dividing line between public and private goods, as well as between the public and private sectors, is often blurred, and that the provision of private (excludable) goods may have social and environmental implications as important or as serious as those arising from the provision of public goods. Much of the past involvement of the State with development in New Zealand was partly inspired by social and environmental considerations, such as the 'uneconomic' planting of forests (in areas such as the East Coast of the North Island) for the purpose of providing employment and controlling erosion. The establishment and maintenance of many 'uneconomic' post offices in small and isolated settlements occurred out of social considerations (providing essential financial and information services to those who are less mobile, an argument now dismissed as 'political'). The provision of many private goods, such as cars, houses, and agricultural products (which may involve a high level of pesticide use), on the other hand, has significant public good aspects and environmental implications.

Hence the corporatization or privatization of State trading activities and the concurrent establishment of agencies with clear, non-conflicting mandates does not necessarily provide better answers to the social and environmental questions associated with those activities. Whether environmental considerations will be given greater weight than under the previous system, where conflicting values were internally 'balanced' within agencies with double mandates, is an open question. The argument that has been advanced is that it is more transparent for governments to 'buy' goods and services considered important from a non-commercial point of view, from those companies, instead of saddling them with conflicting mandates. But more open and transparent balancing does not seem to have resulted in any significant environmental gains. Much still depends on the preparedness of governments to develop and implement policies that address environmental problems, whether they generate from within the State or from the private sector. As the energy policy area demonstrates, there has been a reluctance on the part of governments to 'interfere' with the operations of SOEs, out of fear of upsetting the commercial footing on which these agencies were established. On the other hand, as reflected in the decision by the National Government in 1992 to provide grants to promote extensive planting on the East Coast of the North Island (*National Business Review*, 3 July 1992), and in Prime Minister Bolger's reminder to the SOEs of their social responsibilities (*The Press*, 11 August 1992), it is recognized that these companies, operating on purely commercial grounds, fail to address important social and environmental issues associated with the resources they manage.

This brings us to a third, contradictory, assumption underlying the shift towards market-based resource management. Implicit in this move is the notion that if market-based resource management fails, it is still always possible for the government to jump in and correct such failure. Ministers retain the power to modify the Statements of Corporate Intent of SOEs, and governments can introduce rules and regulations, or provide incentives, to move the private sector into socially and environmentally desirable paths. But it is somewhat paradoxical to expect governments to be willing and able to do this if, in first instance, it is assumed that they do not have any superior motive or the capability to make any wiser decisions than the market with regard to the allocation and management of resources.

But even if governments are prepared to remedy market failure, it may be too late. Responding to market failure is a reactive strategy that allows environmental problems to emerge *before* governments step in. This implies that opportunities to prevent problems from emerging are lost, at potentially great costs. Given the fact that environmental damage may be irreversible and have huge consequences, including the transformation or even loss of life support systems, a reliance on a market feedback strategy, or any reactive strategy for that matter, is in many cases wholly inappropriate. For these reasons—as we pointed out in the Introduction—there is a need for anticipatory environmental policy.

Relying on a market correction strategy also suggests that markets are somehow prior to, and independent from, the social and political system when they are in fact social and political creations. Markets can function only within a political and social order that lays down rules and protects property rights. Markets are only one social choice mechanism among various others, and a very limited one for that matter (Dryzek, 1987). Treating markets as prior to politics 'imprisons' governments in making choices (Lindblom, 1982). A market failure approach therefore greatly constrains social creativity in making societal choices, including the development of other mechanisms, policies, and meta-policies, for dealing with the environmental problematique.

Overall, it can be argued that the shift in resource allocation and management from a 'hands on' approach by the State towards a market-based orientation does not automatically imply that, from an environmental perspective, resources are managed any better. Although the State may no longer be directly involved in environmental 'vandalism', there is no guarantee that such vandalism no longer occurs. Indeed, the State may be responsible for facilitating and permitting such vandalism by the private sector through the mindless promotion of undifferentiated economic growth and development, for example. Whether environmental values are to carry a greater weight in resource management, either in the public or the private sector, depends very much on the political commitment of governments to the introduction of effective environmental policies.

Bringing More Business into Government

A second important plank of the reforms advocated by Treasury and introduced by the Fourth Labour Government was the reorganization and reshaping of the core (non-commercial) public service. Again, the reform was inspired by economic theories about government and bureaucracy, and by an approach to the public service that has been characterized as new managerialism or New Public Management (NPM). The general thrust of the reform was to model the public service on management principles derived from the private sector, with the view to making it more efficient, accountable, and flexible (Boston, 1991a, 1991b; Hood, 1991; Martin, 1990; Treasury, 1987).

By the time these reforms were introduced across the whole of the public service, by way of the State Sector Act 1988 and the Public Finance Act 1989, significant changes had already occurred in the system of environmental administration. Although the initial environmental reform, begun by Labour after the 1984 elections, took place very much in response to the demands of environmentalists, it also foreshadowed the kind of change that was to take place across the public service. Underlying both reforms were the same ideas and principles. Here, we will discuss those ideas and principles and the implications for environmental policy of their application throughout the public service. In Chapter 5, we will focus on the environmental reforms *per se*, and address the question of whether these changes represent an advance in environmental policy making.

Public service reform in New Zealand is not unique, but has reflected an international trend in public administration. What *is* unique about the reform in New Zealand is the speed and 'unusual coherence' with which changes have been introduced (Hood, 1991, p. 6). NPM does not have a unified philosophical basis, but draws on variety of schools of thought and theories, such as institutional economics (also referred to as the new economics of organizations), public choice theory, and new managerialism. Although there is potential conflict between some of these ideas, this did not prevent the programme of reform in New Zealand from being fast, radical, and coherent.

Since the introduction of the State Sector Act 1988 and the Public Finance Act 1989, the public service in New Zealand has been changed beyond recognition from one based on the Westminster model towards a system having much more affinity with the operation of the private sector. Government departments now operate as business-like organizations, with chief executives instead of heads of departments; personnel are no longer appointed on an indefinite (career service) basis, but on a contract basis, with payment dependent on measurable performance; ministers enter into contracts with departments to 'purchase' their services; and departments are required to formulate corporate plans with quantifiable criteria for measuring 'outputs'. The reforms, inspired by principles derived from public choice and other theories which are based on the presumption that public service performance is primarily the result of the self-interested behaviour of individuals, have in many cases led to the separation of conflicting mandates and of policy and delivery functions among agencies, to an emphasis on goals instead of process, and to increased flexibility in the management of departments ('inputs'). Essentially, the reforms break with the tradition of a unified, career-based public service (Martin, 1990; Walsh, 1991; Whitcombe, 1989).

The reforms in New Zealand appear to have served a number of not always compatible objectives, such as consistency, accountability, transparency, contestability, complementarity, co-ordination, economy, efficiency, and the minimization of capture (Boston, 1991b, p. 239). It can be argued, however, that not all of these objectives have been equally important. Some of them, notably efficiency, carried a greater weight than others, giving the reforms a coherence that would not have been feasible if all objectives had been assigned equal importance (Bührs, 1992b).

Although the reforms may have been largely beneficial from the point of view of inducing changes in behaviour and processes leading to improved 'performance' (Steering Group Review of State Sector Reforms, 1991), they are also problematic. Managerialist principles, derived from the private sector, are not simply transferable to the public sector, which is in important respects different from the private sector and requires different structures and arrangements (Boston, 1991a, pp. 21–2). Notably, three difficulties can be identified as being of particular relevance to the environmental policy process. These are associated with the emphasis on goals, especially quantifiable goals, the reinforcement of the vertical nature of the policy process, and the implications of the reforms for the development of a long-term perspective in environmental policy.

The emphasis on goals in the reforms is an illustration of efforts, discussed earlier in Chapter 1, to make the policy process more rational. The idea that the performance of organizations can be improved by introducing clear objectives is nothing new (Simon, 1947). Although Simon explicitly acknowledged the limitations of a purely rational model of decision making, the concept provoked a long-standing debate about its feasibility and desirability (Goodin, 1979, 1982; Gregory, 1989; Lindblom, 1959, 1979). We will not enter here into the debate between rationalism and incrementalism, except to mention that it has led to a recognition by many analysts that an extreme emphasis on either goals or process in policy making is unrealistic and undesirable (Lindblom, 1979; Simon, 1976a). In a complex and diverse world, it is often impossible to set or achieve clear objectives, whereas policy making without goals or intent (apart from the fact that it is a contradiction in terms) may lead to 'drifting' (action without direction) and undesirable outcomes (Etzioni, 1967; Lindblom, 1977). Parties on both sides of the debate seem to have found wisdom in a middle way between both extremes, involving the consideration of ends and means simultaneously, whether identified as 'bounded rationality' (Simon, 1947), 'mixed scanning' (Etzioni, 1967), or 'strategic analysis' (Lindblom, 1979, 1980).

Environmental problems are amongst the most difficult facing society. Many of these issues are highly complex ('science intensive'), interrelated (ecological interdependence), comprehensive (ecological, social, and economic dimensions), and controversial (involving ethical, value conflicts). In such circumstances (characterized by a high degree of uncertainty and disagreement) it is often difficult, if not impossible, to formulate clear or measurable goals in line with the managerialist perspective. Consequently, the criteria for 'good' environmental policy relate as much to the *process* or *direction* as to the formulation of measurable goals. Intentions, efforts, resources, and mechanisms facilitating conflict resolution are in these conditions at least as significant as clear and quantifiable objectives.

Too much emphasis on clear and measurable goals in defining and assessing the role of environmental agencies may lead to goal displacement:

a focus on goals that can be more easily achieved, or to which progress is more demonstrable, at the cost of goals or issues which are more difficult to resolve, or where progress can be hard to measure (such as sustainable resource use, or enhancing the quality of life). Taking the Corporate Statements and Annual Reports of the Ministry for the Environment as an indication of the goals and criteria for the environmental policy performance of the Ministry, one certainly gets the impression that goal displacement has occurred within the Ministry, to the extent that goals and performance are related to rather meaningless and trivial 'outputs'. Examples are the measurement of performance on the basis of such things as the number of briefing papers 'provided on time and accepted by Ministers', the number of research projects completed, 'the provision of advice', and 'Ministerials: Draft responses to all Ministerial correspondence to be provided within 20 working days of receipt of correspondence, with quality such that first drafts are acceptable to the Minister, in 95 percent of the cases' (Ministry for the Environment, 1991b, 1992b). Little, if any, substantive information about the development of policies and strategies to tackle environmental problems can be found in Corporate Statements, nor is there information about their effectiveness in the Annual Reports. The reports seem to suggest that the policy performance of the Ministry can best be measured in terms of the rate at which quantities of paper can be produced.

A second effect of the application of managerialist principles to the public sector is that the co-ordination of policy has become even more problematic than under the previous system. The downside of giving chief executives the 'freedom to manage' in order to achieve the goals set by individual ministers has been a strengthening of the phenomenon of departmentalism, an almost exclusive preoccupation of departments with their own goals and interests. With the abolition of 'dual mandates' and the separation of conflicting roles, departments are no longer confronted with the need to balance conflicting sets of goals. There is little incentive for them to consider goals or interests other than their own, particularly if their performance is assessed on the goals agreed upon with individual ministers. Unless departments are functionally interdependent for the achievement of their goals, they have no reason to give consideration to the effects of their activities on the goals of other departments, or on collective goals.

The Government recognized this problem (Steering Group Review of the State Sector Reforms, 1991), and has tried to remedy it by incorporating a clause in the performance contracts between ministers and chief executives requiring consultation in matters affecting other departments or the collective interests of the Government. The problem has been exacerbated, however, by the erosion of the notion of a unified public service, and a decline in the public service culture (Martin, 1991a). Also, apart from the question of how this requirement is enforced, it is doubtful whether it is adequate to overcome the structural impediments to interdepartmental consultation.

Although these problems affect the performance of the public sector as a whole, they have an especially serious effect in the realm of environmental policy. Given the interdependence of environmental phenomena, fragmentation in policy making has been identified as an important cause of the displacement of environmental problems, and of environmental policy failure in general (Caldwell, 1963; Dryzek, 1987). Many, if not most, sectoral policies (such as economic, agricultural, energy, and transport policies) have important environmental repercussions. Consequently, as we discuss further in Chapter 6, a more comprehensive or co-ordinated approach to environmental policy making has been identified as a condition for improving environmental policy performance (Bartlett, 1990a; Bührs, 1991a, 1991b; Haigh and Irwin, 1989).

The Ministry for the Environment has been given a reporting function, implying that it should be consulted on all proposals with significant environmental implications before they reach the Cabinet table. Although this is potentially an important mechanism in the implementation of the Ministry's co-ordination role, it is regularly circumvented and is dependent on ministerial support to make it work (Bührs, 1992a). The Ministry, not having real powers or a management role, depends primarily on a strategy of persuasion in its efforts to develop and co-ordinate environmental policy (Bührs, 1991b).

Not surprisingly, many policies (such as economic policy, agricultural policy, energy and transport policies) have continued to be developed without adequate consideration being given to environmental implications. Even in policy areas that are usually considered as more directly 'environmental' (such as hazardous substances, packaging, and waste disposal), policy development and co-ordination has been very difficult and slow.

A third problem associated with the reforms is that they may reinforce a short-term view of the policy process. By being made more accountable to ministers whose time horizons extend only to the next election, departments are led towards giving priority to short-term, politically attractive issues. This tendency is reinforced by the prevailing view of recent New Zealand governments that planning is not an important, or even desirable, activity in which to become involved, as it smacks of heavy government intervention and creates unrealistic expectations about the capabilities of governments. Instead, New Zealand governments since 1984 have focused on creating the frameworks, on setting the rules (the 'level playing fields'), within which other people decide what they want to achieve, whether in the short or long run. This (meta-) policy approach has been applied not only to the economic policy area, but also to a whole range of policy areas, including health, education, and environmental policy, although there are differences in the degree of control the central government retains over the parameters in each area (McKinlay, 1990).

This approach of devolution and decentralization appeals to many environmentalists, as it ties in with their doubts about the capability of central governments and bureaucracies to deal with complex environmental problems, as well as with philosophies of giving communities greater control over their resources (Dryzek, 1987; Ophuls, 1977; Paehlke, 1989; Paehlke and Torgerson, 1990). It also raises a number of unresolved issues, such as: the capability of local authorities and their commitment to environmental values; equity with regard to access to resources among and within regions; the traditionally low level of public interest and participation in local government; and the place and role of local government in the play of forces behind the many environmental problems of a national, international, and global nature (such as those related to the energy resources and transport industries). Many, if not most, environmental problems cannot be resolved within a couple of years, but require a long-term view, strategy, and commitment, and need to be addressed globally and nationally as well as at local level. Whether local government and the private sector have the commitment and capability to take on such a role is highly questionable.

The shift towards 'the market' and devolution in resource policy and management may create a policy vacuum in many areas where national governments fail to provide guidance. Local government and the private sector have not yet come to terms with the new responsibilities thrust upon them.

It is ironic that recent New Zealand governments have made themselves highly unpopular by adopting policies that they themselves regard as being in the long-term interests of the country, but that are widely perceived as anything but long-term policies. This is not surprising, as these policies do little more than lay the responsibility for providing solutions to major problems (whether the lack of investment, unemployment, energy conservation, or the sustainable management of resources) somewhere else (with the market or price mechanism, consumers, producers, or local government). In the absence of firm guidance by the central government in these matters it is hard to see how people can interpret this approach as anything other than 'passing the buck'. The abolition of agencies that once provided an institutional basis for policy advice in these matters (such as the New Zealand Planning Council, the Environmental Council, and the Ministry of Energy) has only helped to reinforce that impression.

Overall, the reform of the public service along new managerialist lines may have had a positive effect on environmental management in some respects, and a neutral, or even negative, effect in other respects. Trade-offs between environmental and other values have become more transparent with the separation of conflicting mandates between government agencies, and the degree of technical and economic rationality and accountability in the environmental policy process has been enhanced by the emphasis on goals-based management. Another positive element of the reform is the flexibility that it gives to environmental (and other) government agencies in the allocation of resources for addressing problems. But the reforms mean little in terms of the relative priority given to environmental values in the policy process, and they may have accentuated problems with regard to environmental co-ordination, the development of long-term policies and strategies, and, paradoxically (given the emphasis on goals), the need for central government guidance in environmental issues that are too big or too complex to be handled on a lower level. These findings are not surprising, however, as the reforms were primarily inspired not by a desire to improve *environmental* policy making and management, but by the wish to put government activities on a more efficient footing in line with theories and practices derived from economics and the private sector.

Economic Instruments

A third plank of reform advocated by Treasury relates to a greater use of economic instruments as an alternative to direct regulation ('command and control' mechanisms), particularly in the area of environmental policy (Bührs, 1991a, pp. 208, 371; Treasury, 1985a, 1985b). The idea, of course, originated overseas (Anderson et al., 1977; Baumol and Oates, 1975; Kneese and Schultze, 1975), but has received growing attention in New Zealand in the last decade (Ackroyd et al., 1991; Bromley, 1988; Kerr and Sharp, 1985; Meister, 1990; Sharplin, 1987).

Some of the claimed advantages of using economic instruments rather than direct regulation (standards) are efficiency (achieving goals at fewer costs), enhancement of choice, providing incentives for technological innovation, minimizing bureaucracy (need for control), internalizing real (external, hidden) costs of activities, and generation of revenue (Elkin and Cook, 1985; Kelman, 1981; OECD, 1980b, 1989).

Economic instruments can be classified into several categories, such as charges, subsidies, deposit-refund systems, market creation, and (financial) enforcement incentives. A range of these instruments have been introduced in the environmental policies of various countries, although in a rather piecemeal way and not always for environmental (rather than revenue raising) reasons. In Europe, charges, subsidies, deposit-refund systems, and enforcement incentives are fairly common, whereas market creation has been applied on any significant scale only in the United States (Cairncross, 1991; Majone, 1989; OECD, 1989).

In New Zealand, despite the fact that since the early 1980s Treasury demonstrated a strong interest in the application of economic instruments, little headway has been made in this field. The only significant economic instrument introduced in New Zealand in the area of environmental policy has been the establishment of a system of property rights for fishing quota (Individual Transferable Quota, ITQ) in 1986. Another example of market creation can be found in legislation aimed at reducing and ultimately phasing out ozone depleting substances, under which import licenses have been made tradeable. Apart from that, very little has been achieved. Differential taxation has been introduced to make unleaded petrol a few cents per litre cheaper than leaded petrol. The Resource Management Act 1991 allows for the introduction of economic instruments, but in a very limited way; it stipulates that only means that have been provided for in statute shall be considered (Resource Management Act 1991: section 32; Salmon, 1991a). The Act itself allows but a limited form of trading in water permits (Resource Management Act 1991: section 136). The attempt in 1992 by the Minister for the Environment to sell the introduction of a regional petrol tax as a 'green tax' in support of public transport failed. The measure, which allowed regional councils to impose a maximum levy of two cents on a litre of petrol, was widely perceived not as 'green' but as hypocritical, given that it was accompanied by a forty per cent cut in the government subsidy for public transport. In no way did the tax compensate for the decline in public transport services—or for the higher prices—that resulted from the deregulation of public transport and the move towards a 'user pays' regime. As a measure purportedly encouraging people to use public transport, it was a débâcle. Moreover, as the increase was absorbed by the profit margins of oil companies, it had no effect whatsoever (*The Press*, 29 April 1992, 13 May 1992).

On the other hand, it should be noted that the aversion of New Zealand governments since 1984 to charges or subsidies, inspired by the fear of bringing about 'market distortions', has also had some positive effects on the environment. The Fourth Labour Government abolished a range of subsidies, grants, and tax breaks for land development and farming practices which, in the past, had been responsible for considerable environmental damage—for instance, by promoting the clearance of areas of native forests for farming or exotic forestry plantation, by encouraging an intensive use of pesticides, and by enabling farming on marginal and erosion prone land (land development grants, price subsidies, subsidies on fertilizers).

Against this, however, must be weighed the abolition or reduction of subsidies that had a positive environmental impact, such as the public transport subsidies referred to above, subsidies to promote energy efficiency and conservation and, more recently, grants for research in the field of organic agriculture. This supports the conclusion that the abolition of subsidies and grants that had a negative environmental effect was inspired not so much by government commitment to the environment as by a rather purist conception of the beneficial effects of the market.

Belief in the role of the 'invisible hand' of the market in producing common goods is, however, only one reason why New Zealand governments have not been more aggressive in introducing economic instruments in the environmental policy area. It is possible to identify at least three other categories of problems attendant upon the introduction and application of economic instruments in this field, each providing its own explanation as to why such instruments have not been introduced much more extensively. The three categories are: implementation problems, political-economic problems, and moral and philosophical problems (Elkin and Cook, 1985).

Problems with the implementation of economic instruments stem in part from the complexity of determining the correct level of economic instruments, and in part from enforcement problems. For instance, if charges are to achieve the desired effect, they should be set at a level where they provide sufficient incentive without 'overkill' (imposing unnecessary costs). Ideally, levels should be set on the basis of information about each company's production-cost function and on the marginal cost imposed per unit of undesirable effect—obviously a huge task if numerous companies are involved in the particular industry (apart from the fact that all the necessary information may not be available). To meet this problem, charges can be set for a whole industry on a trial and error basis, but this is rather unsatisfactory as it may mean that in quite a number of cases the target behaviour may not be achieved.

An example of an implementation problem related to the property rights approach can be found in the Quota Management System (QMS) for fisheries in New Zealand. As the total allowable commercial catch for some fish species, in particular orange roughy and hoki, appeared to be unsustainably high (a problem arising partly because determining the maximum sustainable level is a highly complex matter, and partly because politicians ignored the advice of officials), ITQs had to be reduced. But as the quotas had been set at an absolute level (and not as a relative proportion of the total allowable catch), the Government was forced into an expensive compensation deal with ITQ owners in order to make the reductions (Lambert, 1991a; *National Business Review*, 29 November 1992). Although the complexity of the problem would have been the same under a non-property rights system, the costs to the Government of making such a mistake would have been much less.

Other implementation problems arise because economic instruments are not self-enforcing, despite the assumptions often made to that effect. The argument that active policing or control can be avoided by substituting economic instruments for bureaucratic regulation (standards), as financial incentives will guide self-interested individuals towards the desired goal or behaviour, does not hold. Self-interested individuals will pollute more than they are allowed to on the basis of a right allocated to them, and they will manipulate information, if adequate monitoring and policing mechanisms have not been put in place, or if the risks of being caught (including the chances of prosecution and level of penalties) are not very high.

Again, an example of this problem in New Zealand can be found in the fisheries QMS system. Numerous cases of illegal fishing (non-reporting) and misreporting of catches have come to light in recent years (*Conservation News*, February 1992). Given that there are not enough observers to monitor all fishing boats, and the chances and costs of being caught can be considered relatively slight (confiscated boats have been returned to their owners), these cases could well be just the tip of an iceberg.

Available evidence is that economic instruments do not work as well as claimed by enthusiasts. In countries where they have been introduced, they have tended to serve a revenue-raising or cost-saving function, but have had in many cases little or no significant impact on environmental quality (Hahn, 1989; Majone, 1989). Their desirability, feasibility, and effectiveness have to be judged not only on (theoretical) economic grounds, but in a political, social, cultural, and moral context.

Political-economic problems associated with economic instruments relate to such issues as the lack of public support for economic instruments (among environmentalists and existing polluters alike), the question of to whom to allocate the initial rights (existing polluters/users, other interested parties, or all members of public?), ownership and decision making in relation to public resources (should individuals have the right to own and decide on public goods?), and the costs for the economy (inflationary effects of charges). Altogether, these difficulties mean that there is little or no 'political bread' in introducing economic instruments. The difficulties are often sufficient to dissuade even the most interested politicians from pursuing the idea.

Political and social factors also go some way towards explaining the lack of headway made with economic instruments in New Zealand. Although the notion has gained ground in recent years (Ackroyd et al., 1991), support has been largely confined to academic and business circles. In general, environmentalists have been much less enthusiastic about the idea, and many eye the initiatives of the Maruia Society in this direction ('Green Economy Programme'; Salmon, 1991a; 1991b) with suspicion.

Opposition to the introduction of economic instruments has also come from other groups in New Zealand. Since the 1970s, industries in New Zealand have consistently and successfully opposed the introduction of compulsory deposit systems and product charges (Bührs, 1991a). Māori have mounted fierce opposition to the introduction of tradeable property rights for resources (such as fisheries) which they claim under the Treaty of Waitangi.

Despite the fact that the introduction of economic instruments may lead to efficiency gains (Elkin and Cook, 1985), they also encounter economic obstacles. The imposition of new charges (such as a carbon tax) has inflationary consequences, and is therefore not likely to be popular with governments that, as in New Zealand since 1984, have been obsessed with getting inflation down (in line with monetarist policies).

But the most important objections are of a moral or philosophical nature. It has been argued that using economic instruments in environmental policy (in particular in pollution control) reflects indifference towards the motives of polluters, fails to stigmatize polluting behaviour, degrades environmental values (by subjecting them to pricing or market forces), and raises equity questions (allowing choice only to wealthier people). The use of economic instruments is not, as some advocates seem to imply, a neutral matter (related to the efficiency of means in achieving given goals), but has important ramifications for the type of society people (want to) live in. Whether or not economic instruments should be used is a political and ethical question, involving debate about values and processes (Elkin and Cook, 1985; Kelman, 1981; Majone 1989; Sagoff, 1988).

In New Zealand, however, very little explicit consideration has so far been given to the moral or philosophical implications of the introduction of economic instruments (Environmental Council, 1987), although it is likely that the lack of enthusiasm for these instruments on the part of environmentalists, notably with regard to the creation of property rights and markets in environmental goods, also stems from those moral reservations. Yet many environmentalists in New Zealand are keeping an open mind on these matters, in particular on the potential usefulness of environmental charges, as reflected in calls for the introduction of a carbon tax.

Altogether, there are many good reasons why economic instruments have not yet made much headway in environmental policy in New Zealand. Despite their philosophical attractiveness to Treasury, and the existence of a number of other strong proponents in New Zealand (Ackroyd et al., 1991), it has become clear from overseas experiences that economic instruments are not the panacea for environmental problems that some may initially have thought. Their claimed advantages are often exaggerated. Economic instruments still require government intervention and control to be effective, and in many cases they are no substitute for regulation (Elkin and Cook, 1985; Hahn, 1989; Hula, 1988; Mitnick, 1982; Rose-Ackerman, 1977).

So far, economic instruments, unlike other New Right reforms, have failed to capture the imagination of most politicians in New Zealand. With the departure of their most ardent advocate within Cabinet, Simon Upton, from the environmental portfolio, and the débâcle of the 'green' petrol tax in 1992, the National Government seemed to lose much of its interest (if it had any) in this field. Given also that both other main parties (Labour and the Alliance) do not display a strong enthusiasm for the use of economic instruments in environmental policy, it is likely that the rate of their introduction in New Zealand will remain slow.

Towards a Market-led Environment?

Given New Zealand's political system, governments can move fast and radically, as demonstrated between 1984 and 1990 by the Fourth Labour Government. In many areas, including that of environmental policy, the policy landscape has been completely altered. After 1990, under the National Government, reforms continued in a very similar ideological mould, albeit at a slower pace.

Over a period of about nine years, the main thrust of reform was to reduce the role of the State in the allocation and management of resources, whether for economic, social, or environmental purposes. In the economic sphere, the changes have been most radical, designed to release the forces of the market towards a return of growth and prosperity. The split between responsibilities for development on the one hand, and environmental protection on the other, was inspired as much by a desire to make State trading activities more efficient as by environmental demands and promises. Similar efficiency motives dominated the reform of the public service, and underlay Treasury's interest in economic instruments for implementing environmental policy.

In key areas of resource management, such as energy, the changes have brought about a definite shift towards decision making on purely commercial grounds, without government 'interference' (apart from setting an expected rate of return on investments). Although governments still have the right and power to direct activities in these areas (in so far as assets have not yet been sold) for social or environmental reasons, they have proved to be very reluctant to use this option. Governments seem to have adopted Treasury's view that commercial decision making in these matters will also lead to the most desirable outcomes from a social and environmental point of view. Consequently, government policy in these areas lacks direction in terms of the purpose or rate of resource use.

This does not imply that, from an environmental point of view, decisions about these resources are any better or worse than before. Heavy direct government involvement in the energy sector in the past has been perceived by many as an environmental (as well as economic) disaster. Nevertheless, as the failure of market-based decision making to produce environmentally desirable outcomes in an area such as energy is well documented, guidance by governments seems inevitable. In the absence of an immediate crisis, however, the form of that guidance will depend at least as much on a government's commitment to economic growth as on the strength of environmental demands. There is little reason to believe that, without greater commitment of governments to environmental matters, the restructured public service is conducive to an 'integration' of economics and environment that gives more weight to the latter than in the past, and even less cause to believe that the environment will be given overriding or 'lexical' priority (Dryzek, 1987,p.59).

The move towards a market-led environmental policy becomes most problematic with regard to the use of economic instruments, where a low level of political support combines with technical complexity and potential economic costs. In a political climate where New Right and monetarist policies still dominate efforts to restore economic growth, governments are more likely to reduce or eliminate forms of government intervention (economic incentives, regulation) that involve government expenditure than to pursue environmental policies that incur an increase in costs, inflation, or regulation. In other words, governments of this ideological orientation are more inclined to adopt environmental policies 'on the cheap', despite the potentially high environmental, social, and economic costs of such policies in the long term.

The drive to get government out of business and to get more business into government has led to the virtual elimination of direct 'State vandalism' with regard to the environment, although such vandalism may still be sponsored by the State through policies which blindly promote economic growth and resource use. It has not, in itself, created a shift towards a more positive approach in environmental policy. Instead, it has opened the door more widely for environmental vandalism by others, notably in the private sector. Given that potential, the question of how environmental decision making outside central government, at the level of local and regional government and in the private sector, will be guided, becomes vital. In that context, it is important to assess whether, and to what extent, the reorganization of national environmental administration, the reform of local government, and the introduction of new environmental legislation, in particular the Resource Management Act, provide a framework for the future development of sound and effective environmental policy.

5
INSTITUTIONAL REFORM
Environmental Policy and Resource Management

The restructuring of national environmental administration, the comprehensive reorganization—indeed, virtual re-creation—of local government in New Zealand, and the comprehensive reform of environmental statutes through the Resource Management Act 1991 are three profound and remarkable reforms in their own right, but they also complement and amplify those discussed in Chapter 4. The Resource Management Act and Local Government Amendment Acts assigned major responsibilities for environmental policy—both recently identified responsibilities and latent responsibilities formerly resting with central government—to newly created local and regional councils. Together with the reorganization of national environmental administration, these reforms established a comprehensive new framework for management of water, land, and other resources—a framework with potentially far-reaching consequences for environmental policy development in New Zealand.

This new institutional framework is potentially of tremendous consequence for the way in which the environmental problematique is defined, interpreted, and addressed through politics. And a set of reforms more significant for environmental policy beyond New Zealand—whether in terms of theoretically based insight into strategic design or practical experimentation with institutional arrangements—can scarcely be imagined.

To what extent has reform of local government and the institutional arrangements for environmental resource management contributed to an improvement of environmental policy? It is too early in the implementation of the reforms to be able to assemble much evidence of concrete outcomes. But a truly serious answer to this question will require more than just measurement of outcomes and the evaluation of those outcomes against specified goals and prior conditions. A full assessment will require an appreciation of the dynamics of reform that led to the particular institutional arrangements chosen, an understanding of how policy change will be driven in the policy processes still being created, and an acknowledgement of the 'classic difficulties associated with making sensible, intentional changes in complex institutions' (March and Olsen, 1989). These reforms, like all policy reforms, were born of politics and their ultimate effect on environmental quality is mediated by politics. So, in evaluating them we want to know how they were influenced by the bias mobilized to produce them and how they, in turn, may improve environmental policy by structuring bias in ways that will lead to better grappling with various dimensions of the environmental problematique.

Major reorganization of national environmental administration took effect in 1987, the Local Government Amendment Acts became law in 1988 and 1989, and the Resource Management Act was passed in 1991. New Zealand will be working through the implementation of these particular reforms throughout the 1990s. But all this ambitious legislation and its consequences and significance can only be understood in the context of the many other sweeping reform efforts begun by the Labour Government during its six years in power (1984–90) and continued by the subsequent National Government. Most of these reform initiatives, which collectively constituted 'a period of radical change in New Zealand that has left no aspect of life untouched' (Wilson, in Holland and Boston, 1990, p. 8), did not address environmental policy in particular but rather considered the structure and operation of government in general. As discussed in Chapter 4, they were nevertheless profoundly consequential for environmental policy development.

Some of the substance and character of the major environmental policy reforms since 1984 can be attributed to efforts of organized environmental groups and to the commitment of government towards strengthened environmental policy. But these environmental reforms were all cast, shaped, and limited so as to be consistent with the theoretical and ideological underpinnings of the overall reform programme of the Government. As Boston, Martin, and Walsh (1991, p. 392) note:

> Regardless of how one evaluates their content, a striking feature of the public sector reforms between 1984 and 1990 was their consistency. In general, each new policy initiative built on and supported the previous policy shift.... All the major reforms were guided by a similar body of theory and a common analytical framework.

Thus the New Right principles that informed and guided most Labour and National reforms since 1984 are, not surprisingly, reflected in the reform of national environmental administration from 1984 to the present. They also inspired and directed both local government reform and resource management reform. At the same time, environmental policy reforms were influenced by environmental policy ideals that had been evolving since the 1970s and had earlier found expression in the activities of environmental activists, various initiatives of the Commission for the Environment and other advisory bodies, an external review (OECD, 1981), the manifestos of both major political parties, and the abortive efforts to develop a New Zealand Conservation Strategy (Bührs, 1991a, pp. 216–58).[1] The Resource Management Act, therefore, is partly systemic environmental policy and partly 'enabling legislation' that extends other New Right government reforms. Understanding this mixed heritage is crucial to understanding the potential, peculiar character, and limitations of the new environmental policy system created by the Resource Management Act and the preceding Local Government Amendment Acts.

Linkages Among the Reforms

Complementing New Right principles in many of the reform initiatives of the Fourth Labour Government were the objectives of better policy co-ordination, greater accountability of the bureaucracy and politicians, protections against exercise of government power, and constitutional, electoral, and Parliamentary reform to improve the political process. Prominent in pursuing these latter objectives within the Fourth Labour Government was Geoffrey Palmer, Deputy Prime Minister from 1984 to 1989 and Prime Minister from 1989 to 1990. Palmer, a former (and future) law professor, had long been prominent in advocating the establishment of more checks and balances against the exercise of power by government (Palmer, 1987, p. 22). In the Fourth Labour Government's first term, 1984–87, Palmer had been Attorney-General and Minister of Justice and he was particularly associated with the Labour Party's 1984 election promises for parliamentary reform, constitutional reform, electoral reform, and introduction of a Bill of Rights. Following the August 1987 election, however, Palmer also took on the Environment portfolio. Philip Woollaston was named as Minister Assisting the Deputy Prime Minister, Associate Minister of Justice, and Associate Minister for the Environment. Woollaston had been Parliamentary Under-Secretary for Local Government and Environment in Labour's previous term and had played a central role from the beginning in the restructuring of national environmental administration and in initial efforts to reorganize local government.[2] Labour had promised a major review of resource statutes in its 1984 manifesto, and in 1986 Woollaston indicated that

---

1. What we refer to as principles and ideals can also be analysed as policy myths in which theory, fact, fiction, and value come together to simplify complex and contentious issues (Murray and Swaffield, 1992).
2. Later Palmer would refer to Woollaston as 'my friend and mentor on environmental questions for years' (Palmer, 1990, p. 7).

Labour intended to proceed with such a review, presuming a return to government in the 1987 elections (Bührs, 1991a, p. 252).

After Labour's re-election, a comprehensive reform of local and regional government was announced in December 1987, and in January 1988 the Government publicly committed itself to a concurrent resource management law reform effort. A single special Cabinet Committee chaired by Palmer, the Cabinet Committee on the Reform of Local Government and Resource Management Statutes, was established to be responsible for policy development for both reform efforts.

Agenda status for both local government reform and resource management reform was achieved in part because of the consistency of these reforms with the broader reform thrust of the Labour Government, in part because the logic of the broader reforms suggested that they should also be entrenched in local government (not only New Right efficiency reforms but also accountability, procedural, and checks and balances reforms), and in part because of commitments that Labour had made to reform the structure of environmental decision making. The reorganization of local government and the review of resource statutes gained recognition as problems deserving serious attention at about the same time that policy ideas linking them began to be cultivated in reform proposals. Political processes and events were propitious for reform too, as Labour had been returned for a second term, seemingly with a mandate (however ambiguous) for further reform. Some of the potential bureaucratic saboteurs of reform—the Department of Lands and Survey, the New Zealand Forest Service, and the Ministry of Works and Development—had been or were soon about to be either dismantled or disabled by reorganizations of central government.[3] Treasury, with its anti-planning and anti-regulation philosophy, was in favour of rationalizing local government structures and functions and of reviewing existing Environmental Protection and Enhancement Procedures (requiring environmental impact assessment), the Town and Country Planning system, and other resource statutes, all of which were seen as impediments to economic efficiency, investment, and growth. Treasury, in its privileged political position, could reasonably expect to influence any reforms that might emerge.

Even for an extraordinarily ambitious, energetic, and determined government, there are always more potential issues, problems, and policies than can possibly be addressed. But a particular policy window (Kingdon,

---

3. According to Palmer (1990, p. 91): 'It [the Resource Management Law Reform project] was only possible because the old Ministry of Works and Development was abolished.'

1984) was open during the Fourth Labour Government's second term, an opportunity to make something big happen in local government restructuring and in environmental and resource policy. Geoffrey Palmer and Philip Woollaston had helped open the policy window and, as policy entrepreneurs committed to comprehensive, co-ordinated reforms in these areas, they were in a position to link problem recognition, policy ideas, and political events to achieve dramatic policy change.

Reforming National Environmental Administration

A review of the organizational arrangements for environmental administration was commenced by the new Labour Government in 1984 and, as discussed in Chapter 4, the first of many reorganizations undertaken by Labour were in the area of environmental administration. Originally, environmentalists had advocated the establishment of a Ministry for the Environment that would combine all the major conservation responsibilities scattered over a wide range of agencies. On top of that, the proposed Ministry would become the principal planning and regulatory agency for the environment, combining functions held by various other departments. This proposed Ministry would have real clout, replacing the 'toothless' Commission for the Environment (Royal Forest and Bird Protection Society of NZ et al., 1982, 1985).

Treasury, however, was not in favour of combining all these responsibilities in one agency, nor did it support the allocation of a planning and regulatory role to a Ministry for the Environment. Instead, Treasury saw a Ministry for the Environment's role as primarily that of a policy agency, leaving regulatory functions (e.g., pollution control) with other agencies (such as the Department of Health) and the responsibility for the implementation of environmental policies with local government. This reflected Treasury's view that policy, regulatory, and delivery functions should be separated in order to avoid capture of the policy process (a principle which would later be applied throughout the public service, as discussed in Chapter 4).

Treasury saw the task of a Ministry for the Environment as primarily one of developing a framework within which those involved in environmental decision making would find incentives to arrive at solutions themselves. For this reason, Treasury was also not in favour of allocating a planning function to the Ministry, as the word 'planning' was associated with undesirable bureaucratic control (Treasury, 1985a, 1985b).

Therefore, although the establishment of the new Department of Conservation as an 'advocate for conservation' can in part be interpreted as a major victory for the environmental lobby, it was also an outcome reflecting the Treasury line. Consequently, the mandate of the Ministry for the Environment—characterized as the 'Ministry in the Middle' (Establishment

Unit, 1986)—is much harder to explain on the basis of the demands of environmentalists. It mirrors, rather, an aversion to bureaucratic regulation and planning (both associated with a 'command and control' approach to environmental policy) by Treasury and key Labour ministers.

Less directly attributable to either the efforts of environmentalists or Treasury was the creation of the office of the Parliamentary Commissioner for the Environment. The Commissioner was allocated the role of independent watchdog over the system of environmental administration, and is responsible for investigating issues and areas in which the environmental policy process may not be functioning properly. The office combines elements of the roles of ombudsman and auditor, and has significant investigative, but no decision-making, powers. Given its role, the Commissioner's office was also the obvious place to locate responsibility for the environmental assessment procedures (Environmental Protection and Enhancement Procedures), a residual function of the former Commission for the Environment that did not fit in nicely with the Ministry for the Environment's policy advisory role. Although Treasury considered the procedures to be unnecessary—just another layer of bureaucratic control—the Government decided that they would remain in place until new arrangements for environmental assessment were introduced (Bührs, 1991a).

So, by mid-1987 the New Zealand Forest Service, the Department of Lands and Survey, the Wildlife Service of the Department of Internal Affairs, and the Commission for the Environment had been abolished. Created in their places were a Forestry Corporation, a Ministry of Forestry, a Land Corporation, a Department of Survey and Land Information, a Department of Conservation, a Ministry for the Environment, and a Parliamentary Commissioner for the Environment. Commercial activities were concentrated in the Land Corporation and the Forestry Corporation; the Ministry of Forestry and the Ministry for the Environment became policy advisory agencies, with some servicing and regulatory functions; the Department of Survey and Land Information was established as a servicing agency; the Parliamentary Commissioner for the Environment was created to serve as an auditor-ombudsman-system guardian; and the Department of Conservation was established as a resource management agency with a conservation advocacy role.

The principle of sustainability in the management of resources and reference to the intrinsic value of ecosystems were included in the Environment Act 1986 establishing the Ministry for the Environment and the Parliamentary Commissioner for the Environment. Also particularly significant for environmental policy was the retrenchment of government involvement in construction and development activities, reflected in the abolition in April 1988 of the once-powerful Ministry of Works and

Development and the incorporation of its remaining commercial activities in the Works and Development Corporation. The responsibilities of the Ministry of Works and Development for Town and Country Planning and Water and Soil Conservation were transitionally transferred to the Ministry for the Environment, pending further reform generated by the ongoing review of resource statutes.

Developing a new policy on environmental impact assessment procedures was an early project undertaken by the new Ministry for the Environment. A discussion paper was produced (Ministry for the Environment, 1986) and public comment was solicited, with a proposed new policy published in 1987 (Ministry for the Environment, 1987a). This proposal was never enacted, as reform of environmental impact assessment procedures was soon incorporated into a much more ambitious reform effort (Murray, 1990, pp. 37–9) that would entail a review of dozens of environmental and resource management statutes.

Local Government Restructuring and Reform

In the Fourth Labour Government's first term, 1984–87, local government reform had been a low priority and had been undertaken largely through appointment of an energetic Local Government Commission, a permanent quasi-judicial organization charged with producing an effective system (Bush, 1990, pp. 234–5). Some incremental reforms were achieved by this process—opening decision processes to the public, modification of the electoral system, some relatively easy amalgamations, and revision of land tax statutes (p. 236). But traditional resistance, and the limited power of the Commission, made it impossible to achieve comprehensive reform not mandated by Parliament.

A much more ambitious programme of reform was announced after Labour's re-election in 1987, with the Minister of Local Government, Michael Bassett, promising 'a fundamental review of all aspects of local government function, structures, organization and funding' (Martin, 1991b, p. 273). Although closely co-ordinated with the concurrent review of resource and environmental statutes, the local government reform process moved to the stage of legislative enactment much more quickly than did the resource management reform effort. The published schedule called for the Local Government Commission to approve final reorganization schemes in time for new local authorities to be elected in 1989.

A discussion document was produced by the Officials Co-ordinating Committee on Local Government in early 1988, followed shortly by Parliamentary direction in the form of the Local Government Amendment (No. 3) Act. This legislation directed the Local Government Commission to prepare final schemes for both regional and local units of government in one year, in accordance with specified objectives. The Commission solicited several rounds of submissions and published indicative reorganizational schemes before issuing its final proposed arrangement of new regional and local authorities in early 1989. Further measures implementing local government restructuring were passed by Parliament in the Local Government (No. 2) Act 1989, and the new units of local government were established in November 1989 after local elections, although many matters of funding and function remained to be resolved.

This local government reform effort resulted in substantial reduction of the number of local and regional units of government. Thirteen regions, seventy-four local districts, and seven special purpose boards were created to replace 625 existing units of local government, which had included authorities, united councils, counties, municipalities, districts, and special purpose boards. Most of the New Right principles that had guided central government reform could also be seen in the new system of local government. There was the same kind of emphasis on separation of regulatory functions from operational activities, contract appointment of executives and objective-based planning and performance measurement, transparency of accounting practices, and limitation of the size and functions of government.

Although hardly an example of incremental policy or incremental politics, neither can local government reform be understood as an example of apolitical, analycentric, 'big' decision making. Decree by legislation of the fundamental purposes of local government was a product rather than a beginning of the reform process. Along the way, the purity of some of the principles of state sector reform was diluted (Martin, 1991b, p. 273). No single choice can be identified as the policy decision; rather, the policy evolved over several months and years beginning in 1984. In the haste to have the new system in place well before the 1990 parliamentary elections (to minimize electoral retribution and to make repeal or reversal more difficult), the overall reform programme was incomplete when the new system began legal operation in November 1989. Substantial unfinished business remained with regard to funding and, for regional governments particularly, assignment of functions. Many details were left to be worked out during implementation. Certainly what Bush (1990) calls 'the back-to-front approach of determining form ahead of function' is one that derives from political considerations, not from those of analysis and instrumental rationality. The particular process of policy selection—using an energetic, activist Commission, which was empowered by a bold Parliament and directed by resolute ministers—determined how the policy was shaped and channelled as well as whether it ultimately could be 'made'.

Especially significant for reform of resource and environmental policy was the establishment of thirteen new regional authorities which were given boundaries that roughly followed catchment boundaries. Regional councils were to be directly elected and were expected to be assigned significant regulatory and co-ordinative functions by legislation resulting from concurrent reform efforts in transportation and resource management.[4]

By itself, this wholesale re-creation of local government undoubtedly has innumerable consequences for environmental policy. Elimination of most special-purpose units of government (except, initially, area health boards and electric power boards, which were addressed by separate legislation) certainly has consequences for policy formulation, implementation, and co-ordination. Many of the special purpose boards that were abolished, such as catchment, drainage, river, and pest destruction boards, had significant environment-affecting missions. General purpose territorial districts, which had environmentally significant responsibilities for urban planning, land use, and waste disposal, were reduced in number from more than two hundred to seventy-four, making possible, in theory anyway, the application of resources to better co-ordinated policy strategies and service delivery.

But unquestionably local government reform's greatest significance for environmental policy was in establishing the structures, organizations, and basic processes that would be used by the Resource Management Act to assign functions and redesign policy processes and institutions. Always a subordinate, secondary, constrained subset of the broader political system (Bush, 1989), local and regional government would thus be 'enabled' in a significant way. Through the Resource Management Act, front-line responsibility for environmental policy would be largely delegated and decentralized, although not devolved (as ultimate power, authority, and responsibility would still be reserved by central government for itself).[5]

---

4. The Transit New Zealand Act 1989 and the Transport Services Licensing Act 1989 did assign to local and regional government key functions in transportation policy. These too have environmental implications as, for example, bus services are now competitively bid for, with transport authorities owned by local districts treated like any other bidders. User confusion and operations downsizing has led to reduced services in several districts.
5. There is a real irony here, as the Resource Management Act authorizes the centralization of powers that under the Town and Country Planning Act were vested in local communities. Thus the Resource Management Act could potentially be used to establish a 'fast track' procedure for central government consideration and approval of consent applications deemed to be of national importance—accomplishing the same end as the National Development Act 1979, a keystone of the 'Think Big' programme of the Muldoon Government, which had been severely criticized by the Labour Party and later repealed by the Fourth Labour Government.

The Resource Management Act

In January 1988, Minister for the Environment Geoffrey Palmer announced that the Labour Government would undertake a comprehensive review and reform of the major laws pertaining to natural resources. This would include an integrated review of the Town and Country Planning Act, water and soil legislation, minerals legislation, and environmental assessment procedures. From the beginning this reform effort was closely co-ordinated with the concurrent local government reform effort, with a single ad hoc Cabinet Committee responsible for both reforms. A core group of four people (two from the Ministry for the Environment, one from Treasury, and one from a private law firm) were appointed to manage the resource management law reform project—a departure from the usual officials committee approach to creating new law, but similar in some respects to the approach that had been used earlier in developing the proposals for reorganizing national environmental administration. In September 1988 the ongoing coastal legislation review was merged with the resource management law reform as well.

The way the Labour Government had formulated and adopted many of its other reforms of the public sector and of New Zealand society—by emphasizing the formulation of detailed policies within the Cabinet and among a closed group of policy advisers followed by speedy adoption by a Labour-controlled Parliament—was not the strategy or process used to formulate and enact the Resource Management Act. For many of the reforms undertaken by the Labour Government from 1984 to 1990, the public had either been excluded from consultation, or not even informed about the Government's intentions (Boston, Martin, and Walsh, 1991, p. 390). Even though several rounds of submissions were solicited during the work of the Local Government Commission, for example, the tight timetable imposed by the government limited the extent and meaningfulness of the formalities of consultation. By contrast, the reform and reorganization of environmental administration that had begun in 1984 had been characterized by a remarkably high level of openness and public participation (Bührs, 1991a, pp. 263–7). Reports had been published as discussion papers with submissions sought, an Environmental Forum was staged, non-government officials were appointed to the Working Party on Environmental Administration, Environment Minister Russell Marshall and Under-Secretary for the Environment Philip Woollaston held meetings in each of twenty-two regions, and the Establishment Unit for the Ministry for the Environment and the Parliamentary Commissioner consulted widely and held meetings in various parts of the country.[6]

---

6. Philip Woollaston claimed that this had been 'the most thorough consultation on

Likewise, the resource management law reform project also entailed extensive programmes of public information and consultation—publication of discussion documents and a newsletter, numerous public meetings, and receipt of thousands of written submissions in several rounds and comments by toll-free telephone. These comments and submissions, by individuals, organized interest groups, industry, Māori and community groups, and local authorities, probably had more influence on the evolving resource management reform proposal than public consultation had had with other reform initiatives of the Labour Government, although more by way of changing the wording of specific clauses than in changing the fundamental structure of the draft legislation. The initial timetable of two years was demanding but generous by contrast with the tight schedules imposed on other reform initiatives such as local government reorganization. (Subsequently the timetable for the resource management law reform project proved to be more flexible as well.) The guidelines issued for the review by the supervising Cabinet Committee were also extraordinarily general by contrast with those that had governed most other Labour reform initiatives; the warrant given the co-ordinating Review Group was virtually open-ended. The first phase of the review entailed a so-called 'zero based' (i.e., nothing taken for granted) examination of the purposes, objectives, and priorities for reform. The initial phases of the review entailed consideration of a significant body of policy analysis—evaluations and reviews done for earlier reforms, recent reports done for the Ministry for the Environment, Treasury, and other agencies (e.g., Hearn, 1987), and policy research commissioned by the Core Group and the Ministry for the Environment (many of which were published by the Ministry as working papers).[7] The specification of reform objectives was a product not a beginning of the process and did not begin to emerge in a firm form (Ministry for the Environment, 1988b) until nearly a year into the review.

Preliminary proposals were issued in December 1988 and a draft bill was introduced in December 1989. It was referred to a select committee, which undertook further extensive public consultations and considered 1325 new written submissions. The select committee did not report back to Parliament until August 1990, leaving too little time for debate and passage before election adjournment. In November, the new National Government announced that it intended to pass the bill into law and appointed a review group to consider and report on the bill before Parliamentary reconsideration.

---

machinery of government ever conducted in New Zealand' (Bührs, 1991a, pp. 366–7).

7. The Ministry for the Environment published 32 resource management law reform working papers in 1988.

Following that group's report, the government proposed changes to the bill and, following further select committee consideration, it was passed by Parliament in its modified form in July 1991, to take effect on 1 October. The most substantial change made in the bill in this final review was to divert Part 9 into a separate act, the Crown Minerals Act, thereby exempting allocation of mining and prospecting rights and access to Crown-owned minerals from the principle of sustainable management.

The resource management law reform project had not been highly controversial, although it did provoke extensive debate. Unlike most of the other Labour reforms, it did not kindle resentment or generate tension or predispose individuals, major interest groups, or the National Party to oppose it (which proved crucial to the ultimate adoption of the Act, largely unchanged, after the Labour Government failed to secure passage before the 1990 election). Controversies and debate were generally limited to details and specifics, with the broad thrust of the proposals enjoying at least the lukewarm support of environmentalists and of both the Labour and National parties. Because of the emphasis on consultation and the solicitation of a wide range of contributions to the review process, the public and various groups felt included in the process (rather than feeling overrun and deceived, as with other reforms).

But there was also another reason why the resource management law reform project and the subsequent draft legislation never engendered the same degree of resentment and opposition as other Labour initiatives. The ad hoc Cabinet Committee, the Core Group, and the legislative drafters fashioned an Act, although comprehensive in scope and seemingly radical in its departure from past policy, that had wide appeal because it was written in such a way as to leave many issues undecided. Characterized by the Ministry for the Environment as 'a framework rather than a blueprint', the Act was written according to the 'plain English' and 'general principle' approaches to drafting statutes (Ministry for the Environment, 1989a, p. 2; Palmer, 1987, pp. 150–4). The less detail included, the less opportunity for dispute at the formulation and selection phase of the policy process and the greater the inclination of disparate individuals, interests, and parties to embrace the reform in principle, seeing in it what they wanted to see. Contention over details of policy was thus postponed until the implementation phase (Morgan, Memon, and Miller, 1991). Agreement was achieved on goals and objectives, but only as expressed in general, precatory language. Concrete, operational goals and objectives of the reform would be worked out over time, in the course of a political struggle over means, as forewarned by Environment Minister Palmer in a statement on the occasion of introduction of the bill into Parliament:

The law is only a beginning. The Bill sets up a sound framework. How effective it is in achieving sustainable management practices will be over to local communities, professionals and politicians (Ministry for the Environment, 1989a, p. 1).

Overview of a New Policy Process

The structure of the Resource Management Act is complex, as is the framework for environmental policy making it creates. It also is tightly integrated, with a linked series of relationships among and between several management instruments. Achievement of the Act's purpose is made fundamental to each. In most respects, however, it is not a revolutionary departure from previous law, as it builds, for example, on the Water and Soil Conservation Act 1967 and particularly the management planning approach developed in the Town and Country Planning Act.

The Act has a single stated purpose: 'to promote the sustainable management of natural and physical resources'. Sustainable management is defined as

> managing the use, development, and protection of natural and physical resources in a way, or at a rate, which enables people and communities to provide for their social, economic, and cultural wellbeing and for their health and safety while—
> (a) Sustaining the potential of natural and physical resources (excluding minerals) to meet the reasonably foreseeable needs of future generations; and
> (b) Safeguarding the life-supporting capacity of air, water, soil, and ecosystems; and
> (c) Avoiding, remedying, or mitigating any adverse effects of activities on the environment.

In achieving the purposes of the Act, all persons exercising functions and powers under it are enjoined to recognize and provide for matters of national importance, such as protection of outstanding natural features, landscapes, and significant indigenous vegetation and fauna; to have particular regard to other matters such as the intrinsic value of ecosystems and maintenance and enhancement of the quality of the environment; and to take into account the principles of the Treaty of Waitangi.

The Act sets out the duties and restrictions of all persons with respect to use of land, the coastal marine area, beds of lakes and rivers, water, discharges, and noise, and declares that every person has a duty to avoid, remedy, or mitigate any adverse effect on the environment.

The functions, powers, and duties of district and city councils, regional councils, and the Ministers of Conservation and the Environment are specified by the Act. District and city councils have primary responsibility for management of land use, noise, and surface water. A particularly important role is assigned to regional councils, who are given responsibility for management of water, soil, geothermal resources, pollution control, hazardous substances, and natural hazards. The Minister of Conservation has special responsibilities with respect to coastal management. The Minister for the Environment has an overview and monitoring role, and may directly determine policy by setting national environmental standards by regulation for noise, contaminants, water, soil, and air; by issuing national policy statements to direct and guide local government decisions; and by 'calling in' any application for a resource consent in order to make a decision about it at a national level.

A policy and planning framework is specified by the Act, to provide a 'tiered, cascading' hierarchy of standards, policy statements, and plans. A national coastal policy statement, issued by the Minister of Conservation, is mandatory; other national policy statements may be issued by the Minister for the Environment. National environmental standards, or regulations, are also optional. Any national environmental standards and policy statements are binding on regional and district councils.

Each regional council is required to prepare a single regional policy statement that will provide the basis for integrated resource management for that region. A region may also issue more detailed regional plans, including implementation methods and rules that prohibit, regulate, or allow activities, in order to achieve its (and central government's) policies. Only a regional coastal plan is mandatory.

A district, in turn, is required to prepare a single plan that must be consistent with national policy statements, the regional policy statement, and regional plans, and must focus on managing effects of activities on the environment. District plans may contain rules that prohibit, regulate, or allow activities.

Where any activity contravenes the restrictions specified in the Act or where a plan so specifies, a resource consent must be sought. The Act provides for a standard consent process for land use consents, subdivision consents, coastal permits, water permits, and discharge permits.

The Act places a general duty on the Minister for the Environment, the Minister for Conservation, and every regional and district authority, before adopting any objective, policy, rule, or other method, to have regard to alternative means for achieving the purposes of the Act and to evaluate the costs and benefits of the principal alternative means. A general obligation is imposed on applicants for resource consents to undertake environmental impact assessment in advance of an application. All district and regional councils are required to state, with respect to policies and plans, the environmental results anticipated from implementation of those policies and methods. In issuing any rules, the regional and district councils are required to have regard to the actual or potential effects on the environment. An obligation is imposed on local and regional authorities to monitor the state of the environment, the suitability and effectiveness of policies and plans, and the exercise of resource consents. The Act requires public consultation in the preparation of all policy statements and plans, and permits any person or organization to make submissions on most consent applications.

The Planning Tribunal continues in its established role of dealing with appeals, inquiries, and disputes, and is given a stronger enforcement role. The Act sets out a range of enforcement mechanisms, such as enforcement orders, abatement notices, excessive noise and water shortage directions, and criminal sanctions, including fines and possible imprisonment for more serious crimes (Grinlinton, 1992).

In sum, the new framework and institutionalized policy process established by local government and resource management reform is distinctive and comprehensive. But what are its certain substantive implications for environmental policy? Is it biased towards the production of 'greener' outcomes in the physical, social, and economic environment? Towards the cultivation and elaboration of environmental values, norms, and meaning in the political culture? Towards imbedding ecological rationality in social and political institutions by providing 'opportunities for individuals to develop and affirm environmental values and to press for innovative adaptation of structures and processes to a changing political world' (Bartlett, 1990b, p. 92)? Questions of this kind require that we think of these reforms not as straightforward environmental policies but as environmental meta-policies, as discussed in Chapter 1.

Environmental Meta-policy
Like any government, the Labour Government from 1984 to 1990 was responsible for a large number of ordinary environmental policy changes and developments, for example with respect to protecting indigenous forests or regulation of ozone depleting chemicals (and with respect to policies not ordinarily thought of as environmental, such as agriculture subsidies or transportation regulation). Most governments engage in a certain amount of rearranging of agencies as part of their effort to put a distinctive stamp on policy—redrawing lines of authority, shuffling components from one part of a bureaucratic hierarchy to another, creating new units to carry out pet initiatives. But many of the reforms of the Labour Government, including all of those described in Chapters 4 and 5 of this book, went far beyond ordinary policy making. These policies—meta-policies—were more fundamental in

character, being policies about *whether*, *how*, and *by whom* future ordinary policies would be made.

The environmental policy system New Zealand has in the 1990s is markedly different from the system it had in the first half of the 1980s. Some of the changes, such as the privatization, corporatization, and commercialization of many government operations, the reform of the public service, the emphasis on economic incentives in lieu of direct regulation, and the redesign of local government, apply across the board to all of politics and government including environmental policy. The environmental policy system, however, is further changed by the reorganization of national environmental administration and the recasting, through the Resource Management Act, of environmental policy structures, processes, rules, opportunities, responsibilities, roles, duties, resources, interests, powers, and language.

Given the minimal penetration of environmental values into New Zealand law, politics, and administration by the early 1980s, merely to say that all this institutional reform has contributed to an improvement of environmental policy is not claiming a great deal. In the early 1980s, environmental policy was severely disadvantaged in a highly bureaucratized, centralized system that had few environmental advocates or even friendly ears. Its policy agenda was tightly controlled and only a few crude means were available to force consideration of environmental values. Certain features of this system remain familiar today, of course, such as the relatively unfettered policy dominance of the Cabinet over the national legislature and executive. But by contrast, environmental policy is now formulated in a political system that is institutionally rich in opportunities for the advance of environmental values. At the national level, some of the most powerful bureaucratic opponents of environmental values have disappeared, shrunk, or been redirected. The Ministry for the Environment, the Parliamentary Commissioner for the Environment, and the Department of Conservation enjoy a degree of bureaucratic autonomy and a potential for policy influence that was not possible under the previous system. At the regional level, whole new authorities have been created with primary responsibility for environmental quality and resource management. Positive obligations for realizing environmental values are now part of the organic missions of all general purpose local authorities (and most special purpose local authorities have been abolished). Defining environmental concerns as policy problems, and getting those problems onto policy agendas at some level of government, is now much easier.

As a consequence, the nature of citizen action and the character of organized environmentalism has changed and will continue to change. In this more complex landscape, environmental groups must diversify and target, taking advantage of many more opportunities to force action and policy innovation and to generate publicity. Many more opportunities exist for individuals to exert a direct influence on environmental policy, through election to local and regional councils, through employment by local and regional councils, through involvement in the various new policy and decision processes (policy statements, district plans, consent applications, and so on) established by the new system and, finally, through hands-on involvement in resource use and management.

But this multiplication of opportunities for policy influence has a price. The same access is also available to those whose first interests are not environmental quality and environmental values. Indeed, the resources of environmentalists and environmental groups are likely to be stretched thin, making it impossible to keep tabs on every policy forum, process, or institution. Likewise, press scrutiny may be less consistently focused. The unified consent system established under the Resource Management Act is intended to improve economic efficiency by reducing the time and costs to developers.

In spite of the injunctions and directives of the Resource Management Act with respect to sustainability, avoiding adverse effects, and the intrinsic value of ecosystems, environmentalists should not be surprised to find local government councils and staff only marginally sympathetic to policy arguments anchored in broad claims about the public interest, nature preservation, future generations, or green lifestyles. Business has a generally privileged place in politics (Lindblom, 1977; Lindblom and Woodhouse, 1993; McConnell, 1966). In New Zealand as well as in other developed western nations with stronger traditions of robust local government than New Zealand, business is most privileged at the local level (Nice, 1987; Schattschneider, 1960; Wilson, 1985). Local politics tends to revolve around matters of land use and economic development, dominated by informal networks of local builders, developers, bankers, lawyers, retail merchants, and politicians. To the extent that environmental values can be made congruent with the values of these vested interests, they will flourish; to the extent that they can be painlessly afforded, they will be tolerated and indulged. But to the extent that they challenge local development and economic growth, the power of the vested interest will swing against them in most places (Petulla, 1988, p. 172).

There are at least three ways that business is even more privileged under the Resource Management Act than under preceding legislation. First, the Act creates a strong presumption favouring individual property rights by expressly permitting all land uses unless prohibited by a rule in a plan or unless a consent is specifically required. The procedures for granting consents are aimed at facilitating private development. Second, activities can be controlled only with respect to adverse or detrimental effects; the Act places the burden on government and opponents of development to specify the effects that are not allowed and to prove that any rules or other measures are necessary to achieve particular environmental goals.[8] Preventive, anticipatory policy directed at the sources of environmental problems is discouraged, whereas business risk and uncertainty are minimized and flexibility is enhanced. Third, the Act requires evaluation of the costs and benefits of principal alternative means before adopting any objective, policy, rule, or other method. This general requirement will provide an advantage to those activities whose costs are uncertain, intangible, and long-term but whose benefits are immediate, obvious, and easily calculated in terms of money, such as those of business. It will disadvantage activities like environmental protection that have long-term, often unquantifiable benefits but sometimes substantial immediate monetary costs (Swartzman, Liroff, and Croke, 1982).

There is, of course, the potential for this bias to be counterbalanced by the active, assertive involvement of central government in this process, notably through the significant powers reserved to the Minister for the Environment to issue national policy statements, to set national environmental standards, and to issue guidance for implementation of the Resource Management Act. The Minister also has responsibility to monitor implementation and, where local authorities are not performing their functions, may even appoint people to exercise those functions.

The Resource Management Act is not self-implementing; its ultimate influence on environmental policy development and environmental quality is not predetermined by the language of the Act only. Should environmental policy become a high priority agenda item of some present or future Cabinet or influential Environment Minister, the opportunity will exist for policy entrepreneurs to contribute to significant policy development *under* the Resource Management Act, in addition to the usual statutory route.

In any event, the Resource Management Act is not so comprehensive that anyone has claimed it is the last environmental statute that will ever be needed to assure a clean and green New Zealand environment. Among other things, its dominant concern with resources (a concept that can only be defined and understood in a utilitarian context) greatly limits its relevance to much of the

---

8. This will be especially difficult for regional and local governments, with their limited resources and technical capabilities. Moreover, a focus on effects alone will make it particularly difficult to adopt anticipatory policies to cope with two kinds of effects that are often most significant environmentally—threshold and cumulative effects.

ecological dimension of the environmental problematique, in spite of the non-utilitarian language in its statement of purpose and principles (e.g., 'intrinsic value'). Moreover, it virtually ignores the social dimension of environmental policy as well; as such it has limited significance for the urban environment where most New Zealanders live.

Nor were the reforms of national environmental administration the last word in institutional design. For example, an inadequacy of New Zealand's administrative structure that was identified well before the resource management law reform effort was lack of a national environmental regulatory agency (OECD, 1981). New Zealand is one of a few developed nations without such an agency. The initial Labour Government proposals for resource management law reform included establishment of an Environmental Protection Agency and a Hazardous Substance Advisory Board. As introduced, and in its final enacted form, the Resource Management Act included provision for establishment of a more narrowly named Hazards Control Commission. But that part of the Act did not come into force on 1 October 1991, requiring instead development in further legislation. Not until October 1992 did the National Government issue proposals for hazardous substances regulation, promising to introduce legislation in Parliament in 1993 (Ministry for the Environment, 1992a).

Whatever the final disposition of the Hazards Control Commission, there are other inadequacies of the new environmental policy system. For example, there is little requirement or provision that energy consumption policy be considered in conjunction with environmental and resource management policies. There are many remaining questions of structure and process too. The Environment Act 1986, for example, left room for some confusion about the role of the Ministry for the Environment, in spite of the reform's underlying principle that new agencies were to have clear, non-conflicting mandates. This has been a confusion that the Ministry for the Environment has been unable to resolve for itself. The Ministry is by default New Zealand's central co-ordinating agency for environmental policy, but it has no clear mandate to require other agencies to co-operate or provide information and expertise (Bührs, 1991a, pp. 386–90). It is primarily a policy advisory and reporting agency, but with some management and regulatory responsibilities assigned to it as well (a few transitionally). In relation to the importance of its limited responsibilities, it has a small budget and few resources compared to other agencies. Unlike the Department of Conservation, which has a role as advocate for conservation, it was not explicitly assigned a role as a policy advocate for the environment.

Instead, a role emphasized by the Ministry for the Environment has been one of finding balance, as the agency in the middle, a system reformer—a role that Ministry officials have embraced in public statements and in published annual Corporate Plans. This was the role publicly acknowledged by the Ministry as it served as the principal agency providing analysis and support for the massive resource management law reform project. Thus from this perspective, the Resource Management Act was not primarily environmental policy; rather, it was enabling legislation for local government, a continuation of reforms to improve the overall policy and legislative framework of the system. A second role assigned to the Ministry for the Environment, however, is that of a policy agent, responsible for developing environmental policies—in fact, and again by default, an advocate for better environmental policy. The incompatibility of these two roles, advocate and balancer, remains, and to some extent it hamstrings the Ministry's vision of its mission. Although the Ministry for the Environment continues to eschew a description of itself as an operational department (obvious regulatory, co-ordinative, and management responsibilities notwithstanding), in its 1992–93 Corporate Plan it acknowledges 'a greater responsibility for implementation', having redefined its purpose as '[t]o achieve sustainable management of the environment' (Ministry for the Environment, 1992b, p. 5). Such a mission would seem to require a range of hands-on management and directive activities inappropriate for a 'Ministry in the Middle'.

We can say, then, that New Zealand has attempted to improve environmental policy primarily through reform of organizational structures and policy processes, but that a meta-policy analysis reveals some significant contradictions, deficiencies, and confusions. New Zealand, through institutional reform, has greatly increased its policy emphasis on anticipatory as opposed to reactive policy making, and is now in some respects a world leader in some of the procedures and requirements it has adopted; but the new environmental policy system still is unbalanced and reflects an earlier dominance of nature protection issues over those of, for example, energy, pollution control, and urban development. The new institutionalized policy system is forcing some degree of comprehensive and integrated attention to these areas (a matter we shall explore at greater length in Chapter 6), but environmental policy development, as reflected by the major reforms achieved to date, is still uneven. This should not be surprising, nor is it necessarily damning, given that substantive environmental policy was not the primary purpose of the reforms, and that they were not driven primarily by environmental values or principles. The reforms were supported for a variety of reasons, including a general commitment to 'better decision making'; for the most part substantive environmental policy goals emerged as *products* of the reform processes.

Evaluation and Conclusions

In terms of declared purposes and principles, the Resource Management Act is an eloquent extension of earlier New Zealand environmental initiatives of the 1980s, notably the reorganization of national environmental administration. This restructuring was achieved in part through the Environment Act 1986 which endorsed the principle of sustainability in the management of resources, the mutuality of environmental relationships, and the intrinsic value of ecosystems. The Environment Act defined environment in an encompassing way and enabled consideration of the environment in policy formulation (Fisher, 1991, p. 4). Likewise the Resource Management Act establishes a succinct and compelling purpose—to promote the sustainable management of natural and physical resources. The Act also lists a cogent set of principles to be applied to management of all resources in achieving its purpose. It is by declaration, then, a national environmental policy act (albeit one focused largely on resources).

But statements of aspiration and direction, however noble, are no more than symbolic unless some means are provided to ensure compliance with the direction. The Resource Management Act also establishes a framework for environmental policy making, assigns authority and power to local and regional government for policy planning and decision making, directs that certain processes be used in that planning and decision making, and authorizes various means by which local government and the Planning Tribunal may enforce regulations, plans, and consents. Every part of the Act is linked with its statement of purpose, giving it an impressive integrated coherence directed at a single notable objective of sustainable environmental quality. It seems to devolve—but really only delegates—authority, power, and responsibility to local and regional government. Yet a hierarchical structure is established, with central government in a privileged place at its apex having a reserve of powers. The kinds of intergovernmental relations anticipated by the Act are solely vertical authority relationships. The Act contains but few explicit incentives or penalties designed to induce local and regional councils to comply with its spirit, few concrete or specific policy directives, and few action-forcing mechanisms directed at government at any level.

An appreciation of this overall context, and of the split purpose and focus of the Resource Management Act, is essential for understanding the new institutional processes established by the reforms of local government and resource management law. On the one hand, the Resource Management Act is an extension and continuation of earlier policy initiatives to extend and improve environmental administration and to adopt further substantive policies. So the Resource Management Act as environmental policy endorses sustainable management as a fundamental purpose of resource and environmental policy and provides for comprehensive application of the concept in all processes and outcomes provided for in the Act. It further defines sustainable management to include maintaining and enhancing the quality of the environment, recognizing and avoiding or mitigating the adverse effects of irreversible change, and not endangering the ability of renewable resources to yield long-term benefits. The Act requires that all persons acting under the legislation have regard to principles including actual and potential effect on ecosystems, ecological processes, and biological diversity; potential advantages and disadvantages to the environment; and the maintenance and enhancement of natural, physical, and cultural features. It establishes duties and responsibilities for all persons to avoid, remedy, or mitigate adverse effects, and restricts the use of common property resources such as air and water unless expressly allowed. It provides for the integrated management of land, air, water, and minerals by replacing more than seventy statutes, passed at different times, with a single coherent framework.

On the other hand, the Resource Management Act is an extension and continuation of the reform of government generally as influenced by New Right thinking; in particular it is an important second stage of local government reorganization and reform. Consequently, it is 'principally enabling', providing a purpose and delegating authority and responsibilities to restructured local government and a reason for existence for newly created regional government. But it provides surprisingly few directives, few provisions for intergovernmental guidance or co-ordination, and few action-forcing mechanisms. And it provides little vision and few substantive goals for society. How it works as environmental policy will depend on how the opportunities it provides are exploited by local and regional governments and also, especially, on how the policy gaps and ambiguities it leaves are filled by central government in the 1990s.

6
COMPREHENSIVE ENVIRONMENTAL POLICY
Obstacles and Prospects

Victor Hugo wrote (1852) that 'greater than the tread of mighty armies is an idea whose time has come'. More recently, sociologist Robert Nisbet (1982) concluded that 'It is entirely possible that when the history of the twentieth century is finally written, the single most important social movement of the period will be judged to be environmentalism'. The profound influence environmentalism has had on politics and policy suggests that there is more to it than merely a label for a particular policy orientation. The environmental movement and environmental policy are both responses to the pressures of a set of particular problems that have gained political saliency and also responses to a number of ideas that have tied these problems together—while defining additional ones—in a politically potent package. Environmental policy development has been consistent with Kingdon's (1984) finding that two major influences on how all political agendas are set and alternatives specified are 'the inexorable march of problems' and the content of ideas.

One of the 'ideas whose time had come' in the 1960s was the concept of the environment itself. Even before governments began enacting large numbers of new laws, establishing agencies, and inaugurating programmes to deal with environmental effects, existing policy segmentation was identified as an environmental problem. Compartmentalization of government programmes, institutions, and analytical effort facilitated the taking of actions that degraded the environment, with no agents being responsible either for side effects or for overall consequences. Attempted remedies were partial and often counterproductive. Fragmentation inhibited recognition of sources, causes, and interrelationships, particularly those that might be counter-intuitive. The environment was thus taken for granted as policies dealt 'with its various elements without regard to their interrelated totality' (Caldwell, 1963, p. 136).

Ironically, most environmental policy action of the past three decades has not ameliorated fragmentation but has added to it through the creation of thousands of laws, agencies, positions, and programmes, each narrowly directed at one environmental problem or effect. Most environmental policy has proceeded by way of compartmentalized and unco-ordinated, if not conflicting, attacks on specific issues and problems (Bartlett, 1990a, p. 235).

Yet using the term environment should force a consideration of the whole, of the future, and of basic relationships—all of which are implicit in the environment concept itself. These were the profound reasons why the very term environment was initially promoted in the 1960s and why a new social movement found it so appealing to use in defining itself. By suggesting and advocating use of 'environment', Caldwell and others were doing more than merely offering a new subject for policy making—more even than proposing a reorientation of politics and policy to favour environmental protection and enhancement. The idea of environmental policy, from the beginning, implied something fundamental about both the *processes* and *ends* of policy making (Bartlett, 1993b). Among other things, truly environmental policy would have to be anticipatory; its success would ultimately require radical changes in social values and practices; it could be accomplished only through systemic reform of government institutions; and truly environmental policy would need to be both comprehensive and integrated. (These are, not accidentally, the four themes around which this book is organized.)

Theodore Lowi (1972) has argued that 'policy determines politics' in the sense that the nature of problems affects the kind of treatment they get. To the extent that this is true, the particular nature and demands of environmental problems—and of the idea of environmental policy *per se*—inescapably push environmental policy to take up the challenges of anticipation, changing the way we do things, institutional reform, and making policy more comprehensive and integrated. As noted in the Introduction, in spite of some of the real accomplishments of environmental policy since the 1960s, these four challenges are still recurring themes in the debates and literature on environmental policy. Indeed, they underlie frequent characterizations of environmental policy achievements as inadequate (Bührs, 1991a, pp. 14–16). In Chapters 2 to 5 we assessed New Zealand's environmental policy development in light of the first three of these challenges. In this chapter we analyse whether, and to what extent, the developments described in preceding chapters have led or are likely to lead to more comprehensive and integrated environmental policy in New Zealand.

Needs and Obstacles

Although claims and findings of environmental policy failure have become widely fashionable, they do not always bear up under closer scrutiny (Bartlett, 1993a). Nevertheless, unambiguous success has been equally hard to document, and there is a growing consensus that the approaches taken to date have been inadequate given the nature and magnitude of the environmental problematique. A key reason, according to a growing number of analysts (Bartlett, 1990a; Bührs, 1991a, 1991b; Davies, 1991; Guruswamy, 1989, 1991; Haigh and Irwin, 1989; Irwin, 1991; Lowrey and Carpenter, 1984; OECD, 1991; Rabe, 1986), is that policies do not adequately recognize the complexity and interrelatedness of environmental phenomena.

Policy is fragmented in at least three important ways (Guruswamy, 1991, p. 83). First, the environment itself is treated as consisting of separate and distinct resources, media, and systems (air, water, wildlife, energy, soils, hazardous substances, and so on). Second, the three dimensions of the environmental problematique are often understood and dealt with separately. Those government institutions responsible for economic and social policy operate with narrow mandates independently of those responsible for environmental and natural resources policy. Third, policy traditionally focuses on alleviating effects immediately and restrictively defined, rather than on the sources or causes of those effects (Brundtland Commission, 1987). The result is policy that is frequently reactive, piecemeal, unreasonably costly, and 'too little too late'. Rather than solving or resolving problems, severely fragmented environmental policy as often as not overlooks problems, displaces problems, and causes problems.

Based on the work of the Conservation Foundation and others in the 1980s, Irwin (1991, pp. 12–18) identifies seven reasons for taking steps towards integrating environmental policy:

1. Fragmentation encourages use of control methods that transfer problems to other parts of the environment.
2. Existing problems are often not accurately identified and therefore cannot be effectively managed.
3. What is often the best solution—prevention—is ignored.
4. Fragmentation decreases the likelihood that new and more complex problems will be identified and prevented or controlled.
5. Fragmentation makes it difficult to set priorities among problems.
6. Fragmented environmental programmes hinder more effective integration of environmental policy into other policy sectors.
7. Fragmentation results in an excessively complex and inconsistent administrative structure.

Although recognition of the need for better co-ordinated, more comprehensive, and better integrated environmental policy is growing, there are very real obstacles that hinder and complicate such policy development. One of the most serious obstacles has been semantic confusion and ambiguity in the language used in analysis of, and debate over, comprehensive or integrated environmental policy.

Few concepts have been used in more muddled and even duplicitous ways in policy discourse. Contrary to the guidance provided in dictionaries, 'comprehensive' is often used as though it meant *including all* or *including everything*, and 'integrated' is used as an exact synonym of comprehensive or to mean *fully incorporated into an indivisible whole*. These absolute meanings are usually implied in arguments against integrated, comprehensive policy of whatever kind; unless the definitions are challenged, then, the case becomes simple and persuasive. If comprehensive environmental policy making refers only to discrete decisions each of which deals with everything at once, then it is indeed impossible. So also is perfectly co-ordinated or wholly integrated environmental policy.

But co-ordination, comprehensiveness, and integration are far from absolute, all-or-nothing concepts.[1] Policies are social processes and commitments that involve many people over time; comprehensiveness refers to greater degrees of consideration of matters of importance (or 'thinking broadly and prospectively about consequences'—Wilson and Harris, 1991, p. xvii); and 'integrated' merely suggests some degree of weaving together and merging. There is significant scope for coping with environmental problems more effectively if policies are developed and implemented with a greater *degree* of comprehensiveness, integration, and co-ordination (Bührs, 1991a).

The practical difficulties of institutionalizing greater capability for comprehensive, integrative environmental policy should not be underestimated. The very characteristics of environmental concern that make reliance on decomposition, trial-and-error, and feedback unwise also threaten the success of attempts at more comprehensive, integrated policy making. Characteristic of policies having significant impact on the environment

---

1. This, of course, does not keep some analysts from dredging up old arguments about discredited models of rational comprehensive decision making to attack a straw man (e.g., Krier and Brownstein, 1991). The misleading claim continues to be made that, because comprehensive rationality is impossible, 'it is silly to conclude that "we are compelled to treat the environment as a whole"'. Comprehensive rationality, in the sense of knowing everything, is indeed impossible, and rational comprehensive decision making, in the sense of making decisions based only on logical processing of complete information, is also hopelessly idealistic and infeasible. But because 'comprehensive' does *not* mean including all or including everything, the conclusion that comprehensive environmental policy is impossible does not hold. The question is not so much whether a comprehensive, integrated approach to environmental policy is feasible or not (it is), but whether and how a higher degree of comprehensiveness and integration can be achieved (Bartlett, 1990a).

are consequences that are often irreversible and impacts that may be geographically or temporally dispersed or may appear at the end of a long causal sequence. Some environmentally important outcomes will only result if a (usually unknown) threshold is exceeded. Sometimes actions have effects that would be unremarkable if the actions occurred independently in isolation, but are noteworthy as the product of more than one action (that is, cumulative, interactive, and synergistic effects) (Bartlett, 1986a, p. 107).

However substantial the need may be for thinking broadly[2] and protecting against the tyranny of small decisions, the means for accomplishing this are not obvious or easy. Even if the case for more comprehensive and integrated environmental policy is compelling, it is not widely understood or appreciated, and its complexity and abstractness make it difficult to explain and 'sell' to politicians and the public.

Nor is there consistent support for comprehensive, integrated policy among policy analysts, in academia, or even among environmentalists. Comprehensiveness and integration run counter to the modern nature of expertise, which almost always means narrow, specialized, disciplinary expertise. Environmentalists tend to favour more immediate, visible objectives, and worry about the uncertainty and political risks of untried approaches to policy making. As discussed earlier in Chapters 2 and 3, in New Zealand (as elsewhere) there is scarcely a consensus about the *substantive* elements of good comprehensive environmental policy among environmentalists, and much less agreement in the broader political arena.

In addition to complexity and interrelatedness, the public good nature of many environmental problems raises obstacles for policy action. Environmental problems affect everyone (often in immeasurable and intangible ways, such as with issues of genetic diversity and the quality of life), so there is potentially a very wide basis of support for addressing them. But people usually give a higher priority to their more specific interests, and incentives to organize to secure broad public goods are weak. Even in a unitary political system like New Zealand's, the emergence of a clear constituency in favour of comprehensive, integrative policy is likely to be temporary and unusual.

Indeed, the existing structural institutional contexts within which comprehensive, integrative environmental policy must develop are heavily biased against it (although perhaps less so in New Zealand than in some other

---

2. 'Thinking big' would be a better term except for its unfortunate association in New Zealand with the Think Big policies promoted in the late 1970s and early 1980s by the National Governments headed by Robert Muldoon.

developed nations). Formal and informal power structures favour *ad hoc* bargaining, short-term pragmatism, and powerful private interests such as business, often at the expense of public goods. Policy processes are far from neutral; all organizational structures work as agenda-setting procedures, affecting the choice of action alternatives. It is not possible to design a structure that excludes bias and strategic behaviour (Hammond, 1986), and any attempt to create a structure to bias strategic behaviour towards comprehensive, integrated environmental policy must contend with the variety of other interests already embodied in existing institutions. Any efforts to institutionalize comprehensive, integrated environmental policy are likely to be costly in the short run, which greatly limits their appeal in the face of overall budget pressures and the pressing needs of existing environmental programmes.

Moreover, institutional reform involves much more than government organizational change. Further, even more formidable, obstacles exist in economic structures and processes and in the broader socio-cultural context. Sponsoring economic growth, for instance, is a key function of the modern State. The imperatives of capitalist economics combine with the 'much deeper pressures of the competitive multi-state system' to impose limits on the freedom of the State in determining policy—requiring that economic growth and development always take priority over environmental protection (Walker, 1989).

Successful institutionalization of comprehensive, integrative environmental policy is ultimately dependent upon a supportive foundation of interests, values, and norms—a political culture that espouses and practises ecological rationality rather than finding it threatening. Truly comprehensive, integrative environmental policy requires extensive public participation, co-operation, and support; almost by definition it cannot be successfully imposed on an unwilling, antagonistic, or even merely indifferent public.

Given these constraints and obstacles, it is hardly surprising that most environmental policy falls short of the integrated, comprehensive ideal. But the formidability of obstacles to change does not mean that policy inadequacies should be accepted as inevitable and unavoidable. Current environmental policy is unnecessarily *ad hoc*, fragmented, and narrowly focused, and there is considerable scope for coping with environmental problems more effectively by addressing them in a more comprehensive, integrated way. More comprehensive, integrated environmental policy is possible and desirable—as demonstrated by many past efforts (all insufficiently studied), traditional arrangements, and ongoing policy experiments that can be found around the world.

Policy Developments Outside New Zealand

Worldwide, along with a second wave of environmental concern and demands in the late 1980s, came a renewed interest from governments in making environmental policy more comprehensive and integrated. This interest was prompted in large part by analyses and criticisms of the kinds of environmental policies that had been adopted in the 1970s. In particular, the World Commission on Environment and Development, better known as the Brundtland Commission, focused considerable attention on comprehensiveness and integration with its immensely influential report *Our Common Future*. The Commission argued that, although

> existing environmental protection policies and agencies must be maintained and even strengthened, governments now need to take a much broader view of environmental problems and policies. . . . Environmental protection and sustainable development must be an integral part of the mandates of all agencies of governments, of international organizations, and of major private-sector institutions. . . . The ability to choose policy paths that are sustainable requires that the ecological dimensions of policy be considered at the same time as the economic, trade, energy, agricultural, industrial, and other dimensions—on the same agendas and in the same national and international institutions (1987, pp. 311–13).

The Brundtland Report subsequently served as a catalyst for action by a number of non-governmental organizations, by international agencies in the United Nations system, and by many national governments, most notably Norway, Canada, and the Netherlands (McChesney, 1991a). In several countries the Report helped provide political support for initiatives and experiments that were already under way.

Probably the strongest response has come from the Netherlands, which began shifting its framework for policy planning to a more integrated approach in the early 1980s, before publication of the Brundtland Report (Bennett, 1990). Rather than separate plans for air, water, and waste, an indicative plan for the environment was introduced in 1984 and the first National Environmental Policy Plan, *To Choose or to Lose*, was released in 1989.

In Canada, a major step towards integration occurred with the 1988 Environmental Protection Act, which consolidated and strengthened previous legislation (Rabe, 1990).

In the United Kingdom, the Royal Commission on Environmental Pollution had proposed in 1976 that pollution control be integrated; in 1987 the suggested solution, a unified Inspectorate of Pollution, was finally created (Owens, 1990).

In the United States, several studies of integrated, multi-media approaches to pollution control were undertaken by the Conservation Foundation in the 1980s. The Environmental Protection Agency (itself an early experiment in achieving integration by reorganization) sponsored several limited policy experiments in integrated pollution control, established an Office of Pollution Prevention, and began a debate on the merits of 'prevention of unreasonable risk' as a standard for action that would foster a unified system for regulating substances (Davies, 1990; U.S. EPA, 1987, 1990). The appointment in 1989 of the President of the Conservation Foundation, William Reilly, as Administrator of the Environmental Protection Agency, resulted over the next four years in further agency initiatives aimed at pollution prevention and more unified, risk-based goals and programmes.

Not surprisingly, much of the effort to make environmental policy more comprehensive and integrated has been invested in a variety of technical tools to improve information and analysis capabilities. Among the tools being developed in recent years are materials accounting and engineering mass balance, multimedia inventories, multimedia monitoring and modelling, product life-cycle assessment, ecological risk assessment, and geographic information systems (Irwin, 1991, pp. 46–50). But whereas creating needed data and making it usable and available may be a necessary condition for comprehensive and integrated environmental policy, it is hardly sufficient by itself as it surmounts few of the obstacles discussed in the previous section.

There have also been a number of experiments with policy instruments, or means, for achieving greater comprehensiveness or integration. Policy planning has been emphasized by the Netherlands and Canada. The United Kingdom has named ministers charged with environmental portfolios in all ministries (p. 51). The European Community is developing a directive on auditing of environmental performance at the facility level. In the United States, pollution prevention legislation at both the national and state levels requires reporting and the establishment of standard source reduction methods. Several nations in Europe use multimedia or co-ordinated pollution permit systems and, again, the European Community is developing a directive on these matters. Sweden uses trained multimedia inspectors for pollution control enforcement, and the United Kingdom and the United States have developed plans to move towards this approach. All of these initiatives build upon earlier efforts, such as environmental impact assessment systems, that have also been receiving new attention. The European Community has adopted a directive on impact assessment that pushes its member nations to a greater degree of integration (Wathern, 1989), and Canada in particular has been considering a substantial reorientation and extension of its assessment process (Gibson, 1993).

This brief review of policy development outside New Zealand supports the conclusion that more comprehensive, integrated environmental policy is increasingly being seen by governments as necessary and possible. Given reasonable evaluation standards derived from realistic theoretical conceptions rather than idealistic criteria based on extreme definitions, more comprehensive and integrated policy can be and has been successful in providing improved capability for addressing the environmental problematique. 'Integration has begun' (Wilson and Harris, 1991). But possibilities and potential are far from exhausted. To what extent have the developments and reforms in New Zealand, described in the preceding chapters, resulted in a more comprehensive or integrated environmental policy? What, if anything, is distinctive about these developments and reforms in the international context, and what should be learned from them?

The New Zealand Experience

In the face of the attention given to the need for comprehensiveness and integration in environmental policy development in North America and Europe in the 1980s, New Zealand's reforms since 1984 could hardly be judged positively if, altogether, they had resulted in no greater capabilities for more comprehensive, integrated environmental policy. Indeed, we can identify some capabilities that have been created deliberately as explicit goals of policy reform, as in the case of the Resource Management Act and the reorganization of national environmental administration. For other reforms and developments, such as the restructuring of local governments, the corporatization and privatization of many government functions, and the growth of strong environmental organizations and third parties committed to green values, improved capabilities for comprehensive or integrated policy have been an incidental consequence of policy development, albeit no less significant.

Some reforms and developments, however, appear to be at least partially counterproductive with respect to developing a more integrative approach to environmental policy. In particular, a dogmatic reliance on the market in economic, ecological, and social dimensions of environmental policy and aspects of the reform of the public service have negative implications for the achievement of greater integration and comprehensiveness in environmental policy. Whereas some of the reforms of recent years distinguish New Zealand as an innovator and world leader with respect to comprehensiveness and integration, there is much that current New Zealand environmental policy does not integrate or comprehend, as mentioned earlier in Chapter 2. New Zealand's achievements in making policy more comprehensive and integrated, however significant, have been accomplished while putting off consideration of many serious, readily identifiable omissions and inadequacies in national environmental laws, programmes, and organizational structures.

Reorganization of National Environmental Administration
The first of many reorganizations of national government undertaken by the Labour Party after 1984 were in the area of environmental administration, as discussed in Chapter 5. The reason Labour turned to environmental matters first was simply that environmentalists had succeeded in putting reorganization of environmental administration on the agenda that Labour brought with it to power. Environmentalists had advocated, among other things, the creation of a 'super-ministry'—a Ministry for the Environment that would combine major environment planning, management, and regulatory responsibilities in a single powerful agency. This organizational approach would thus, presumably, have achieved a comprehensive view and functional integration of policy responsibilities.

The structure actually established by Labour, however, was considerably more fragmented than what environmentalists had proposed, and more fragmented in some ways even than the previous structure which had had the Commission for the Environment as the central co-ordinating agency. But the Commission had been in a weak and difficult position from which to live up to its responsibilities. The Ministry for the Environment established in 1986 was established on a statutory basis, was given more resources and staff, and was clearly allocated a policy advisory role for environmental concerns broadly defined. It was also assigned a reporting function whereby departmental proposals considered to have important environmental impacts were to be submitted to it before being presented to Cabinet—a function that, if ever fully implemented, would have significant potential for achieving greater integration and comprehensiveness (Bührs, 1992a).

But the Ministry was assigned limited regulatory, planning, or advocacy authority, and this greatly circumscribes the integrative role it can play.[3] It cannot give directives to other national government agencies, nor can it require other agencies to co-operate or even to provide information and

---

3. The Ministry has often disavowed its role as advocate (while nevertheless practising it), adopting instead a position of 'declared neutrality', as the 'agency in the middle.' This seems to be as much a preferred agency interpretation as a statutory or Cabinet mandate. In its 1992–93 Corporate Plan, the Ministry did redefine its mission and purpose in the direction of greater advocacy ('To achieve sustainable management of the environment') and more operational responsibility ('a greater responsibility for implementation').

expertise needed for the development of more integrated environmental policies. Although it has more resources than the Commission it replaced, it is not able to play an assertive role in the development and evaluation of a wide range of legislative proposals in areas such as economic growth, energy, transport, or agriculture, or to act as an effective counterweight to Treasury in that regard. The reporting function assigned to the Ministry has been an important mechanism, having been invoked more than 200 times up until the end of 1991, but it has not lived up to its potential (Bührs, 1992a). Moreover, strengthening the reporting function by itself would still be insufficient to ensure integration of environmental considerations into the policy process as a whole.

The creation of the Department of Conservation also established a better, albeit still limited, basis for more integrated environmental policy. The Ministry for the Environment is not the only voice for the environment in the policy process; since 1987 there have been two Ministers with major environmental portfolios. Although the responsibilities of the Department of Conservation are more narrowly focused than those of the Ministry for the Environment, it also has an explicit formal mandate to be an advocate for the environment. Conservation concerns are functionally integrated in a single agency. Rather than suffering in the internal balancing processes in agencies with 'dual mandates' (combinations of development, regulatory, and management functions), environmental values are now more strongly represented and weighed against other interests in a more open decision process (Bührs, 1991b, p. 24).

Likewise, the creation of the Parliamentary Commissioner for the Environment, an independent officer of Parliament responsible for overseeing the system of environmental administration, adds a third environmental voice to the functioning of national government. The Parliamentary Commissioner's role as a system guardian and 'environmental auditor general' should also foster a comprehensive view and an integrative perspective through the contributions that office makes to policy development, notably in providing advice for improving the capabilities of environmental structures and processes as a whole.

These three agencies, however, hardly exhaust the functional needs of integrated, comprehensive policy at the national level. The most glaring deficiency—also the most likely to be remedied, however belatedly or adequately—is the absence of a national pollution control regulatory agency. By the end of the 1980s New Zealand was one of the few OECD countries that did not have a central agency charged with pollution and hazardous substance control (responsibilities were instead fragmented among the Department of Health, the Ministry of Agriculture and Fisheries, the

Department of Labour, the Ministry for the Environment, and local government). The initial government proposals for the Resource Management Act included establishment of an Environmental Protection Agency, but in the introduced bill the authority of this prospective agency was narrowed and it was renamed the Hazards Control Commission. Nominally included with the Resource Management Act, Part VIII represented only the government's commitment to developing legislation and did not come into force with the rest of the Act. The actual proposals for hazardous substances law reform, issued in October 1992, yet again renamed the (still prospective) agency the Environmental Risk Management Authority. The legislation as proposed would continue a distinction made in few other countries between hazardous substances and pollution, with pollution control still not being acknowledged as a primary responsibility of New Zealand national government because the effects are claimed to be only local or regional in scope or magnitude (Ministry for the Environment, 1992a, p. 10).

Of course, the Resource Management Act does provide for optional national environmental standards or regulations, but the agency charged with determining the need for and developing any such standards is the Ministry for the Environment. The Ministry for the Environment is also the only candidate for *administering* any such regulations or standards, which brings into sharp relief the conflicts the Ministry for the Environment faces in its roles as long-term system reformer, policy advocate, balancer, manager, and regulator. Given its resources, corporate ideology, and political context, it is likely to continue to give the roles of manager and regulator short shrift. To the extent that comprehensive, integrated environmental policy, particularly with respect to the ecological and social dimensions, depends on central agency direction and co-ordination, New Zealand's current organizational structures leave gaping holes.

The Resource Management Act and the Re-creation of Local Government
It is with respect to new mandates, processes, and organizational structures created in the linked local government and resource management law reforms that the potential for more comprehensive, integrated environmental policy has been most extended. Although, with respect to other countries' policy, scholars have concluded that 'the enactment of a new, integrated act is a near impossibility' (Guruswamy, 1989; Davies, 1991, p. 140), the unique political system of New Zealand (Palmer, 1987) has made the near impossible possible. A fundamental objective of the reforms that produced local government restructuring and the Resource Management Act was to make environmental policy more comprehensive and integrated. The reforms sought to accomplish this in several ways.

In the course of rationalizing the structure and functions of local government, the reforms abolished many smaller and special purpose units of local government, reassigning responsibilities to more territorially encompassing general purpose units. In theory anyway, part of the aim of this reorganization was to increase the comprehensiveness of the scope of local government and to make it possible for policy generally to be integrated administratively and politically within each district. For the first time since the nineteenth century, autonomous regional governments were established, again in part to provide a more comprehensive perspective and to play a role in integrating general policies that transcend district boundaries.

With respect to environmental policy *per se*, the Resource Management Act represents an attempt to achieve greater comprehensiveness and integration by several means. Although the impetus for the reform was primarily on rationalizing structures and processes, to some extent the Act achieves and provides for substantive co-ordination, or co-ordination by common principles or purposes (Bührs, 1991b; Minnery, 1988). As discussed earlier in Chapter 5, the Act has a single stated purpose, to promote the sustainable development of natural and physical resources. The rest of the Act is directed at achieving that purpose:

> The purpose of the Act as directly enacted by Parliament plays an articulated role in the preparation of all policy, planning and regulatory instruments. The purpose of the Act moreover is related directly to its associated statutory principles. The relationships among the range of resource management instruments formulated executively, that is policy statements through to rules in plans, are themselves described clearly and precisely. There is an unambiguous hierarchy. At the apex of the system is the purpose of the Act. Every other instrument is dependent upon it, driven by it, prescribing by it, or otherwise founded upon it (Fisher, 1991, pp. 10–11).

Because of its limited applicability to much of the economy, not to mention most of national government policy making, the Resource Management Act can hardly be considered an adequate overall environmental policy. But, building on the Environment Act 1986, it further entrenches in legislation a number of principles and values by which a broader (more comprehensive) range of policies are to be made henceforth. One of the most remarkable aspects of the reform effort that culminated in the Act was the near-consensus achieved, even if at a very general level, regarding the purpose of sustainable management and the principles that underpin it. This agreement, notwithstanding the still shallow nature of support for environmental policies in the wider New Zealand society (Chapter 3), provides a foundation for local and national government to pursue more integrated policy development both under the Act and beyond it.

The Act, moreover, provides a variety of procedural means through which a greater degree of integration and comprehensiveness can be achieved. Implementation of the Act revolves around the development of policy statements and plans that by definition must be to some extent comprehensive and integrative in their effect. Plans and statements, as well as local and regional rules, must be consistent with (co-ordinated by) higher level plans and statements. The public participation provisions, duties to consult, and mandated openness of decision processes establish mechanisms that facilitate co-ordination and integration by information gathering and mutual adjustment. The Act provides for a standard, integrated system of permits and consents for all discharges specified in the Act or for all situations where a policy or plan so requires. This permitting system thus, in theory anyway, integrates environmental protection regulation not only across pollution media but also across other resource and social impact concerns (e.g., water use, land use, subdivision, coastal activities).

The Act also imposes on local and regional councils analytical duties that require them to augment their analytical capabilities and be more comprehensive in their approach to developing policy. Costs and benefits of alternative actions must be evaluated. An extensive obligation is imposed on local and regional authorities to monitor the state of the environment, the suitability and effectiveness of plans, and the exercise of resource consents. Finally, a key means of accomplishing the purpose of the Act is through a pervasive requirement for assessing impacts, imposed not only on local and regional government but also on applicants for resource consents.

The impact assessment provisions are of particular significance, as, through the Resource Management Act, New Zealand has adopted the most thoroughgoing and comprehensive effort in the world to achieve integrated environmental policy through impact assessment (Bartlett, 1993b). Rather than having separate impact assessment processes and procedures, impact assessment under the Resource Management Act is integrated with planning and decision making procedures to an unusual, if not unique, extent. Also, the practice of impact assessment is defined in a comprehensive way, thus integrating environmental impact assessment with what are usually considered distinct forms of impact assessment, such as risk assessment, social impact assessment, and technology assessment. And rather than focusing exclusively on projects, the traditional approach in most countries (and in New Zealand previously), the Resource Management Act requires impact assessment of all projects needing consents as well as the policies, plans, and programmes of regional and local councils.

In sum, the Resource Management Act is a landmark achievement in providing a *basis* for more comprehensive and better integrated environmental policy. Much of its potential is as yet unrealized, however. Much depends on the adequacy of resources—not just money but also the qualifications of personnel—that ultimately will be dedicated, for example, to the tasks of systemic monitoring and impact assessment. Given the often unimpressive record of local government in environmental matters in many other countries, there is considerable reason to be concerned about how much of the potential of the Act will be realized.

The Act does not provide any guarantee that the economic, ecological, and social dimensions of the environment will be integrated in policy development. In its restricted focus on environmental effects, the Act may even direct attention away from the sources of those effects, contrary to the approach recommended by the Brundtland Report. Moreover, in drafting the Act, Parliament exempted most of central government from many of its provisions; the duties to monitor, to do impact assessment, and to issue integrated policy statements, which are mandated for local and regional government, are not imposed on all agencies and authorities of central government. Indeed, full realization of the integrative potential of the Act even with respect to local and regional government is dependent on central co-ordination and direction through issuance of optional environmental standards and national policy statements. Under the National Party Government of 1990–93, which enacted the Resource Management Act, no optional policy statements or standards were forthcoming to guide the Act's early implementation. The strong commitment of the Government to economic growth and leaving market forces unfettered meant that even the national coastal policy statement, mandatory under the Act and finally reissued by the Department of Conservation in draft form in October 1992,[4] offered little firm direction. The difficult and extended gestation of that policy statement posed problems for regional and local authorities in drafting their own policies and plans in a timely way.

Corporatization, Privatization, Commercialization
Those institutional reforms that have put government in New Zealand on a more commercial basis present a very mixed picture with regard to the comprehensiveness and integrativeness of environmental policy. On the one

---

4. An earlier draft coastal policy statement had been issued in August 1990, anticipating that the Resource Management Bill would be passed by the Labour Government before election adjournment of Parliament. Work on a draft statement began again under the new National Government for the revised Resource Management Act actually enacted in July 1991.

hand, 'the unfettered market possesses, in negative feedback and co-ordination, some claims to ecological rationality' (Dryzek, 1987, p. 71). Markets can be integrative mechanisms, as extraordinarily effective and encompassing co-ordination is possible in free, well-functioning markets through adjustment and exchange. Corporatization and privatization and other organizational and accounting reforms that separate commercial functions from the rest of government clearly make it more difficult for government in New Zealand to subsidize environmental destruction ('State sponsored vandalism'). Elimination of dual mandates requires integration through a more open decision-making process. Because resources and human capabilities are limited, and totally comprehensive and completely integrated policies are not possible, one of the best ways of coping more effectively with various aspects of the environmental problematique is to reduce and circumscribe, where possible, the need for means—other than local initiative and ordinary mutual adjustment—to achieve comprehensiveness and integration. Some reliance on markets and market-like mechanisms, as well as greater reliance on self-organization and self-governance (Ostrom, 1990), may free up scarce attention, resources, and creativity for grappling with policy problems that do require more directive co-ordination.

On the other hand, however, perfect markets are rare and difficult to create and maintain (and they do not create and maintain themselves). Even for the economic (resource) dimension of environmental policy, the potential for market failure is enormous. There are virtually no private (excludable) goods that have no public good characteristics, as discussed in Chapter 4. Healthy markets may be superb at co-ordinating and integrating economic values, but their usefulness in integrating across ecological and social values is more than questionable (Dryzek, 1987, pp. 71–87). Using markets alone to provide a comprehensive approach to the social or ecological dimensions of environmental policy is a prescription for disaster. Precarious social and ecological values are not readily accommodated by markets and are necessarily given short shrift by them, leading to fragmentation and aggravation of problems rather than resolution. Market approaches alone can only go so far in 'shifting the focus to the policy sources'. In New Zealand, corporatization and privatization have dealt with the problem of dual mandates by setting loose a number of new organizations freed of their former obligations to protect the environment—obligations which have been replaced by vague injunctions to be good corporate citizens. New ideological barriers have been erected to any consideration of how to incorporate environmental values into the very fabric of business decision making—the kind of intra-organizational environmental policy at the heart of some of the integrated environmental policy initiatives being undertaken in Europe.

Reform of the Public Service

Even though 'service to the government as a whole as the focus of official loyalties' (Martin, 1990, p. 124) was an integrative force under the old system, there is little evidence that it contributed positively to better *environmental* policy making. Nevertheless, as discussed in Chapter 4, the transformation of the core public service to a system modelled on business organizations is problematic for environmental policy in several ways. Each of these problems has particular implications for the need to make environmental policy more comprehensive and integrated.

An emphasis on goals might, in theory, be used as a strategy for improving environmental co-ordination and integration by establishing common environmental goals across all agencies, committing administrators to substantive ecological rationality (Bührs, 1991b). But there are enormous difficulties inherent in the task of specifying and agreeing on a set of such goals. And neither Labour nor National governments have evinced much interest in using these kinds of goals in this way or, for that matter, in using goal setting as broad policy planning to develop a coherent overall 'substantive' environmental policy. Rather, the emphasis has been on formulating and stating clear, measurable, short-term, operational objectives. The result, not surprisingly, is that in setting objectives, agencies have steered away from addressing long-term considerations, controversies, processes, the difficult and complex, and matters requiring negotiation, persuasion, and joint action. Instead, they have emphasized the trivial, the short-term, and matters over which they exercise considerable autonomy and control (see, for example, any recent Corporate Statement of the Ministry for the Environment—although these are by no means more egregious than those of other agencies in this respect). The result is a system that offers more than the usual impediments to greater comprehensiveness and integration and strong incentives militating against any agency advocating or attempting it.

This tendency towards a short-term perspective and departmentalism (a preoccupation of departments with their own objectives and interests) is further encouraged by the managerial freedom given chief executives, the reduction of the balancing required by dual mandates, changes in the culture of a unified, non-partisan, career public service, and greater accountability to Ministers (Martin, 1991c). The full effects of the public sector reforms will take years to work themselves out fully, however, and what they necessarily portend for comprehensive and integrative environmental policy is not entirely clear. There is a need for further research and analysis that pays 'attention to values relevant to governance other than economic rationality' (Martin, 1990, p. 136).

International Environmental Policy

When many New Zealanders, including Cabinet Ministers, thought of environmental policy in the late 1980s they thought first of highly visible, well publicized initiatives that involved New Zealand's relationships with other nations. One of the issues that proved most enduringly popular for the Labour Government was its opposition to nuclear testing in the South Pacific and to the visit of nuclear-powered ships to New Zealand ports. Especially after the Environment portfolio was assigned to Geoffrey Palmer, who simultaneously served first as Deputy Prime Minister and then Prime Minister, the Labour Government undertook a number of high-profile international initiatives with respect to driftnet fishing, ozone depletion, Antarctica, and global warming, among other matters. Few of these initiatives had much significance in terms of the need to make environmental policy more comprehensive or integrated, except to demonstrate the necessity on some issues for a view and a policy approach extending far beyond the territorial waters of New Zealand. An exception is the global warming issue—if New Zealand governments were ever to take seriously the formal commitments made by both Labour and National to reduce carbon dioxide emissions by 20%, they could only do so by considering new domestic policies that span and integrate ecological, economic, and social dimensions.

To some extent, the unusual dominance of international environmental issues in New Zealand, through their occupation of some of the limited space on public and government agendas, may have served to divert attention from defining and addressing domestic environmental problems. If politicians, in focusing on international issues, helped convince themselves and the public of the truthfulness of their rhetoric about the cleanness and greenness of New Zealand, then further efforts to make domestic environmental policy more integrated and comprehensive were rendered even more difficult as problems continued to be defined away by denial.

Evaluation and Conclusions

Beyond the policy initiatives analysed here, there were a great many others undertaken since 1984, across a wide spectrum of policy domains—health, taxes, education, justice, economic performance, labour, housing, social welfare, constitutional revision, and so on. Many of those do not impinge directly on environmental policy as traditionally defined, and they are beyond the scope of this book and certainly of this chapter. But indirectly they may in the long run be of importance to the task of making environmental policy more comprehensive and integrative, as they constitute some of the policies (policy sources) with which environmental policies ultimately need to be integrated.

There also have been changes in New Zealand society that must be taken into account in evaluating achievements and obstacles. Some of these—changes such as the high level of distrust and the lack of faith that New Zealanders have in their current electoral system and in the two major political parties—are not the intentional result of public policy *per se*, but nevertheless are among the unintended consequences of the adoption of unpopular policies by governments that lacked mandates to make sweeping and bold changes. As much as anything, these changes in the political landscape have made possible the rapid transformation of the Green Party from its formal establishment in 1990 into a potent political force. Although Green activists and supporters are far from having arrived at any coherent and precise policy agreement with their partners in the Alliance, or even with each other (they are no different in that respect from any other political party), they are nearly unanimous in their adherence to the principle that environmental concerns should be integral to all other policy development. Depending on whether the Alliance partners are able to make electoral success possible by resolving their differences regarding social, economic, and environmental policies, the Green Party may well become a significant contributor to comprehensive, integrated environmental policy development in the 1990s.

Also since 1984, general dissatisfaction with government policies and the circumstances under which they were imposed (that is, the adoption of policies contrary to published manifestos, by governments supported by only a minority of the electorate) has contributed to further growth of a strong sentiment for electoral reform. The depth of this sentiment was reflected in the overwhelming vote in a 1992 referendum in favour of a mixed member proportional system (MMP), despite the support expressed by the leaders of both the Labour and National Parties for the current system. If the current 'first past the post' electoral system (which is what makes possible the control of the national legislature and executive by single parties) is scrapped, then, depending on the details of the design of a new system (both subject to confirmation in another referendum), the implications for the integrative and inclusive nature of New Zealand politics and policy making could be profound. The ramifications would certainly extend to environmental policy.

More integrative politics may make it far more difficult to 'get things done' quickly, so periods of radical redirection of policy, such as New Zealand saw from 1984 through 1991, may never occur again. The enactment of integrative environmental legislation such as the Resource Management Act may not become impossible, but the pace of change will become a great deal slower and more deliberate. The speed and ease of achieving change notwithstanding, if policy processes and the politics that informs them become more inclusionary, more participative, more collaborative, and more co-operative, then perhaps the kinds of environmental policies that transcend economic, ecological, and social dimensions may be more likely.

Aside from these broader issues, a number of general conclusions about how New Zealand has so far addressed the recurring theme of the need for more integrated and comprehensive environmental policy are justified. Although basic institutional deficiencies remain, with respect to basic structures, processes, and conceptual issues New Zealand has been ahead of the rest of the world in grappling with what Davies (1991, p. 139) calls 'internal integration', that is, 'the integration of programs and policies dealing with air, water, and land pollution'. Questions remain about the adequacy of problem definition, problem identification, responsibility assignment, standard setting, and enforcement, but not with respect to the degree that the environment is treated as an integrated whole in dealing with pollution under the Resource Management Act. New Zealand is also ahead of much of the rest of the world in integrating pollution control at the local and regional level with some other aspects of environmental policy, particularly natural resources policy. There are exceptions, however, such as energy policy, as well as anomalies, such as aspects of waste reduction and pollution that cannot be tackled effectively except at the national level.

Irwin (1991, p. 30) argues that integrated pollution control decision making must have three focuses: 'the *substance*, or pollutant, as the agent of change; the *source* of the pollutant as cause, whether a facility, product life-cycle, or activity; and the region or *ecosystem* as the level to assess and control effects'. Certainly the Resource Management Act establishes ecosystem-based regions as a level to assess and control effects. Although the mechanisms for dealing with ecosystem effects that encompass more than one region are less well established, New Zealand may nevertheless be as well prepared legally and institutionally as any country in the world to deal effectively with locally and regionally diffuse (non-point source) pollution problems—problems that everywhere have proven particularly intractable.

The Resource Management Act, however, stresses regulation to control effects rather than controlling activities *per se*. It severely limits regulation of economic, social, and cultural matters. Moreover, both analytical and control responsibilities are weighted heavily at the local and regional, rather than national, level. The result is a lack of focus on either substances or sources. The still prospective hazardous substances legislation is intended to remedy that partially by creating an integrated focus on substances. To some extent pollution prevention may be an effective focus of regional policies and plans, but regional and local government is severely constrained, not only by legal barriers to its involvement in economic decisions 'reserved' to the private sector, but also, with respect to fostering economic growth and development, by the competitive position of each local authority. New

Zealand governments, under the free market policy regime of both Labour and National, have remained ideologically committed to limiting any policy focus on sources to one of exhortation only.

With respect to 'external integration' (Davies, 1991)—the incorporation of environmental policy into other types of policy, identified by the Brundtland Report as a necessary basis for sustainable development (Brundtland Commission, 1987)—New Zealand has taken steps to integrate pollution policy with aspects of resources policy, but beyond that has been far less innovative. It has done little to inject environmental considerations into key central government processes such as budget decisions, nor has it done much, if anything, to strengthen the environmental forces in all major agencies (what Davies calls the 'fifth-column' approach). As in all other countries, the knowledge basis for comprehensive, integrated environmental policy making in New Zealand remains weak. Scattered experimentation is taking place with a variety of technical tools, such as corporate environmental audits, product standards, and ecological risk assessment, but mostly independent of any strong policy push from central government. Nor has the idea of 'full social cost pricing'—making the price of goods reflect the full environmental and social costs (Davies, 1991; Tietenberg, 1991)—moved much past the preliminary discussion phase in New Zealand. Parliament has exempted central government from many of the mandatory integrative provisions of the Resource Management Act. Economic and other social policies continue to be formulated and implemented independent of environmental considerations, even more so under the free market policy regime than under the previous 'interventionist' regime.

There is no political commitment for integrating environmental values into key policy areas such as economic policy, agriculture policy, or transportation policy—either through procedural means or through the development of an overall substantive environmental policy. But, at the same time, the content of ideas and the inexorable march of problems both continue to push for making environmental policy more comprehensive and more integrative. Integration is an idea whose time has come. We can fairly say that in New Zealand as in other developed countries, 'integration has begun' (Wilson and Harris, 1991, p. xx)—but only begun. The enshrinement of the principle of sustainability in wide reaching legislation, and the various procedural and structural changes resulting from the reorganizations of national and local government and the Resource Management Act, have established an opportunity for New Zealand to become a world leader in integrative, comprehensive environmental policy. Whether New Zealand exercises such leadership will depend on the political commitment that is reflected in implementation throughout the rest of the 1990s.

CONCLUSION

In the Introduction we promised to shed light on four central themes or challenges by analysing developments in New Zealand with the help of perspectives and insights derived from public policy and environmental policy analysis. The themes were: the need for anticipatory environmental policy making; the need for changing our ways; the need for institutional reform to enhance environmental policy performance; and the need for more integrated or comprehensive environmental policy development. For a number of reasons, New Zealand offers a particularly interesting case in environmental policy development. Perceived as a relatively 'clean and green' country, it has been in the enviable position of being able to avoid some of the serious environmental problems that have emerged elsewhere. As the country that gave birth to the first green party in the world, it could possibly be in the vanguard of a change of values and lifestyles that many argue is required to save the world. Bold institutional reforms that have drastically changed New Zealand's policy-making framework, including that of environmental policy, may offer inspiration to those who seek 'roundabout' ways of enhancing environmental policy performance. And if all these changes are leading to more integrated or more comprehensive environmental policy development, New Zealand could be among those leading the world in this respect.

Paradoxes and Discrepancies

How does New Zealand's record stack up against these claims or expectations? The picture is one of paradoxes and discrepancies. Out of an unimpressive environmental record before 1984, a situation has emerged in which the environment has a much more prominent place in the policy process. Despite the narrow focus of mainstream environmental demands on conservation issues in the past, New Zealand has introduced one of the most integrated approaches to the management of natural resources in the world. Although support for the environmental movement has sky-rocketed in the last decade, there are as yet few signs of a fundamental change in New Zealand values and lifestyle.

Closer scrutiny of these developments reveals that some environmental problems, notably those with regard to the natural environment, have received considerable political attention for a long time. This has resulted in the establishment of an extensive network of protected areas and in a significant strengthening of conservation advocacy within the institutional—legislative and bureaucratic—framework.

Yet, although some of the major conservation issues have been resolved, there are still significant problems in this area. Many ecosystems, and with them many species, continue to decline, as a result of introduced pests, poor management, and development. In large part this reflects a widespread, traditional, and fundamental weakness in conservation policy not unique to New Zealand, namely the notion that only some ecosystems need protection and that these can be protected by 'setting them aside'. But the very interdependence of ecosystems, and of ecosystem policy with economic (resource) and social (quality of life) policy, makes a mockery of this notion.

Setting aside some ecosystems for protection may engender the idea that somehow ecosystems outside those areas do not need protection, or need much less protection. Yet forests, wetlands, and other ecosystems that are not officially protected are, of course, just as important as protected ecosystems for the preservation of species and resources, natural processes (such as carbon dioxide absorption), and climatic conditions. Ecosystems deserve protection whatever their formal ownership status. Although setting aside natural areas for 'total' protection has its value, this should be complemented by a broader conservation policy that recognizes the need for protection, and as far as possible restoration, of all natural ecosystems. Despite the Resource Management Act, which makes the consideration of ecological effects mandatory in all resource management decisions, this issue remains controversial, as illustrated by the continuing debate regarding New Zealand forests in private ownership.

The importance of integrated resource management for ecological, economic, and social reasons has also recently found recognition in New Zealand's Resource Management Act. Yet, as before, policies affecting the use of resources, such as energy policy, transport policy, agricultural policy, and broad economic policy, continue in many cases to be developed independently of environmental considerations, or with such considerations added on after the 'core' of these policies (Majone, 1989) has been determined on other grounds. With the shift towards market-based resource allocation, in particular in the energy sector, the sustainable management of resources in New Zealand still is a long way off.

Other weaknesses in New Zealand's environmental policy as it has developed thus far relate to the social or quality of life dimension. Urban expansion and (re)development has been driven by economic (including speculative) processes. The nature and effects of these developments have been weakly controlled by an approach to planning that involved little more than imposing zoning restrictions (and which now, under the Resource Management Act, must be based wholly on a defensible assessment of effects rather than on any proactive focus on sources of environmental degradation).

Social and environmental problems related to transport, the quality of housing, the decay of some city areas, pollution and waste disposal, and depopulation and the loss of resources in other areas, have not been adequately addressed, let alone made the subject of anticipatory policy making. Under the Resource Management Act these issues are unlikely to be dealt with more effectively than in the past because of the Act's focus on effects instead of sources, and because of the lack of an overarching government policy regarding human settlement.

If some environmental problems, notably pollution problems, are of a smaller scale in New Zealand than in many other countries (and this is a big 'if'), this is not because of anticipatory policies followed by governments, but because of the relatively small size of the industrial sector and the population. The extent of pollution in New Zealand, however, is still largely unknown because of inadequate research and monitoring. Occasional systematic studies of the scale and severity of pollution problems in New Zealand have not been encouraging. For example, a 1993 study commissioned by the Ministry for the Environment found that there could be 7800 contaminated sites in New Zealand, of which approximately 1580 could be high risk (Ministry for the Environment, 1993)—hardly comforting figures for an allegedly clean and green country.

Significant gaps continue to exist in New Zealand's pollution control policy. Much of the responsibility has been shifted from central government to local government without ensuring adequate capability, including expertise and other resources, at that level. Pollution continues to be dealt with as though it is primarily a local or regional problem, and little guidance, co-ordination or technical support is provided by central government. In the management of substances, an artificial distinction is maintained between hazardous and non-hazardous substances. Although a central government agency is likely to be established to co-ordinate control over hazardous substances, and the Resource Management Act has laid the basis for a more integrated approach to the control of pollution, New Zealand does not yet have a central agency charged with integrated pollution control. By focusing on effects, the Resource Management Act may direct attention away from the sources of pollution and allow regional disparities in tolerance of pollution levels to emerge. In the absence of strong guidance or control by central government, and given the limited capabilities and incentives on the local level, there are few reasons to expect that the control of pollution in New Zealand will be any more effective than in the past.

Altogether, New Zealand has not set a good example with regard to the development of anticipatory environmental policies, despite the opportunities that have presented themselves. The weakness of demands in those areas where New Zealand's environmental problems have generally been perceived as minor, notably pollution and other quality of life issues, has provided little incentive to governments to develop anticipatory policies. Until recently, the direct involvement of the State in resource development has been another factor working against the introduction of stringent controls. Vested interests in resource development found strong support in the overall political institutional framework, in legislation, in advisory organizations, and in the mandates of government agencies. By contrast, environmental values related to resource conservation, pollution, and quality of life in the context of human settlement were given much weaker advocacy within the institutional framework, often within development oriented agencies ('dual mandates').

To what extent have these barriers to the development of anticipatory and more integrated environmental policy been overcome as a result of the institutional reforms undertaken? The answer to this question, as we discussed in Chapter 6, is far from straightforward.

Some barriers to the consideration of environmental values have been overcome by way of the reforms undertaken since 1984. In most cases, dual mandates have been abolished, and responsibilities for development and environmental protection separated. This has exposed the political nature of the 'balancing act' between development and environment values and brought the political process of achieving balance or integration further into the open.

Within the institutional framework, environmental values have been considerably strengthened with the establishment of the Department of Conservation as an advocate for conservation, the creation of the Ministry for the Environment as a central environmental policy agency, and the establishment of a Parliamentary Commissioner as a system guardian for the environment. With the devolution of many development activities to the private sector or to government corporations operating on a commercial basis, some of the principal actors that shaped government policy have moved away from the centre of the policy process. Finally, with the introduction of the Resource Management Act, environmental values have been given centre stage in the resource planning process, notably on the local government level. Altogether, environmental considerations now have a much better chance of being considered and incorporated in the policy process compared to the pre-reform situation.

Yet, as mentioned above, important gaps remain, notably with regard to the advocacy of environmental values related to pollution control, human settlement, and other quality of life (social) issues. And the institutional means for achieving co-ordination remains weak (Bührs, 1991a). The mandate of the Ministry for the Environment regarding these matters is ambiguous and its resources remain very limited. In areas such as energy policy, transport policy, agricultural policy, and economic policy, the formal basis for the Ministry's input lacks 'teeth'. Sustainability has not been incorporated into the mandates of all government agencies and State owned enterprises that manage natural resources, nor has it been made a cornerstone of government economic policy.

Explaining Paradoxes and Discrepancies

The paradoxes and discrepancies in New Zealand's environmental policy development defy an explanation on the basis of any single policy model or perspective. The change of government in 1984, and the rise in support for environmental demands, are illustrative of developments in the problem and politics streams in Kingdon's agenda-setting model discussed in Chapter 1. But the growing support for environmental issues cannot explain the scale or the radical nature of the reforms, nor can these be explained purely on the basis of the solutions advanced by policy entrepreneurs in the various policy communities, the environmental community included. In many ways the agenda-setting process for the reforms, which could be characterized as a revolution from above, seems to better fit the 'mobilization' model identified by Cobb, Ross, and Ross (1976) in which governments take the initiative in developing proposals and putting them on the public agenda.

Although many of the reforms, notably those in economic policy and the public sector, were pushed through with little public consultation, this was not the case with the environmental reforms, which were subjected to extensive public input and debate. Nevertheless, as discussed in Chapters 4 and 5, the environmental reforms reflect the general principles that underlay the government's agenda of reform and cannot be explained simply on the basis of environmental demands.

Institutional factors have also been of prime importance in the reform process. If the capability of government officials to push through their own preferences despite significant societal opposition is a measure of State autonomy (Nordlinger, 1981), then the radical reforms reflect a very high degree of autonomy of the State in New Zealand. This conclusion, of course, is not surprising given the extraordinary concentration of power that is vested in New Zealand governments (Palmer, 1987). Without this, it is unlikely that these reforms would have taken place—at least in the same form and at the same pace.

The fact that the reform process has been led from above may explain some of the paradoxes and discrepancies in environmental policy developments referred to above, as well as some of the remaining gaps and limitations of the environmental reforms in New Zealand. Although local and regional authorities have been given a greater role in the management of resources, they still must manage on the terms and conditions set by the central government. For instance, the options open to local and regional authorities for dealing with energy issues are extremely limited, given their lack of formal powers and resources in these areas and the retention of control by central government over the energy reform process (of which the move towards the privatization of the electricity industry is a core element). With regard to transport issues, regional authorities have been given responsibility while the public transport sector has been deregulated and government support for public transport significantly cut. As a result of these moves, policy vacuums have been created as the central government has shed responsibility onto local government without having put in place adequate support structures and resources to facilitate further development in these vital environmental policy areas.

Another factor behind these gaps and discrepancies is the dramatic shift in the role of the State in New Zealand from one of direct involvement in most areas of resource management towards market-based resource allocation and minimalist government intervention. Although this has eliminated some forms of 'State sponsored vandalism', it has also brought about a governmental reluctance to intervene in commercially based resource decisions. Even when State owned enterprises disregard the social and environmental implications of their decisions, central government has done nothing more than remind them of their vaguely assigned responsibilities in this regard. As a result of this reluctance, the balancing of economic and environmental values, although more open and explicit with the separation of commercial and environmental responsibilities, does not necessarily lead to more favourable outcomes from an environmental point of view. In the end, it is the relative priority assigned by the government to often conflicting values that determines their weight in the policy process.

Future Environmental Policy

Given the political, economic, social, and international context in which environmental policy develops, at least three questions arise with regard to the future development of New Zealand's environmental policy. First, does the shift towards market-based resource management mark a return to nineteenth-century free-market vandalism and laissez-faire environmental policy, or should it be interpreted as a starting point in the direction of a more efficient allocation of resources and the development of more efficient, and perhaps more effective, instruments for government intervention? Second, in what direction will further value change in New Zealand occur, and what will be the political implications of this for future developments in environmental policy? Third, to what extent will future environmental policy in New Zealand be shaped by international and global environmental pressures?

A New Role for the State?

The answer to the question of whether the shift to market-based resource allocation marks the revival of free-market environmental vandalism or the beginning of more efficient and effective State intervention in environmental matters does not simply depend on an assessment of whether the private sector is more efficient than the State, or on whether economic instruments are more efficient than other forms of government intervention, such as regulation. The question is ultimately political and ideological. Why is the State doing what it does? And what is the proper role of the State?

If the ultimate rationale for State action is to ensure economic growth and development—for reasons rooted in the imperatives of capitalist accumulation as well as in the international system of competing states (Walker, 1989)—then a shift towards market-based resource allocation and indirect State intervention is unlikely to bring about any significant environmental improvement. From this point of view, only the means by which economic growth is promoted changes, whereas environmental interests continue to be of secondary importance in government policies.

For instance, market-based resource allocation and economic instruments—even if they do increase the efficiency of resource use and mitigate environmental impact—are introduced primarily for economic reasons, namely, the promotion of economic growth and the alleviation of the costs of government intervention. But increased economic growth may very well negate any environmental gains that are made. In times of economic recession or frail economic growth, on the other hand, governments are reluctant to use instruments (such as a carbon tax) that may impose additional financial strain on the economy, as the New Zealand experience illustrates.

To suggest that government policies with regard to the environment are restrained by economic imperatives should not, however, be taken to imply that governments do not have a choice with regard to economic policy. Some economic problems, such as high inflation and unemployment levels, may be fairly obvious, but that does not mean that there is only one way to address them. In the 1980s, the presentation (by governments in New Zealand, Britain, and the United States) of neoclassical solutions for the plight of the economy as 'inevitable' remedies masked the political nature of economics. The political demise of Keynesianism and the political weakness of alternative economic approaches does not prove the validity of New Right recipes. Similarly, there is scope for debate as to what the economic constraints on environmental policy are.

Ultimately, the question about the degree and form of State intervention is not economic but political. What should the role of the State be? Both nineteenth-century liberal-minimalist answers and twentieth-century socialist-maximalist answers have proved their inadequacy in terms of environmental performance in all three dimensions: the protection of ecosystems, the protection of the quality of life, and long-term resource availability. States that have followed a course somewhere in between these two extremes—that is, most countries—have also failed to halt or reverse many forms of environmental deterioration. Somehow, new ways must be found for dealing with the environmental problematique.

Environmental analysts have had few problems in identifying the failings of the State with regard to the challenges posed by the environmental problematique (see, for example, Dryzek, 1987; Ophuls, 1977; Paehlke and Torgerson, 1990). But both in their analyses and prescriptions, important differences have surfaced, with some advocating a stronger role of the State (Hardin, 1968; Ophuls, 1977), and others in favour of decentralization and a transfer of State powers towards smaller communities (Dryzek, 1987; Schumacher, 1973). When it comes to identifying how to achieve such radical political change, however, we find little guidance from these authors.

Neither do we pretend to have the answers. But two things are, in our view, of prime importance. First, that the political debate about the role of the State—not only in environmental matters, but in general—be revived. Second, that this debate, and any consequent steps towards institutional changes, involve as many members of the public as possible. It is of no small concern that in recent years significant changes in the role of the State have occurred, particularly in New Zealand, without any prior meaningful political debate about that role. Many of these changes were not part of a formal government programme, but were introduced with instrumentalist justifications suggesting that 'there was no choice' and that these changes 'had to be done'. Highly political choices regarding the role of the State were presented and enacted under the guise of technocratic remedies for enhancing efficiency and productivity. Many of these measures were adopted without debate about their very significant implications for the kind of society that New Zealanders live in or wish to live in.

Our second concern is obviously related to the first. Choices regarding the role of the State, and the kind of society which it serves, can only be legitimately made and successfully implemented if they are carried by a very large proportion of the population. In these matters, it is not just the economic, technical, or political experts who should have a say. If democracy is to mean anything, then all citizens should have an opportunity to say what the role of the State should be. In that sense, the State should be 'given back' to the people.

For New Zealand, these comments point in the direction of significant political reform. The scale and pace of the reforms in New Zealand during the last decade would not have been possible without the extraordinary concentration of political power in the central government. That many of these reforms were imposed on New Zealand by two subsequent governments without public debate and against significant public opposition has given rise to widespread disillusionment about New Zealand's prevailing political system. It will therefore come as no surprise if a majority of New Zealanders vote for a change in the electoral system in the 1993 referendum. If anything, it would be a sign that New Zealanders wish to claim their government back by demanding more participatory, democratic processes of policy development—similar to those that central government has required of local and regional governments, but not of itself, through the Resource Management Act.

Future Value Change?
We found no evidence for the claim that New Zealanders are leading the world in a paradigmatic change towards a 'postmaterialist' society in which environmental values are given greater weight than economic growth. Support for nature conservation is strong, but should not be confused with radical changes in values, lifestyle, or behaviour. In many respects, including attitudes towards materialist values, New Zealand is still a conservative society.

Nor have we found much support for the view that the environmental movement in New Zealand is somehow of a deeper green nature than its counterparts in European countries (Hay and Haward, 1988). Environmentalists in New Zealand have generally been very pragmatic in their approach to environmental protection, including nature conservation. Their orientation has been more towards finding political openings to achieve protection—mostly through *ad hoc* campaigns—instead of developing and spreading an environmental philosophy. They have developed considerable skill in playing the political game—including the art of compromise. Some of them have not shied away from entering into 'unholy alliances' with the architect of many of the reforms in New Zealand since 1984, Treasury, in order to achieve goals such as the establishment of the Department of Conservation. Overall, environmentalists have predominantly focused on a rather narrow range of issues—in particular ecological and resource issues— and devoted little attention to the social dimension of environmental policy, for instance, as related, to the urban environment, the distribution of resources, and broader quality of life issues. In approaching environmental issues, they have neither been particularly 'deep green' nor very 'holistic'.

One of the reasons for this—apart from the often proclaimed pragmatic and anti-ideological attitude of New Zealanders in general—can be found in New Zealand's political system. The strong concentration of executive power in New Zealand has left pressure groups few options for achieving their goals other than through lobbying. Philosophical debate or navel-gazing has not been the greatest strength of environmentalists in New Zealand, nor has it been the most useful in advancing environmental interests. Having until recently had very little chance of entering Parliament themselves, and very little opportunity for significant policy influence outside Wellington, they have not had to worry about designing an overall political or government programme; to do so would require a broader view of how environmental, social and economic needs and demands can be integrated. Only recently, with the creation of the Alliance of smaller parties, have the Greens been confronted with the need to participate in the development of a broad government programme. Given the diversity of views within the Alliance, this proves to be not an easy process, and one which stretches the art of compromise to the extreme.

Environmentalists in New Zealand, apart from perhaps a small segment within the Values Party and the later Green Party, have always put more emphasis on their political role than on their role as a social movement. Although spreading green values has not been totally neglected, it has mostly been a by-product of political campaigns directed at achieving environmental protection on concrete issues. More recently, they have become more successful in influencing policies and effecting institutional change. And overall, environmentalists in New Zealand have been increasingly effective politically—despite the obstacles inherent in the political system.

Paradoxically, the pragmatic and less ideological orientation of the green movement in New Zealand may actually prove to be more effective in contributing to value change than its more ideologically oriented counterparts overseas. By confronting politicians, bureaucrats, and increasingly also industrialists time and again with concrete demands, and by focusing on institutional change, environmentalists have already considerably strengthened 'instrumental ecological rationality' within New Zealand society—forcing decision makers to address the environmental implications of their decisions. This may well be a more effective—although 'roundabout'—way of also promoting substantive ecological rationality and the adoption of environmental or green values than a strategy emphasizing environmental education, 'missionary' activities, or exemplary behaviour. Although the importance of these last forms of action should not be underestimated—in particular in stimulating debate about possible directions for change—they may be less effective in achieving it.

One other force that may contribute to the further development of environmental or 'postmaterialist' values in New Zealand is that which stems from Māori values. Until recently, Māori views or demands have not played a major role in the development of New Zealand's environmental policy. But with increasing pressure from Māori on governments—notably through the Waitangi Tribunal—to repair past wrongdoings and to honour Treaty of Waitangi obligations, Māori interests and views have found greater political recognition. This finds reflection in specific agreements between the Crown and Māori on Māori claims regarding resources—such as land and fisheries—but also in the requirement embedded in much legislation to consider Treaty of Waitangi obligations in consultation with Māori.

The incorporation of 'Māori rationality' into resource management legislation also promotes a view of the environment that is not predominantly instrumental but holistic, and assigns intrinsic value to the natural environment (Marsden, 1988). In that respect, the increasingly important role of Māori values in the policy process is likely to strengthen further the already strong conservation ethic in New Zealand while forcing a reconsideration of the foundations of that ethic, as the basis for Māori affirmations of intrinsic values differs fundamentally from that offered by most non-Māori preservation advocates.

Environmentalists have expressed some concern about the possible environmental implications of specific Māori claims—notably with regard to land in national parks. It is felt that these parks should be managed on the basis of primarily preservationist values and ecological principles in the interests of all New Zealanders, and it is feared that the management of such protected areas by Māori may lead to problems regarding public access or even to undesirable developments within national parks. The fears are fed by the socio-economic plight of many Māori, which, it is argued, makes them vulnerable to the temptation to exploit, with the aid of foreign capital, regained resources that are seen as needing preservation. Precedents can be found in the exploitation of remaining indigenous forests in private Māori hands. The situation is a complex one that requires environmentalists and Māori to work towards solutions that integrate ecological, social, and economic concerns on both sides.

In conclusion, there is little ground for the argument that New Zealand is leading the world towards a new 'postmaterialist' paradigm. Yet, that does not mean that attitudes in New Zealand towards the environment have not changed. Nor do we exclude the possibility that in the future environmental values will receive an even higher priority than economic values in New Zealand society. The institutional changes that have occurred are likely to further spread and strengthen environmental values in New Zealand society and politics, but the scope and magnitude of value change can be only imperfectly anticipated.

Many of the reforms we have analysed have a catalytic character: they prod, stimulate, and require innovation by forcing action. We might reasonably expect that new institutions created in the 1980s will be shaping environmental policy in the 1990s not just through specific decisions but, even more importantly, through the construction and elaboration of preferences.

And value changes may be prompted by more than institutional changes. As New Zealand undertakes more systematic efforts to assess and monitor its environmental quality, we can expect that there will be more environmental problems discovered and the seriousness of known problems will be reinforced. This march of problems will continue to influence values (and agenda setting). Just as the ideas of the 1980s will have influence for a long time, new ideas, too, will continue to mould values as institutions and language together provide the framework within which environmental conditions and ideas have meaning. Environmental values will continue to change as New Zealanders try to live up to the adopted rhetoric of sustainability which the Resource Management Act will force them to do, just as, for example, New Zealand society has also been fundamentally changed by use of the language of New Right policy reforms in the 1980s. In sum, further extensive environmental value change in New Zealand is inevitable (regardless of the validity of theories of postmaterialism), although the exact form and direction of that evolution is unpredictable.

International Demands and Challenges

Even though a new role for the State in managing the environment has not yet been found, and the kind of value change that many see as necessary has not yet occurred, there may be another factor that will push New Zealand further along the path of environmental policy development: international pressures and demands. Increasingly, the making of environmental policy has become an international and even global affair. To a large extent, the reason for this can be found in the spill-over among countries of the effects of resource management and the treatment of the environment. Many environmental problems have no political boundaries and need international collective action to be dealt with effectively.

In Chapter 2 we noted that in a number of cases New Zealand's environmental policy has been influenced by demands and policy developments in other countries. This is most notable with regard to international issues such as the depletion of the ozone layer, the greenhouse effect, and the Antarctic. But also in other, traditionally more domestic areas of environmental policy making, ideas for policy development may come from innovations abroad, and the influence of pressures and policies from other countries can be significant, such as those concerning the use of pesticides, the management of hazardous substances, and packaging. In New Zealand, policy development in these areas may indeed be inspired more by such external demands—often trade-related—than by domestic demands.

One would also expect external influences to become more important in the management of energy resources, given their vital role in the greenhouse effect. Already, New Zealand has bound itself to agreements to reduce the emission of greenhouse gases that will require significant policy shifts with regard to energy conservation, transport, and the development of renewable energy resources other than hydro-electric power, all areas where policy development in this country has been slow, insubstantial, and inconsistent.

The complexity of the greenhouse problem, however, and the fact that the search for solutions potentially raises profound social, economic, moral, political, and technical questions, makes it one of the most formidable and intractable issues facing modern societies. So far, no government has been able to deal with these challenges very effectively, and it is therefore unrealistic to expect that external demands or pressures will play a major role in the development or implementation of the greenhouse policies of individual countries, despite international agreements.

Substantial progress in New Zealand's greenhouse policy is therefore unlikely to result from international demands or agreements alone. Barring technological breakthroughs in energy technology, progress in this area will depend foremost on the creativity of policy entrepreneurs within and outside government, the relative strength of domestic environmental demands, and the vision and courage of politicians.

So far, New Zealand's principal strength in environmental policy has lain in the ecological dimension—the conservation of nature—and not in resource conservation and quality of life issues. The country is fortunate to be able to rely on a renewable energy resource—hydro-electric power—for the larger part of its present electricity needs. The quality of life in New Zealand is still very high compared to that in many other nations. The image of the New Zealand as 'clean and green', although dented, still prevails. For these reasons, it is unlikely that New Zealand will take the lead on such issues as global pollution.

But even the clean and green image, which has been used to ignore serious environmental problems, has had a positive influence on policy as well. Much of the activity of New Zealand in international forums and negotiations has been encouraged because of the authority New Zealand carries internationally as a presumably clean and green country. Ministers and even opposition politicians have been inspired to take actions, such as promising to reduce emissions of greenhouse gases, to try to live up to that reputation. Much of the progress in regulating pesticides, however slow and still inadequate, has come about because of a concern that without some action the clean and green image of New Zealand—so important to international marketing—might be blemished. As the quality of the New Zealand environment and the policies that collectively impinge upon it come under more systematic and sophisticated scrutiny by the public and interest groups, living up to the clean and green image, even minimally, will become a greater and greater challenge. But the image has such universal appeal in New Zealand society that no government will be able to disavow it, so we can expect it to be a continuing influence on policy development.

Regardless of any overt role played by New Zealand in the future development of international environmental policy, domestically it has already adopted innovative institutional reforms for dealing with environmental problems that should be of great interest to policy entrepreneurs and scholars in other countries. These reforms will be of even greater interest if they can be shown to work. But making them work—which is a political question—will require that the social and economic aspects of the environmental problematique be given greater weight than in the past.

Despite the significant progress that has been made, New Zealand—and for that matter the whole world—still has a long way to go to come to terms with the environmental problematique. The developments in environmental policy during the last two decades should be seen as only the first steps in a highly demanding learning process. The lessons are difficult, and it is not surprising that mistakes have been made and the need for learning sometimes questioned. Nevertheless, if New Zealanders wish to maintain their precarious status as world leaders in environmental policy, they will need to accomplish much more innovation than has been realized so far. Equally importantly, they will need to realize the promise of policies already adopted. What is most significant about the bold reforms in New Zealand is not whether they provide answers to the environmental problematique, but rather that they provide exciting opportunities for grappling with the environmental challenges through learning and through further policy development at home and abroad.

REFERENCES

Ackroyd, Peter, et al. (1991) *Environmental Resources and the Market-Place*. Sydney: Allen & Unwin.
Anderson, Charles (1977) *Statecraft: An Introduction to Political Choice and Judgment*. New York: John Wiley.
Anderson, James E. (1979) *Public Policy-Making*. 2nd ed. New York: Holt, Rinehart, and Winston.
Andersen, Jørgen Goul (1990) '"Environmentalism", "New Politics" and Industrialism: Some Theoretical Perspectives' *Scandinavian Political Studies* 13 (2): 101–17.
Anderson, Frederick et al. (1977) *Environmental Improvement Through Economic Incentives*. Baltimore: The Johns Hopkins University Press.
Auckland Regional Water Board (1988–1991) *Newsletters* 1–13. Auckland: Auckland Regional Water Board.
Auckland Regional Water Board (1990) *Manukau Harbour Water Quality Management Plan*. Auckland: Auckland Regional Water Board.
Bachrach, Peter and Morton S. Baratz (1961) 'Two Faces of Power' *American Political Science Review* 56: 947–52.
Bachrach, Peter and Morton S. Baratz (1963) 'Decisions and Nondecisions: An Analytical Framework' *American Political Science Review* 57: 632–42.
Barrett, Susan and Colin Fudge (eds) (1981) *Policy and Action: Essays on the Implementation of Public Policy*. London: Methuen.
Bartlett, Robert V. (1986a) 'Rationality and the Logic of the National Environmental Policy Act' *The Environmental Professional* 8: 105–11.
Bartlett, Robert V. (1986b) 'Ecological Rationality: Reason and Environmental Policy' *Environmental Ethics* 8: 221–39.
Bartlett, Robert V. (1990a) 'Comprehensive Environmental Decision Making: Can It Work?' in Vig, Norman J. and Michael E. Kraft (eds) *Environmental Policy in the 1990s: Toward a New Agenda*. Washington, D.C.: CQ Press.
Bartlett, Robert V. (1990b) 'Ecological Reason in Administration: Environmental Impact Assessment and Administrative Theory' in Paehlke, Robert and Douglas Torgerson (eds) *Managing Leviathan: Environmental Politics and the Administrative State*. Peterborough, Ontario: Broadview Press.
Bartlett, Robert V. (1993a) 'Evaluating Environmental Policy Success and Failure' in Vig, Norman J. and Michael E. Kraft (eds) *Environmental Policy in the 1990s*, 2nd ed. Washington, D.C.: CQ Press.
Bartlett, Robert V. (1993b) 'Integrated Impact Assessment as Environmental Policy' *Policy Studies Journal*, forthcoming.
Baumol, William J. and Wallace E. Oates (1975) *The Theory of Environmental Policy: Externalities, Public Outlays, and the Quality of Life*. Englewood Cliffs, N.J.: Prentice Hall.
Benedick, Richard Elliot (1991) *Ozone Diplomacy*. Cambridge, Mass.: Harvard University Press.
Bennet, Colin J. (1991) 'Review Article: What is Policy Convergence and What Causes It?' *British Journal of Political Science* 21 (2): 215–33.
Bennett, Graham (1990) 'Policy Planning in the Netherlands' in Haigh, Nigel and

Frances Irwin (eds) *Integrated Pollution Control in Europe and North America*. Washington, D.C.: Conservation Foundation.
Bobrow, Davis B. and John S. Dryzek (1987) *Policy Analysis by Design*. Pittsburgh, Penn.: University of Pittsburgh Press.
Bookchin, Murray (1980) *Toward an Ecological Society*. Montreal: Black Rose.
Boston, Jonathan (1991a) 'Theoretical Underpinnings of Public Sector Restructuring in New Zealand' in Boston, Jonathan, John Martin, June Pallot, and Pat Walsh (eds) *Reshaping the State: New Zealand's Bureaucratic Revolution*. Auckland: Oxford University Press.
Boston, Jonathan (1991b) 'Reorganizing the Machinery of Government: Objectives and Outcomes' in Boston, Jonathan, John Martin, June Pallot, and Pat Walsh (eds) *Reshaping the State: New Zealand's Bureaucratic Revolution*. Auckland: Oxford University Press.
Boston, Jonathan and Fiona Cooper (1989) 'The Treasury: Advice, Coordination, and Control' in Gold, Hyam (ed) *New Zealand Politics in Perspective*. 2nd ed. Auckland: Longman Paul.
Boston, Jonathan and Paul Dalziel (1992) *The Decent Society? Essays in Response to National's Economic and Social Policies*. Auckland: Oxford University Press.
Boston, Jonathan, John Martin, and Pat Walsh (1991) 'Conclusion' in Boston, Jonathan, John Martin, June Pallot, and Pat Walsh (eds) *Reshaping the State: New Zealand's Bureaucratic Revolution*. Auckland: Oxford University Press.
Boston, Jonathan, John Martin, June Pallot and Pat Walsh (eds) (1991) *Reshaping the State: New Zealand's Bureaucratic Revolution*. Auckland: Oxford University Press.
Braybrooke, David and Charles E. Lindblom (1963) *A Strategy of Decision: Policy Evaluation as a Social Process*. New York: The Free Press.
Brewer, Garry D. and Peter deLeon (1983) *The Foundations of Policy Analysis*. Chicago, Ill.: Dorsey Press.
Brittan, Samuel (1983) *The Role and Limits of Government: Essays in Political Economy*. London: Temple Smith.
Bromley, Daniel W. (1988) *Property Rights and the Environment: Natural Resource Policy in Transition*. Wellington: Ministry for the Environment.
Brown, Lester R. (1991) 'The New World Order' in Brown, Lester R. et al. *State of the World 1991*. Sydney: Allen & Unwin.
Brown, Lester R. et al. (1984–1992) *State of the World; A Worldwatch Institute Report on Progress Toward a Sustainable Society*. New York: W. W. Norton.
Browne, Angela, and Aaron Wildavsky (1984) 'What Should Evaluation Mean to Implementation?' in Pressman, Jeffrey and Aaron Wildavsky *Implementation*. 3rd. ed. Berkeley, Calif.: University of California Press.
Brundtland Commission [World Commission on Environment and Development] (1987) *Our Common Future*. Oxford: Oxford University Press.
Bührs, Ton (1987) 'Environmental Policy Development: The Case of New Zealand', Paper presented at the Australasian Political Science Conference, University of Auckland.
Bührs, Ton (1991a) 'Working Within Limits: The Role of the Commission for the Environment in Environmental Policy Development in New Zealand.' Ph.D. thesis, University of Auckland.
Bührs, Ton (1991b) 'Strategies for Environmental Policy Co-ordination: The New Zealand Experience' *Political Science* 43 (2): 1–29.

Bührs, Ton (1992a) 'Giving the Environment the Swerve' *Terra Nova* 14 (March): 33–5.
Bührs, Ton (1992b) [Review of Boston, Jonathan, John Martin, June Pallot, and Pat Walsh (eds) (1991) *Reshaping the State*] *Political Science* 44 (1): 60–1.
Bush, Graham (1980) *Moving Against the Tide*. Palmerston North: Dunmore Press.
Bush, Graham (1989) 'Local Government: Politics and Pragmatism' in Gold, Hyam (ed) *New Zealand Politics in Perspective*. 2nd ed. Auckland: Longman Paul.
Bush, Graham (1990) 'The Historic Reorganization of Local Government' in Holland, Martin and Jonathan Boston (eds) *The Fourth Labour Government: Politics and Policy in New Zealand*. 2nd ed. Auckland: Oxford University Press.
Bush Telegraph. Various issues. Nelson: Maruia Society.
Cairncross, Frances (1991) *Costing the Earth*. London: Business Books.
Caldwell, Lynton K. (1963) 'Environment: A New Focus for Public Policy?' *Public Administration Review* 23 (3): 132–9.
Caldwell, Lynton K. (1990a) *International Environmental Policy: Emergence and Dimensions*. Durham, N.C.: Duke University Press.
Caldwell, Lynton K. (1990b) *Between Two Worlds. Science, the Environmental Movement, and Policy Choice*. Cambridge: Cambridge University Press.
Caldwell, Lynton K. (1990c) 'International Environmental Politics: America's Response to Global Imperatives' in Vig, Norman J. and Michael E. Kraft (eds) *Environmental Policy in the 1990s: Toward a New Agenda*. Washington, D.C.: CQ Press.
Capra, Fritjof and Charlene Spretnak (1984) *Green Politics: The Global Promise*. New York: E. P. Dutton.
Carter, Vernon Gill and Tom Dale (1974) *Topsoil and Civilization*. Norman: University of Oklahoma Press.
Cartner, M. (1991) 'An Analysis of the Importance of Management Research Topics for Academics and Chief Executives in New Zealand and Canada'. Wellington: Victoria University Graduate School of Business and Government Management, Working Paper 12/91.
Castles, Francis G. (1985) *The Working Class and Welfare: Reflections on the Political Development of the Welfare State in Australia and New Zealand, 1890–1980*. Wellington: Allen & Unwin.
Catton, William R. Jr. (1980) *Overshoot: The Ecological Basis of Revolutionary Change*. Urbana, Ill.: University of Illinois Press.
Catton, William R. Jr. and Riley E. Dunlap (1980) 'A New Ecological Paradigm for Post- Exuberant Sociology' *American Behavioral Scientist* 24: 15–47.
Chisholm, Donald (1989) *Coordination Without Hierarchy: Informal Structures in Multiorganizational Systems*. Berkeley, Calif.: University of California Press.
Cobb, Roger W. and Charles D. Elder (1972) *Participation in American Politics: The Dynamics of Agenda-Building*. Boston: Allyn and Bacon.
Cobb, Roger, Jennie-Keith Ross and Marc H. Ross (1976) 'Agenda Building as a Comparative Political Process' *American Political Science Review* 70: 126–38.
Cohen, Michael D., James G. March, and Johan P. Olsen (1972) 'A Garbage Can Model of Organizational Choice' *Administrative Science Quarterly* 17: 1–25.
Colby, Michael E. (1990) *Environmental Management in Development: The Evolution of Paradigms*. Washington, D.C.: The World Bank.
Colmar and Brunton Research (1989) *Syndicated Survey of Environmental Attitudes in New Zealand*. Auckland: Colmar and Brunton Research.

Commission for the Environment (1984) *A Guide to Environmental Law in New Zealand.* 2nd ed. Wellington: Brooker & Friend for the Commission for the Environment.
Commission for the Environment (1985) *Indigenous Forests of New Zealand, Environmental Issues and Options.* Wellington: Commission for the Environment.
Commission for the Environment (1986a) *The Use of 2,4,5-T in New Zealand, A Report to the Environmental Council.* Wellington: Commission for the Environment.
Commission for the Environment (1986b) *Petrol Lead Reduction: Issues and Options.* Wellington: Commission for the Environment.
Condliffe, J. B. (1959) *New Zealand in the Making.* London: Allen & Unwin.
Conservation News. Various issues. Wellington: Royal Forest and Bird Protection Society of NZ.
Cotgrove, Stephen F. (1982) *Catastrophe or Cornucopia: The Environment, Politics and the Future.* New York: John Wiley.
Dahl, Robert A. and Charles E. Lindblom (1953) *Politics, Economics, and Welfare.* New York: Harper and Brothers.
Dalmer, N. E. (1983) *Birds, Forests and Natural Features of New Zealand.* Wellington: Royal Forest and Bird Protection Society of NZ.
Davies, J. Clarence (1991) 'Some Thoughts on Implementing Integration' *Environmental Law* 22:139–47.
Davies, Terry (1990) 'The United States: Experiment and Fragmentation' in Haigh, Nigel and Frances Irwin (eds) *Integrated Pollution Control in Europe and North America.* Washington, D.C.: Conservation Foundation.
deLeon, Peter (1988) *Advice and Consent: The Development of the Policy Sciences.* New York: Russell Sage Foundation.
Department of Conservation (1992) *Draft New Zealand Coastal Policy Statement 1992.* Wellington: Department of Conservation.
Department of Statistics (1989) *New Zealand Official Yearbook 1988–1989.* Wellington: Department of Statistics.
Department of Statistics (1992) *New Zealand Official 1992 Yearbook.* Wellington: Department of Statistics.
Dery, David (1984) *Problem Definition in Policy Analysis.* Lawrence, Kans.: University Press of Kansas.
Devall, Bill (1980) 'The Deep Ecology Movement' *Natural Resources Journal* 20 (2): 299–322.
Diesing, Paul (1962) *Reason in Society: Five Types of Decisions and Their Social Conditions.* Urbana, Ill.: University of Illinois Press.
Diesing, Paul (1982) *Science and Ideology in the Policy Sciences.* Chicago: Aldine.
Douglas, Mary and Aaron Wildavsky (1982) *Risk and Culture: An Essay on the Selection of Technical and Environmental Dangers.* Berkeley, Calif.: University of California Press.
Downs, Anthony (1972) 'Up and Down with Ecology: The "Issue-Attention" Cycle' *The Public Interest* 28: 38–50.
Dror, Yehezkel (1983) *Public Policymaking Reexamined.* 2nd ed. New Brunswick, N.J.: Transaction.
Dryzek, John S. (1987) *Rational Ecology: Environment and Political Economy.* Oxford: Basil Blackwell.

Dunlap, Riley E. (1989) 'Public Opinion and Environmental Policy' in Lester, James P. (ed) *Environmental Politics and Policy: Theories and Evidence*. Durham, N.C.: Duke University Press.

Dunlap, Riley E. and Kent D. Van Liere (1978) 'The "New Environmental Paradigm"' *Journal of Environmental Education* 9: 10–19.

Dunlap, Riley E., George H. Gallup, Jr. and Alec M. Gallup (1992) *The Health of the Planet Survey*. Princeton, N.J.: The George H. Gallup International Institute.

Dunn, William N. (1981) *Public Policy Analysis: An Introduction*. Englewood Cliffs, N.J.: Prentice-Hall.

Dye, Thomas R. (1987) *Understanding Public Policy*. 6th ed. Englewood Cliffs, N.J.: Prentice-Hall.

Easton, Brian (1981) *Pragmatism and Progress: Social Security in the Seventies*. Christchurch: University of Canterbury.

Easton, Brian (1990) *Policy as Revolution: Two Case Studies*. Paper presented at the New Zealand Political Studies Association, 14–16 May, University of Otago.

Eckersley, Robyn (1989) 'Green Politics and the New Class: Selfishness or Virtue?' *Political Studies* 37: 205–23.

Ehrenfeld, David (1981) *The Arrogance of Humanism*. Oxford: Oxford University Press.

Ehrlich, Paul R., Anne H. Ehrlich, and John P. Holdren (1977) *Ecoscience: Population, Resources, Environment*. San Francisco: W. H. Freeman and Company.

Elkin, Stephen, and Brian J. Cook (1985) 'The Public Life of Economic Incentives' *Political Science Journal* 13 (4): 797–813.

Enloe, Cynthia (1975) *The Politics of Pollution in Comparative Perspective*. New York: David McKay.

Environmental Council (1980) *Urban Concerns 1980: Concerns and Policies for Urban Management*. Wellington: Environmental Council.

Environmental Council (1987) *Environment Meets Economics*. Wellington: Government Printer.

Establishment Unit for the Parliamentary Commissioner and Ministry for the Environment (1986) *Preliminary Draft Strategic Plan*. Wellington: Ministry for the Environment.

Etzioni, Amitai (1967) 'Mixed Scanning: A "Third" Approach to Decision-Making' *Public Administration Review* 27: 385–92.

Fisher, D. E. (1991) 'The Resource Management Legislation of 1991: A Juridical Analysis of Its Objectives' in Shields, Adrian (ed) *Resource Management*. Wellington: Brooker & Friend.

Fitzsimons, Jeanette (1981) *Synthetic Petrol or Sustainable Fuels*. Energywatch Special Publication.

Fitzsimons, Jeanette (1990) 'Energy Efficiency: Ten Reasons Why the Market Will Not Deliver' *New Zealand Engineering* November: 28–31.

Flanagan, Scott C. (1987) 'Value Change in Industrial Societies' *American Political Science Review* 81 (4): 1289–319.

Flavin, Christopher (1990) *Slowing Global Warming—A Worldwide Strategy*. Washington, D.C.: Worldwatch Institute.

Fleet, Harriet (1984) *New Zealand's Forests*. Auckland: Heinemann.

Formby, John (1986) 'Environmental Policies in Australia—Climbing Down the Escalator' in Park, Chris C. (ed) *Environmental Policies: An International*

Review. London: Croom Helm.
French, Hilary F. (1992) 'Strengthening Global Environmental Governance' in Brown, Lester R. et al. *State of the World 1992*. London: Earthscan.
Gibson, Robert B. (1993) 'Environmental Assessment: The Canadian Experience and Process Design' *The Environmental Professional* 15: 12–24.
Gilg, Andrew (1986) 'Environmental Policies in the United Kingdom' in Park, Chris C. (ed) *Environmental Policies: An International Review*. London: Croom Helm
Goggin, Malcolm L., Ann O'M. Bowman, James P. Lester, and Laurence J. O'Toole, Jr. (1990) *Implementation Theory and Practice: Toward a Third Generation*. Glenview, Ill.: Scott, Foresman/Little, Brown.
Gold, Hyam and Alan Webster (1990) *New Zealand Values Today*. Palmerston North: Massey University.
Goldsmith, Edward, et al. (eds) (1972) 'Blueprint for survival', *The Ecologist*. Special issue.
Goodin, Robert E. (1982) *Political Theory and Public Policy*. Chicago: The University of Chicago Press.
Goodin, Robert E. and Ilmar Waldner (1979) 'Thinking Big, Thinking Small, and Not Thinking At All' *Public Policy* 27: 1–24.
Goodwin, D. and O. P. D. Hille (1992) 'Concern for the Environment: Do Annual Reports Reflect This?' Research paper, Lincoln University.
Gormley, William T., Jr. (1987) 'Institutional Policy Analysis: A Critical Review' *Journal of Policy Analysis and Management* 6: 153–69.
Gormley, William T., Jr. (1988) 'Institutional Policy Analysis' *The Political Science Teacher* 1(2): 12–5.
Gormley, William T. Jr. (1989) *Taming the Bureaucracy: Muscles, Prayers, and Other Strategies*. Princeton, N.J.: Princeton University Press.
Gregory, Robert (1987) 'The Reorganization of the Public Sector: The Quest for Efficiency' in Boston, Jonathan and Martin Holland (eds) *The Fourth Labour Government: Radical Politics in New Zealand*. Auckland: Oxford University Press.
Gregory, Robert (1989) 'Political Rationality or "Incrementalism"?' Charles E. Lindblom's Enduring Contribution to Public Policy Making Theory' *Policy and Politics* 17 (2): 139–53.
Grinlinton, David (1992) 'Enforcement Mechanisms Under the RMA' *Planning Quarterly* 105: 15–9.
Guruswamy, Lakshman (1989) 'Integrating Thoughtways: Reopening of the Environmental Mind?' *Wisconsin Law Review* 1989: 463–537.
Guruswamy, Lakshman (1991) 'Integrated Environmental Control: The Expanding Matrix' *Environmental Law* 22: 77–118.
Haas, Peter M. (1990) 'Obtaining International Environmental Protection through Epistemic Consensus' *Millennium* 19 (3): 347–63.
Haas, Peter M. (1992) 'Introduction: Epistemic Communities and International Policy Coordination' in Haas, Peter M. (ed) 'Knowledge, Power and International Policy Coordination'. *International Organization*. Special Issue.
Haigh, Nigel and Frances Irwin (eds) (1989) *Integrated Pollution Control in Europe and North America*. Washington, D.C.: The Conservation Foundation.
Hahn, Robert W. (1989) *A Primer on Environmental Policy Design*. Chur: Harwood Academic Publishers.

Hammond, Thomas H. (1986) 'Agenda Control, Organizational Structure, and Bureaucratic Politics' *Political Science* 30: 379–420.

Hanf, Kenneth (1982) 'The Implementation of Regulatory Policy: Enforcement as Bargaining' *European Journal of Political Research* 10: 159–72.

Hardin, Garrett (1968) 'Tragedy of the Commons' *Science* 162: 1243–8.

Hawke, G. R. (1985) *The Making of New Zealand*. Cambridge: Cambridge University Press.

Hay, P. R. and M. G. Haward (1988) 'Comparative Green Politics: Beyond the European Context' *Political Studies* 36: 433–48.

Hayek, Friedrich A. (1982) *Law, Legislation and Liberty*. London: Routledge & Kegan Paul.

Hearn, A. (1987) *Review of the Town and Country Planning Act 1977*. Wellington: Department of Trade and Industry.

Henning, Daniel H. and William R. Mangun (1989) *Managing the Environmental Crisis: Incorporating Competing Values in Natural Resource Administration*. Durham, N.C.: Duke University Press.

Hirsch, Fred (1977) *Social Limits to Growth*. London: Routledge & Kegan Paul.

Hoberg, George (1986) 'Technology, Political Structure, and Social Regulation, A Cross-National Study' *Comparative Politics* 18 (3): 357–76.

Hofferbert, Richard I. (1990) *The Reach and Grasp of Policy Analysis: Comparative Views of the Craft*. Tuscaloosa, Ala.: University of Alabama Press.

Hoffmann, S. (1982) 'A World of Complexity' in Murray, D. J. and Paul R. Viotti (eds) *The Defense Policies of Nations: A Comparative Study*. Baltimore: The Johns Hopkins University Press.

Hogwood, Brian W. and Lewis A. Gunn (1984) *Policy Analysis for the Real World*. Oxford: Oxford University Press.

Holland, Martin, and Jonathan Boston (1990) 'Introduction' in Holland, Martin and Jonathan Boston (eds) *The Fourth Labour Government: Politics and Policy in New Zealand*. 2nd ed. Auckland: Oxford University Press.

Hood, Christopher (1991) 'A Public Management for All Seasons?' *Public Administration* 69 (1): 3–19.

House, Peter W. and Roger D. Shull (1985) *Regulatory Reform: Politics and the Environment*. Lanham, Md.: University Press of America.

House, Peter W. and Roger D. Shull (1988) *Rush to Policy: Using Analytical Techniques in Public Sector Decision Making*. New Brunswick, N.J.: Transaction Books.

Hugo, Victor (1852) *History of a Crime* [Histoire d'un Crime]. Boston: Jefferson Press.

Hula, Richard C. (1988) 'Using Markets to Implement Public Policy' in Hula, Richard C. (ed) *Market Based Public Policy*. Basingstoke, Md.: MacMillan Press.

Inglehart, Ronald (1977) *The Silent Revolution: Changing Values and Political Styles Among Western Publics*. Princeton, N.J.: Princeton University Press.

Inglehart, Ronald (1981) 'Post-materialism in an Environment of Insecurity' *American Political Science Review* 75: 279–316.

Inglehart, Ronald (1990) *Culture Shift in Advanced Industrial Society*. Princeton, N.J.: Princeton University Press.

Ingram, Helen M. (1990) 'Implementation: A Review and Suggested Framework' in Lynn, Naomi B. and Aaron Wildavsky (eds) *Public Administration: The State of*

the Discipline. Chatham, N.J.: Chatham House.
Ingram, Helen M. and Anne Schneider (1990) 'Improving Implementation Through Framing Smarter Statutes' *Journal of Public Policy* 10: 67–88.
Irwin, Frances H. (1991) 'An Integrated Framework for Preventing Pollution and Protecting the Environment' *Environmental Law* 22: 1–76.
IUCN/WWF/UNEP (1980) *World Conservation Strategy.* Gland: Switzerland.
Jesson, Bruce (1987) *Behind the Mirror Glass: The Growth of Wealth and Power in New Zealand in the Eighties.* Auckland: Penguin Books.
Jesson, Bruce (1989) *Fragments of Labour.* Auckland: Penguin Books.
Jones, Charles O. (1970) *An Introduction to the Study of Public Policy.* Belmont, Calif.: Wadsworth.
Kassiola, Joel Jay (1990) *The Death of Industrial Civilization.* Albany, N.Y.: State University of New York Press.
Kelman, Steven (1981) *What Price Incentives? Economists and the Environment.* Boston: Auburn House.
Kennaway, Richard (1991) 'Environmental Issues: The Growing International Dimension' in Kennaway, Richard and John Henderson (eds) *Beyond New Zealand II: Foreign Policy into the 1990s.* Auckland: Longman Paul.
Kerr, Geoff N. and Basil M. H. Sharp (eds) (1985) *Valuing the Environment.* Centre for Resource Management, Lincoln University.
King, Anthony (1975) 'Overload: Problems of Governing in the 1970s' *Political Studies* 23: 284–96.
Kingdon, John W. (1984) *Agendas, Alternatives, and Public Policies.* Boston: Little, Brown.
Kneese, Allen V., and Charles L. Schultze (1975) *Pollution, Prices and Public Policy.* Washington, D.C.: Brookings.
Koopman-Boyden, Peggy G.(1990) 'Social Policy: Has There Been One?' in Holland, Martin and Jonathan Boston (eds) *The Fourth Labour Government: Politics and Policy in New Zealand.* 2nd ed. Auckland: Oxford University Press.
Krasner, Stephen D. (1984) 'Approaches to the State. Alternative Conceptions and Historical Dynamics' *Comparative Politics* 16 (2): 223–46.
Krier, James E. and Mark Brownstein (1991) 'On Integrated Pollution Control' *Environmental Law* 22: 119–38
Kuhn, Thomas S. (1962) *The Structure of Scientific Revolutions.* Chicago: University of Chicago Press.
Lambert, Ray (1991a) 'Recent Developments in New Zealand's Fisheries Policy: The Emergence of the Quota Management System.' M.Sc. (Resource Management) paper, Centre for Resource Management, Lincoln University.
Lambert, Ray (1991b) 'Environmental Auditing: The New Zealand Response to An Evolving Discipline.' M.Sc. (Resource Management) paper, Centre for Resource Management, Lincoln University.
Lane, Jan-Erik (1990) *Institutional Reform: A Public Policy Perspective.* Aldershot, England: Dartmouth.
Lasswell, Harold (1951) 'The Policy Orientation' in Lerner, Daniel and Harold D. Lasswell (eds) *The Policy Sciences: Recent Developments in Scope and Method.* Stanford, Calif.: Stanford University Press.
Lasswell, Harold (1956) *The Decision Process: Seven Categories of Functional Analysis.* College Park, Md.: University of Maryland Bureau of Governmental Research.

Lasswell, Harold (1971) *A Pre-View of Policy Sciences*. New York: American Elsevier.
LeGrand, Julian (1991) 'The Theory of Government Failure' *British Journal of Political Science* 21 (4): 423–42.
Lindblom, Charles E. (1959) 'The Science of Muddling Through' *Public Administration Review* 19: 79–88.
Lindblom, Charles E. (1965) *The Intelligence of Democracy: Decision Making Through Mutual Adjustment*. New York: The Free Press.
Lindblom, Charles E. (1977) *Politics and Markets: The World's Political-Economic Systems*. New York: Basic Books.
Lindblom, Charles E. (1979) 'Still Muddling, Not Yet Through' *Public Administration Review* 39: 517–26.
Lindblom, Charles E. (1980) *The Policy Making Process*. 2nd ed. Englewood Cliffs, N.J.: Prentice-Hall.
Lindblom, Charles E. (1982) 'The Market as Prison' *Journal of Politics* 44: 324–36.
Lindblom, Charles E. (1990) *Inquiry and Change*. New Haven, Conn.: Yale University Press.
Lindblom, Charles E. and Edward J. Woodhouse (1993) *The Policy-Making Process*. 3rd ed. Englewood Cliffs, N.J.: Prentice-Hall.
Lowe, Philip D. and Wolfgang Rudig (1986) 'Political Ecology and the Social Sciences—The State of the Art' *British Journal of Political Science* 16: 313–50.
Lowi, Theodore J. (1972) 'Four Systems of Policy, Politics, and Choice' *Public Administration Review* 32: 298–310.
Lowrey, Kem and Richard A. Carpenter (1984) *Holistic Nature and Fragmented Bureaucracies: A Study of Government Organization for Natural Systems Management*. Honolulu: East-West Center.
Lundqvist, Lennart J. (1980) *The Hare and the Tortoise: Clean Air Policies in the U.S. and Sweden*. Ann Arbor: University of Michigan Press.
MacIntyre, Angus, Nicholas Allison, and David Penman (1989) *Pesticides: Issues and Options for New Zealand*. Wellington: Ministry for the Environment.
McChesney, Ian G. (1991a) *The Brundtland Report and Sustainable Development in New Zealand*. Centre for Resource Management, Lincoln University.
McChesney, Ian G. (1991b) *From Threat to Opportunity: Moving To A Sustainable Energy Pathway*. Centre for Resource Management, Lincoln University.
McConnell, Grant (1966) *Private Power and American Democracy*. New York: Alfred A. Knopf.
McCormick, John S. (1989) *The Global Environmental Movement*. London: Belhaven.
McCormick, John S. (1991) *British Politics and the Environment*. London: Earthscan.
McCubbins, Mathew, Roger Noll, and Barry Weingast (1987) 'Administrative Procedures as Instruments of Political Control' Working papers in political science, Hoover Institution, Stanford University.
McKinlay, Peter (1987) *Corporatisation: The Solution for State Owned Enterprise?* Wellington: Victoria University Press for the Institute of Policy Studies.
McKinlay, Peter (ed) (1990) *Redistribution of Power? Devolution in New Zealand*. Wellington: Victoria University Press for the Institute of Policy Studies.
Majone, Giandomenico (1986) 'Analyzing the Public Sector: Shortcomings of Current Approaches—Part A. Policy Science' in Kaufman, Franz-Xaver,

Giandomenico Majone, and Vincent Ostrom (eds) *Guidance, Control, and Evaluation in the Public Sector*. New York: Walter de Gruyter.

Majone, Giandomenico (1989) *Evidence, Argument, and Persuasion in the Policy Process*. New Haven, Conn.: Yale University Press.

Majone, Giandomenico, and Aaron Wildavsky (1984) 'Implementation as Evolution' in Pressman, Jeffrey and Aaron Wildavsky *Implementation*. 3rd ed. Berkeley, Calif.: University of California Press.

March, James G. and Johan P. Olsen (1983) 'Organizing Political Life: What Administrative Reorganization Tells Us About Government' *American Political Science Review* 77: 281–96.

March, James G. and Johan P. Olsen (1984) 'The New Institutionalism: Organizational Factors in Political Life' *American Political Science Review* 78: 734–49.

March, James G., and Johan P. Olsen (1989) *Rediscovering Institutions: The Organizational Basis of Politics*. New York: The Free Press.

Marsden, Maori (1988) *The Natural World and Natural Resources: Maori Value Systems and Perspectives*. Wellington: Ministry for the Environment.

Martin, John (1990) 'Remaking the State Services' in Holland, Martin and Jonathan Boston (eds) *The Fourth Labour Government: Politics and Policy in New Zealand*. 2nd ed. Auckland: Oxford University Press.

Martin, John (1991a) *Public Service and the Public Servant: Administrative Practice in a Time of Change*. Wellington: State Services Commission.

Martin, John (1991b) 'Devolution and Decentralization' in Boston, Jonathan, John Martin, June Pallot, and Pat Walsh (eds) *Reshaping the State: New Zealand's Bureaucratic Revolution*. Auckland: Oxford University Press.

Martin, John (1991c) 'Ethos and Ethics' in Boston, Jonathan, John Martin, June Pallot, and Pat Walsh (eds) *Reshaping the State: New Zealand's Bureaucratic Revolution*. Auckland: Oxford University Press.

Mascarenhas, R. C. (1982) *Public Enterprise in New Zealand*. Wellington: N.Z. Institute of Public Administration.

Mascarenhas, R. C. (1991) 'State-owned Enterprises', in Boston, Jonathan, John Martin, June Pallot, and Pat Walsh (eds) *Reshaping the State: New Zealand's Bureaucratic Revolution*. Auckland: Oxford University Press.

Mazmanian, Daniel A. and Paul A. Sabatier (1983) *Implementation and Public Policy*. Glenview, Ill.: Scott, Foresman.

Meadows, Donella H., Dennis L. Meadows, Jørgen Randers, (1992) *Beyond the Limits: Global Collapse or a Sustainable Future*. London: Earthscan Publications.

Meadows, Donella H., Dennis L. Meadows, Jørgen Randers, and William W. Behrens III (1972) *The Limits to Growth*. New York: Universe Books.

Meister, A. D. (1990) *Environmental Regulation and Use of Economic Instruments for Environmental Planning and Management: An Overview*. Palmerston North: Massey University.

Milbrath, Lester W. (1984) *Environmentalists: Vanguard for a New Society*. Albany, N.Y.: State University of New York Press.

Milbrath, Lester W. (1989) *Envisioning a Sustainable Society: Learning our Way Out*. Albany, N.Y.: State University of New York Press.

Miller, Raymond (1991) 'Postmaterialism and Green Party Activists in New Zealand' *Political Science* 43 (2): 43–66.

Milne, Christopher D. A. (1992) 'Resource Management Act 1991' in Milne, Christopher D. A. (ed) *Handbook of Environmental Law*. Wellington: Royal Forest and Bird Protection Society.

Minister for the Environment, Media Statement, 'A Green Choice for Consumers', 18 March 1992.

Minister for the Environment, Media Statement, 'Minister Releases Worley Report on Contaminated Sites', 16 December 1992.

Ministry for the Environment (1986) *Environmental Impact Assessment Procedures: A Discussion Paper*. Wellington: Ministry for the Environment.

Ministry for the Environment (1987a) *Proposed Policy on Environmental Assessment Procedures*. Wellington: Ministry for the Environment.

Ministry for the Environment (1987b) *A Strategy for Managing Hazardous Wastes*. Wellington: Ministry for the Environment.

Ministry for the Environment (1987c) *Packaging in the New Zealand Environment - Issues and Options*. Wellington: Ministry for the Environment.

Ministry for the Environment (1987d) *The Manukau Harbour: A Strategy for Restoration and Future Management*. Wellington: Ministry for the Environment.

Ministry for the Environment (1988a) *Directions for Change: A Discussion Paper*. Wellington: Ministry for the Environment.

Ministry for the Environment (1988b) *People, Environment, and Decision Making: The Government's Proposals for Resource Management Law Reform*. Wellington: Ministry for the Environment.

Ministry for the Environment (1988c) *Pollution and Hazardous Substances Management*. Wellington: Ministry for the Environment.

Ministry for the Environment (1989a) *Introducing the Resource Management Bill*. Wellington: Ministry for the Environment.

Ministry for the Environment (1989b) *The Herbicide 2,4,5-T: Technical Report of an Investigation into Residues of the Herbicide and Its Dioxin Component in Sheepmeats*. Wellington: Ministry for the Environment.

Ministry for the Environment (1989c) *Packaging and the New Zealand Environment: Critical Aspects of Resource Use and Waste Management*. Wellington: Ministry for the Environment.

Ministry for the Environment (1990) *Responding to Climate Change - A Discussion of Options for New Zealand*. Wellington: Ministry for the Environment.

Ministry for the Environment (1991a) *Guide to the Resource Management Act*. Wellington: Ministry for the Environment

Ministry for the Environment (1991b) *Report of the Ministry for the Environment for the Year Ended 30 June 1991*. Wellington: Ministry for the Environment.

Ministry for the Environment (1991c) *Producing Less Waste: An Information Paper on Conserving Resources and Reducing Rubbish and Pollution*. Wellington: Ministry for the Environment.

Ministry for the Environment (1992a) *Hazardous Substances and New Organisms: Proposals for Law Reform*. Wellington: Ministry for the Environment.

Ministry for the Environment (1992b) *Corporate Plan 1992–1993*. Wellington: Ministry for the Environment.

Ministry for the Environment (1993) 'Study Looks at Probable Scale of Site Contamination Problem' *Environment Update* 31: 1–2.

Ministry for the Environment and Department of Statistics (1990) *State of the Environment Reporting in New Zealand*. Wellington: Ministry for the

Environment and Department of Statistics.

Ministry for the Environment and Ministry of External Relations and Trade (1992) *New Zealand's National Report to the United Nations Conference on Environment and Development.* Wellington: Ministry for the Environment and Ministry of External Relations and Trade.

Minnery, John R. (1988) 'Modelling Coordination' *Australian Journal of Public Administration* 47: 253–62.

Mitchell, Robert C. (1990) 'Public Opinion and the Green Lobby: Poised for the 1990s?' in Vig, Norman J. and Michael E. Kraft (eds) *Environmental Policy in the 1990s: Toward a New Agenda.* Washington, D.C.: CQ Press.

Mitnick, Barry M. (1982) 'Incentive Systems in Environmental Regulation' in Mann, Dean E. (ed) *Environmental Policy Implementation.* Lexington, MA: Lexington Books.

Morgan, Richard K., P. Ali Memon, and Mary Anne Miller (1991) *Implementing the Resource Management Act* (Proceedings of a conference, 15–6 August 1991, Dunedin, New Zealand). Dunedin: Environmental Policy and Management Research Centre, Otago University.

Murphy, B. D. (1980) *Attitudes to the Future.* Wellington: Commission for the Future.

Murray, Anne C. (1990) 'Environmental Assessment: The Evolution of Policy and Practice in New Zealand.' M.Sc. (Resource Management) paper, Centre for Resource Management, Lincoln University.

Murray, Jeff and Simon Swaffield (1992) 'The Resource Management Act 1991: Myths for Environmental Management' Lincoln University (unpublished).

Nakano, Takamasa (1986) 'Environmental Policies in Japan' in Park, Chris C. (ed) *Environmental Policies: An International Review.* London: Croom Helm.

National Business Review. Various issues. Auckland: Fourth Estate Holdings.

New Zealand Values Party (1972) *Blueprint for New Zealand: An Alternative Future.* Wellington: New Zealand Values Party.

Nice, David C. (1987) *Federalism: The Politics of Intergovernmental Relations.* New York: St. Martin's Press.

Nisbet, Robert (1982) *Prejudices: A Philosophical Dictionary.* Cambridge, Mass.: Harvard University Press.

Nordlinger, Eric (1981) *On the Autonomy of the Democratic State.* Cambridge, Mass.: Harvard University Press.

Nordlinger, Eric (1988) 'The Return to the State: Critiques' *American Political Science Review* 82 (3): 875–85.

O'Connor, Naomi (1991) 'Guy Salmon—Riding the Third Wave' *Terra Nova* (February): 32–5.

[OECD] Organisation for Economic Co-operation and Development (1980a) *Environment Policies for the 1980s.* Paris: OECD.

[OECD] Organisation for Economic Co-operation and Development (1980b) *Pollution Charges in Practice.* Paris: OECD.

[OECD] Organisation for Economic Co-operation and Development (1981) *Environmental Policies in New Zealand.* Paris: OECD.

[OECD] Organisation for Economic Co-operation and Development (1985) *Environmental Data Compendium.* Paris: OECD.

[OECD] Organisation for Economic Co-operation and Development (1989) *Economic Instruments for Environmental Protection.* Paris: OECD.

[OECD] Organisation for Economic Co-operation and Development (1991) *Integrated Pollution Prevention and Control*. Environment Directorate, Environment Monographs No. 37. Paris: OECD.
[OECD] Organisation for Economic Co-operation and Development (1992) *Economic Surveys. Basic Statistics—International Comparisons*. Paris: OECD.
Ophuls, William (1977) *Ecology and the Politics of Scarcity: Prologue to a Political Theory of the Steady State*. San Francisco: W. H. Freeman.
O'Riordan, T. (1981) *Environmentalism*. London: Pion.
Ostrom, Elinor (1990) *Governing the Commons: The Evolution of Institutions for Collective Action*. Cambridge: Cambridge University Press.
Ostrom, Vincent, David Feeny, and Hartmut Picht (eds) (1988) *Rethinking Institutional Analysis and Development: Issues, Alternatives, and Choices*. San Francisco: International Center for Economic Growth.
Owens, Susan (1990) 'The Unified Pollution Inspectorate and Best Practicable Environmental Option in the United Kingdom' in Haigh, Nigel and Frances Irwin (eds) *Integrated Pollution Control in Europe and North America*. Washington, D.C.: Conservation Foundation.
Paehlke, Robert C. (1989) *Environmentalism and the Future of Progressive Politics*. New Haven, Conn.: Yale University.
Paehlke, Robert C. and Douglas Torgerson (eds) (1990) *Managing Leviathan: Environmental Politics and the Administrative State*. Peterborough, Ontario: Broadview Press.
Palmer, Geoffrey (1987) *Unbridled Power: An Interpretation of New Zealand's Constitution and Government*. 2nd ed. Auckland: Oxford University Press.
Palmer, Geoffrey (1990) *Environmental Politics: A Greenprint for New Zealand*. Dunedin: John McIndoe.
Parkin, Sara (1989) *Green Parties: An International Guide*. London: Heretic Books.
Parliamentary Commissioner for the Environment (1992a) *Sustainable Energy Management in New Zealand*. Wellington: Parliamentary Commissioner for the Environment.
Parliamentary Commissioner for the Environment (1992b) *The Management of Hazardous Wastes Disposal: A Review of Government Systems*. Wellington: Parliamentary Commissioner for the Environment.
Petulla, Joseph (1980) *American Environmentalism: Values, Tactics, Priorities*. College Station, Tex.: Texas A&M University Press.
Pierce, John C., Taketsugu Tsurutani, and Nicholas P. Lovrich, Jr. (1986) 'Vanguards and Rearguards in Environmental Politics: A Comparison of Activists in Japan and the United States' *Comparative Political Studies* 18 (4): 419–47.
Pollock Shea, Cynthia (1989) 'Protecting the Ozone Layer' in Brown, Lester R. et al., *State of the World 1989*. New York: W. W. Norton.
Portney, Kent (1986) *Approaching Public Policy Analysis: An Introduction to Policy and Program Research*. Englewood Cliffs, N.J.: Prentice-Hall.
Postel, Sandra (1992) 'Denial in the Decisive Decade' in Brown, Lester R. et al. *State of the World*. London: Earthscan Publications.
The Press. Newspaper. Various issues. Christchurch: The Press.
Pressman, Jeffrey L. and Aaron Wildavsky (1973) *Implementation: How Great Expectations in Washington are Dashed in Oakland*. Berkeley, Calif.: University of California Press.
Quade, E. S. (1982) *Analysis for Public Decisions*. 2nd ed. New York: North-

Holland.
Rabe, Barry (1986) *Fragmentation and Integration in State Environmental Management*. Washington, D.C.: Conservation Foundation.
Rabe, Barry (1990) 'Overcoming Fragmentation in Canadian Environmental Management' in Haigh, Nigel and Frances Irwin (eds) *Integrated Pollution Control in Europe and North America*. Washington, D.C.: Conservation Foundation.
Rainbow, Stephen L. (1987) 'New Zealand's Values Party—The Rise and Fall of the First Green Party' Paper presented to the 1987 Australasian Political Science Conference, University of Auckland.
Rainbow, Stephen L. (1992) 'Why Did Tasmania and New Zealand Spawn the World's First Green Parties' *Environmental Politics* 1 (3): 321–46.
Rees, Judith (1990) *Natural Resources: Allocation, Economics and Policy*. London: Methuen.
Resource Management Act 1991. Wellington: Government Printer.
Richardson, Jeremy (ed) (1982) *Policy Styles in Western Europe*. London: George Allen & Unwin.
Ripley, Randall (1987) *Policy Analysis in Political Science*. Chicago: Nelson-Hall.
Rippingale, Gen (1992) 'Effectiveness of an International Environmental Regime: The Protocol on Environmental Protection to the Antarctic Treaty.' M.Sc. (Resource Management) paper, Centre for Resource Management, Lincoln University.
Roper, Brian S. (1991) 'From the Welfare State to the Free Market: Explaining the Transition' *New Zealand Sociology* 6 (1): 38–63; (2): 135–76.
Rose, Richard (1984) *Understanding Big Government*. Beverly Hills: Sage Publications.
Rose-Ackerman, Susan (1977) 'Market Models for Water Pollution Control: Their Strengths and Weaknesses' *Public Policy* 25 (3): 383–406.
Royal Commission on Social Policy (1988) *Towards a Fair and Just Society*. Wellington: Government Printer.
Royal Forest and Bird Protection Society of NZ et al. (1982) *Environmental Management in New Zealand: A Strategy*. Wellington: Royal Forest and Bird Protection Society of NZ.
Royal Forest and Bird Protection Society of NZ et al. (1985) *Environmental Administration in New Zealand: An Alternative Discussion Paper*. Wellington: Royal Forest and Bird Protection Society of NZ.
Royal Society of New Zealand (1986) *Lead in the Environment in New Zealand*. Wellington: The Royal Society of New Zealand.
Ryan, John C. (1992) 'Conserving Biological Diversity' in Brown, Lester R. et al. *State of the World 1992*. London: Earthscan.
Sabatier, Paul A. (1986) 'What Can We Learn from Implementation Research?' in Kaufman, Franz-Xaver, Giandomenico Majone, and Vincent Ostrom (eds) *Guidance, Control, and Evaluation in the Public Sector*. New York: Walter de Gruyter.
Sabatier, Paul A. and Daniel A. Mazmanian (1979) 'The Conditions of Effective Implementation' *Policy Analysis* 5: 502–4.
Sabatier, Paul A. and Daniel A. Mazmanian (1983) 'Policy Implementation' in Nagel, Stuart (ed) *Encyclopedia of Policy Studies*. New York: Marcel Dekker.
Sagoff, Mark (1988) *The Economy of the Earth: Philosophy, Law, and the*

Environment. New York: Cambridge University Press.
Salmon, Guy (1982) 'Progress in Forest Conservation in New Zealand' Paper prepared for Australian Conservation Foundation National Activists' Seminar. Nelson: Native Forests Action Council.
Salmon, Guy (1984) 'The Native Forests Action Council: An Alternative Viewpoint' in Gregory, R. J. (ed) *The Official Information Act: A Beginning.* Wellington: The New Zealand Institute of Public Administration.
Salmon, Guy (1991a) 'Resource Management Legislation in New Zealand: The First Step Towards a Green Economy' in Ackroyd, Peter et al. *Environmental Resources and the Market-Place.* Sydney: Allen & Unwin.
Salmon, Guy (1991b) 'New Approaches to Water Management—An Environmentalist's View' Nelson: Maruia Society (unpublished).
Salmon, John T. (1960) *Heritage Destroyed: The Crisis in Scenery Preservation in New Zealand.* Wellington: A. H. & A. W. Reed.
Sand, Peter H. (1990) *Lessons Learned in Global Environmental Governance.* Washington, D.C.: World Resources Institute.
Scharpf, Fritz W. (1986) 'Policy Failure and Institutional Reform: Why Should Form Follow Function?' *International Social Science Journal* 38 (2): 179–89.
Schattschneider, E. E. (1960) *The Semisovereign People: A Realist's View of Democracy in America.* New York: Holt, Rinehart and Winston.
Schick, Allen (1977) 'Beyond Analysis' *Public Administration Review* 37: 258–63.
Schumacher, E. F. (1973) *Small is Beautiful: Economics as if People Mattered.* London: Sphere Books.
Scriven, Michael (1991) *Evaluation Thesaurus.* 4th ed. Newbury Park, Calif.: Sage Publications.
Searle, Graham (1975) *Rush to Destruction: An Appraisal of the New Zealand Beech Forest Controversy.* Wellington: A. H. & A. W. Reed.
Self, Peter (1985) *Political Theories of Modern Government, Its Role and Reform.* London: George Allen & Unwin.
Sharp, Andrew (1990a) *Justice and the Māori: Māori Claims in New Zealand. Political Argument in the 1980s.* Auckland: Oxford University Press.
Sharp, Andrew (1990b) 'The Problem of Māori Affairs' in Holland, Martin and Jonathan Boston (eds) *The Fourth Labour Government: Politics and Policy in New Zealand.* 2nd ed. Auckland: Oxford University Press.
Sharplin, Kathy (1987) *Economic Instruments for Environmental Management: An Overview.* Wellington: Ministry for the Environment.
Shields, Eryn (1991) 'National Sewerage Survey' *Terra Nova* 8 (August): 24–34.
Simon, Herbert A. (1947) *Administrative Behaviour.* Glencoe, Ill.: The Free Press.
Simon, Herbert A. (1976a) *Administrative Behavior: A Study of Decision-Making Processes in Administrative Organization.* 3rd ed. New York: The Free Press.
Simon, Herbert A. (1976b) 'From Substantive to Procedural Rationality' in Latsis, Spiro J. (ed) *Method and Appraisal in Economics.* Cambridge: Cambridge University Press.
Simon, Herbert A. (1978) 'Rationality as Process and as Product of Thought' *American Economic Review* 68 (2): 9.
Simon, Herbert A. (1979) 'Rational Decision Making in Business Organizations' *American Economic Review* 69: 507.
Simon, Herbert A. (1981) *The Sciences of the Artificial.* 2nd ed. Cambridge, Mass.: MIT Press.

Simon, Herbert A. (1985) 'Human Nature in Politics: The Dialogue of Psychology with Political Science' *American Political Science Review* 79: 293–304.
Steering Group Review of the State Sector Reforms (1991) *Review of State Sector Reforms*. Wellington: State Services Commission.
Stevenson, Philippa (1992) 'The Scandal of the PCP Dumps' *Terra Nova* 17 (June): 10–15.
Stokey, Edith, and Richard Zeckhauser (1978) *A Primer for Policy Analysis*. New York: W. W. Norton.
Stone, Deborah A. (1988) *Policy Paradox and Political Reason*. Glenview, Ill.: Scott, Foresman.
Swartzman, Daniel, Richard A. Liroff, and Kevin G. Croke (eds) (1982) *Cost-Benefit Analysis and Environmental Regulations: Politics, Ethics, and Methods*. Washington, D.C.: Conservation Foundation.
Terra Nova (1990–1992). Wellington: Brooker & Friend Ltd.
Tester, Frank J. (1987) 'Losing Ground: A Neo-Existential Critique of New Zealand Environmentalism.' Ph.D. thesis, University of Waikato, Department of Geography.
Tietenberg, Tom H. (1991) 'Managing the Transition: The Potential Role for Economic Policies' in Mathews, Jessica Tuchman (ed) *Preserving the Global Environment: The Challenge of Shared Leadership*. New York: W. W. Norton.
Treasury (1984) *Economic Management*. Wellington: Government Printer.
Treasury (1985a) 'Environmental Policy: the Proposed Ministry for the Environment' in *Environment Forum, Background Papers*. Wellington: State Services Commission.
Treasury (1985b) 'Environmental Assessment Procedures' Paper presented by Treasury to the Commissioner for the Environment. Wellington: Treasury.
Treasury (1987) *Government Management*. Wellington: Government Printer.
Trump, Thomas M. (1991) 'Value Formation and Postmaterialism: Inglehart's Theory of Value Change Reconsidered' *Comparative Political Studies* 24 (3): 365–90.
[UNEP] United Nations Environment Programme (1991) *Environmental Data Report*. 3rd ed. Oxford: Blackwell Publications.
[U.S. EPA] United States Environmental Protection Agency (1987) *Unfinished Business: A Comparative Assessment of Environmental Problems*. Washington, D.C.: Environmental Protection Agency.
[U.S. EPA] United States Environmental Protection Agency, Science Advisory Board (1990) *Reducing Risk: Setting Priorities and Strategies for Environmental Protection*. Washington, D.C.: Environmental Protection Agency.
Vogel, David (1986) *National Styles of Regulation: Environmental Policy in Great Britain and the United States*. Ithaca, N.Y.: Cornell University Press.
Vogel, David (1987) 'The Comparative Study of Public Policy: A Review of the Literature' in Dierkes, Meinolf, Hans Weiler, and Ariane Berthoin Antal (eds) *Comparative Policy Research: Learning from Experience*. Brookfield, Vt.: Gower.
Vogel, David (1990) 'Environmental Policy in Europe and Japan' in Vig, Norman J. and Michael E. Kraft (eds) *Environmental Policy in the 1990s: Toward a New Agenda*. Washington, D.C.: CQ Press.
Walker, K. J. (1989) 'The State in Environmental Management: The Ecological Dimension' *Political Studies* 37: 25–38.

Walsh, Pat (1991) 'The State Sector Act' in Boston, Jonathan, John Martin, June Pallot, and Pat Walsh (eds) *Reshaping the State: New Zealand's Bureaucratic Revolution*. Auckland: Oxford University Press.

Wandesforde-Smith, Geoffrey (1989) 'EIA, Entrepreneurship, and Policy Change' in Bartlett, Robert V. (ed) *Policy Through Impact Assessment: Institutionalized Analysis as a Policy Strategy*. Westport, Conn.: Greenwood Press.

Ward, Jonet C. (1992) *Contributions to a National Set of Environmental Indicators to be Monitored at a Regional Level*. Centre for Resource Management, Lincoln University.

Wathern, Peter (1989) 'Implementing Supranational Policy: Environmental Impact Assessment in the United Kingdom' in Bartlett, Robert V. (ed) *Policy Through Impact Assessment: Institutionalized Analysis as a Policy Strategy*. Westport, Conn.: Greenwood Press.

Weale, Albert (1992) *The New Politics of Pollution*. Manchester: Manchester University Press.

Weber, Max (1946) 'Politics as a Vocation' in Gerth, Hans C. and C. Wright Mills (eds) *Max Weber: Essays in Sociology*. New York: Oxford University Press.

Weidner, Helmut (1986) 'Japan: The Success and Limitations of Technocentric Environmental Policy' *Policy and Politics* 14 (1): 43–70.

Weiss, Carol H. with Michael J. Bucuvalas (1980) *Social Science Research and Decision-Making*. New York: Columbia University Press.

Welch, Denis (1992) 'Welch's Week' *Listener* 11 July 1992.

Whitcombe, Judy (1989) 'The Changing Face of the New Zealand Public Service' in Gold, Hyam (ed) *New Zealand Politics in Perspective*. 2nd ed. Auckland: Longman Paul.

White, Michael J. (1983) 'Policy Analysis and Management Science' in Nagel, Stuart (ed) *Encyclopedia of Policy Studies*. New York: Marcel Dekker.

Wildavsky, Aaron (1966) 'The Political Economy of Efficiency' *Public Administration Review* 26: 292–310.

Wildavsky, Aaron (1974) *The Politics of the Budgetary Process*. 2nd ed. Boston: Little, Brown.

Wildavsky, Aaron (1979) *Speaking Truth to Power: The Art and Craft of Policy Analysis*. Boston: Little, Brown.

Williams, D. A. R. (1980) *Environmental Law in New Zealand*. Wellington: Butterworth.

Williams, R. H. (1986) 'EC Environmental Policy, Land Use Planning and Pollution Control' *Policy and Politics* 14 (1): 93–106.

Williams, Gordon R. and David R. Given (1981) *The Red Data Book of New Zealand*. Wellington: Nature Conservation Council.

Wilson, Graham K. (1985) *Business and Politics: A Comparative Introduction*. Chatham, N.J.: Chatham House.

Wilson, Roger (1982) *From Manapouri to Aramoana: The Battle for New Zealand's Environment*. Auckland: Earthworks Press.

Wilson, Paul S. and Ted K. Harris (1991) 'Integrated Pollution Control: A Prologue' *Environmental Law* 22: i–xxi.

Wolf Jr., Charles (1979) 'A Theory of Nonmarket Failure' *Journal of Law and Economics* 22: 107–39.

World Resources Institute (1987–1992) *World Resources*. Baltimore: World Resources Institute.

INDEX

accords, forest 52
acid rain 46, 63
agenda setting 5, 19–22, 27, 36, 38, 44, 51, 53–5, 58, 62–6, 115, 128, 140, 160, 167
agricultural policy 104, 108, 127, 145, 155, 157, 160
agriculture, *see* farming
Alliance, the 56, 77, 78, 83, 87, 111, 153, 165
analycentric approach 14–19, 22–30, 34, 35
annual reports
 corporations 76
 government agencies 103, 151
Antarctic and Southern Ocean Coalition (ASOC) 65
Antarctica 42, 53, 64–6, 152, 168
anticipatory environmental policy making 3–6, 36, 37, 66, 99, 132, 136, 156, 158, 159
approvals, *see* consents
asbestos 48

Bassett, Michael 119
biodiversity 1, 40
Bobrow, Davis 30
Bolger, Jim 99
Britain, *see* United Kingdom
Brundtland Commission 141, 149, 155

Cabinet 60, 91, 104, 111, 116, 122–4, 128, 130, 144, 152
Canada 76, 86, 141, 142, *see also* North America
capitalism 87, 162
carbon dioxide, *see* CO_2 policy
catalytic controls 35
Caygill, David 91
changing our ways 3, 6, 68, 136, 156
clean and green 5–7, 10–13, 37, 57, 64–6, 68, 130, 152, 156, 158, 168, 169
CO_2 policy 78, 110, 152, 162

Coal Corporation 97
commercialization 128, 149
Commission for the Environment 78, 115, 117, 118, 144
compartmentalization, *see* fragmentation
comprehensive environmental policy 3, 9, 10, 36, 39, 103, 104, 106, 121, 132, 136, 137, 138–59
consents 46, 107, 126, 127, 129, 148
conservation 39, 41, 156, 157
conservation issues 42, 51, 52, 58
conservation movement 41, 52, 56, 66
consumerism, *see* green consumerism
convergence 63
co-ordination, *see* comprehensive environmental policy
cornucopians 6
corporate plans, government agencies 103, 132, 144
corporatization 91–4, 96–8, 128, 143, 149, 150
crises 4–6, 21, 44, 45, 51, 97, 112
Crown Minerals Act 124

decentralization 105, 121, 163
decisionism 19, 22, 27, 28
deforestation 40, 94
delegation 121, 133
Department of Conservation 52, 78, 96, 117, 118, 128, 131, 145, 149, 159, 164
Department of Health 117, 145
Department of Labour 146
Department of Lands and Survey 94–6, 116, 118
Department of Survey and Land Information 118
devolution 105, 121, 133, 159
Diesing, Paul 30
district councils 126, 127
Douglas, Roger 91
Downs, Anthony 21

driftnet fishing 42, 53, 64–6, 152
Dryzek, John 25, 30
dual mandates 94, 95, 99, 103, 150, 151, 159
Dunn, William 31

Earth summit, *see* United Nations Conference on Environment and Development
Eckersley, Robyn 33
ecological (ecosystems) dimension 9, 38, 131, 146, 150, 163, 168
economic (resource management) dimension 9, 39, 53, 150, 157, 163
economic growth 31, 32, 39, 43, 49–51, 74, 79, 80, 87, 100, 112, 116, 129, 140, 145, 149, 154, 162, 164
economic instruments 91, 106–12, 128, 162
economic policy 160, 162
education 49, 105
Electricity Corporation 97
energy
 conservation 51, 97, 98, 105, 108, 168
 issues 44–6
 policy 39, 44, 45, 53, 59, 94, 97–9, 111, 112, 131, 157, 159, 161, 168
 resources 43, 44, 51, 168
Environment Act 118, 131, 133, 147
environmental auditing 69, 77, 155
Environmental Council 105
environmental groups 65, 69–71, 83, 128, 129
environmental impact assessment 8, 35, 116, 118, 119, 122, 142, 148, 149
environmental movement 7, 42, 56, 60, 65, 94, 135, 156, 164
environmental policy research 3, 12–15
environmental problematique 1, 3, 6, 9, 13, 36, 38–40, 53, 55–7, 67, 100, 113, 114, 131, 136, 137, 143, 150, 163, 169
Environmental Risk Management Authority 131, 146

environmentalism 1, 31, 33, 36, 67, 68, 77, 79, 80, 89, 128, 135
erosion 43, 44, 51, 107
Europe 7, 12, 32, 53, 56, 58, 63, 81, 93, 106, 142, 143, 164
European Community 142
evaluation 19, 26–9

farming 94, 107
fisheries 43, 44, 50, 107, 108–10, 166
Flanagan, Scott 79
flora and fauna 5, 40, 44
Forest Service, New Zealand 94–6, 116, 118
Forestry Corporation 96, 118
forests 5, 40, 44, 51, 98, 107, 127, 157, 166
formulation, *see* policy formulation
fragmentation 104, 135, 137, 140, 144, 145, 150

geothermal resources 126
global climate change 1, 38, 42, 152, *see also* greenhouse effect
global environmental issues 6, 42, 44, 53, 64
global warming, *see* global climate change
goals 23, 24, 28, 87, 101–3, 106, 113, 124, 151
Great Britain, *see* United Kingdom
green consumerism 69, 75, 83, 87, 89
green parties 7, 50, 68, 156
Green Party, New Zealand 7, 56, 69, 77, 78, 83, 84, 87, 89, 153, 165
green politics 7
green producerism 76, 87
greenhouse effect 4, 5, 46, 53, 63–5, 68, 167–9, *see also* global climate change
Greenpeace 65, 69–71
green values, *see* values, environmental
hazardous substances 48, 57, 63, 65, 66, 104, 126, 131, 146, 154, 158, 168
Hazards Control Commission, *see* Environmental Risk Management Authority

health 39, 47–9, 57, 105
housing 39, 49, 158
hydro-dams 41, 42, 94, 95
hydro-electric power 43, 168

implementation 19, 25–8, 108, 109, 112, 120, 121, 124, 130, 132
incremental politics 24, 36, 102, 120
industrialization 5, 57
Inglehart, Ronald 32, 33, 79–82, 84–6, 88, 89
institutional analysis 7, 8, 88
institutional change 3, 7–9, 27, 34–6, 53, 59, 66, 80, 87–9, 128, 132, 136, 140, 149, 155, 156, 159, 165–7, 169
institutional framework 8, 33–5, 45, 59, 67, 86–88, 104, 113, 127, 133, 156, 159
institutional rules 34, 35
integration, *see* comprehensive environmental policy
interdependence 64
international environmental policy 65, 152, 167, 169

Kingdon, John 22, 54

Labour Government 44, 45, 78, 85, 90, 92–94, 100, 107, 111, 114–17, 119, 121–4, 127, 131, 152
Labour Party 78, 91, 111, 115, 121, 124, 144, 153
Land Corporation 96, 118
land use 121, 129
Lasswell, Harold 19
leaded petrol 48, 64, 107
limits to growth 44, 47, 53
Lindblom, Charles 23, 24, 31
littering 49
local authorities 48, 119, 120, 123, 128, 130, 149, *see also* district councils
local government 49, 105, 112, 116, 120, 121, 125–30, 132, 133, 146–9, 154, 158, 159, 160, 161, 164
Local Government (No. 2) Act 1989 120
Local Government Amendments Act 113–15, 119
Local Government Commission 119, 120, 122
local government reform 9, 10, 92, 112–14, 116, 117, 119–23, 127, 128, 133, 134, 143, 146

managerialist principles 102, 103
Māori 40, 43, 49, 50, 55, 110, 123, 166
market, the 6, 9, 10, 25, 45, 49, 50, 53, 59, 92, 93, 96–100, 105, 107, 108, 110–12, 143, 149, 150, 155, 161, 162
market instruments, *see* economic instruments
Marshall, Russell 122
Maruia Society 56, 69, 70, 109
materialists 33
meta-policy 100, 105, 127
meta-policy approach 14, 18, 30, 31, 33–6, 132
Milbrath, Lester 32
mineral resources 43, 44, 46
mining 39, 42, 51
Minister for the Environment 107, 125, 126, 130
Minister of Conservation 125, 126
Ministry for the Environment 78, 95, 103, 104, 117–19, 122–4, 128, 131, 132, 144, 145, 146, 151, 158, 159
Ministry of Agriculture and Fisheries 145
Ministry of Energy 105
Ministry of Forestry 118
Ministry of Works and Development 94, 95, 116, 118
monitoring 54, 109, 127, 130, 148, 149, 158, 167
Muldoon, Robert 44, 121, 139

National Development Act 121
national environmental administration 9, 92, 112–14, 122, 128, 131, 133, 143, 144
National Government 44, 45, 78, 85, 92, 93, 96, 99, 111, 114, 123, 131, 139, 149
national parks 5, 41, 51, 52, 58, 95, 166

National Party   78, 91, 124, 153
Native Forests Action Council   42, 95
natural resources   39, 42, 43, 58, 66
nature conservation   10, 55, 61, 62, 164, 168
Nature Conservation Council   62
Nature Protection Council   41
Netherlands, the   82, 86, 141, 142
new environmental paradigm   31, 32
NewLabour Party   78, 84
New Public Management   100, 101
New Right   90, 91, 95, 111, 112, 114–16, 120, 134, 162, 167
new social paradigm   68, 78, 79, 89
New Zealand Planning Council   105
North America   7, 12, 53, 56, 143
nuclear power   4, 45, 47, 51, 69, 152

ozone depletion   1, 4, 5, 11, 38, 42, 46, 53, 63–5, 68, 107, 127, 152, 167

packaging   49, 104, 168
Palmer, Geoffrey   42, 115–17, 122, 124, 152
paradigm shift   7, 31, 33, 68, 78–80, 83, 85, 88, 89, 164, 166
Parliament   60, 77, 88, 115, 119, 120, 122–4, 131, 149, 155, 165
Parliamentary Commissioner for the Environment   78, 118, 122, 128, 145, 159
permits, *see* consents
pesticides   48, 64, 94, 98, 107, 168, 169
Petroleum Corporation   97
Planning Tribunal   127, 133
policy agenda   12, 20, 21
policy analysis   3, 12, 14–18, 28, 30, 31, 35, 123
policy cycle   19, 20, 26–8
policy design   26
policy evaluation, *see* evaluation
policy failure   29
policy formulation   19, 26, 27, 121
policy implementation, *see* implementation
policy process   3, 5, 14, 18–20, 23–5, 27–31, 34, 102, 117, 125, 127, 140, 145, 159

policy process approach   3, 14, 18, 19, 22, 24–9, 35, 36
policy selection   19, 22, 25–8, 120, 124
pollution   4, 5, 9, 37, 39, 40, 44, 46–8, 52, 53, 57, 59, 63–6, 158
pollution control   126, 145, 146, 158, 159
population   5, 37, 39, 44, 57, 65, 66, 158
postmaterialism   32, 33, 164, 166, 167
Prebble, Richard   91
Pressman, Jeffrey   26
privatization   91, 92, 94, 96–8, 128, 143, 149, 150, 161
problem definition   5, 13, 19, 20, 27, 29, 36, 38, 50, 54, 55, 57–9, 65, 66, 115, 128, 154, 167
Public Finance Act   100, 101
public opinion   71–4, 81–4, 89
public service, the   9, 91, 100, 101, 103, 105, 112, 117, 128, 143, 151

quality of life   46, 47, 49, 50, 53, 59, 103, 159, 168
quality of life issues   49–51, 66, 164

rational comprehensive decision making   24, 138
rationality   23–5
  comprehensive   138
  ecological   6, 8, 25, 127, 140, 151, 165
  economic   106, 151
  instrumental   23, 24, 120
regional authorities   107, 121, 125–7, 129, 148
reporting function   104, 144, 145
resource issues   42, 44, 46, 51, 53, 164
resource management   45, 46, 53, 90, 105, 111
Resource Management Act   9, 10, 27, 46, 53, 78, 92, 107, 112–15, 121, 122, 125, 126, 128–34, 143, 146–9, 153–5, 157–9, 164, 167
resource management law
  reform   114, 116, 119, 121–4, 127, 131–3, 146

Index

Royal Forest and Bird Protection Society 41, 69, 70

scenic beauty 5, 37, 41, 42, 55, 65
science 3, 15, 17–19, 26, 30, 39, 102
segmentation, *see* fragmentation
sewage disposal 47, 48
social choice mechanisms 25
social policy 49, 137
social (quality of life) dimension 9, 39, 131, 146, 150, 157, 163, 164
social transformation 6, 7, 32, 82
social welfare 2, 60, 152, *see also* quality of life issues
soil management 126
standard of living 37, 39, 46, 47
standards, national environmental 126, 130, 146, 149
State Enterprises Act 93
State owned enterprises 93, 94, 96, 97, 99, 160, 161
State Sector Act 100, 101
State sponsored vandalism 90, 94, 95, 112, 150, 161
State, the 9, 34, 49, 58, 60, 88, 90–100, 111, 140, 159–63, 167
Stone, Deborah 31
sustainability 39, 43, 52, 53, 77, 79, 97, 103, 108, 118, 124, 125, 129, 132–4, 141, 144, 147, 155, 157, 160, 167

technocentrists 6
technology 39
Think Big policy 44, 50, 58, 96, 121, 139
tourism 5, 37, 58, 92
Town and Country Planning 116, 119
Town and Country Planning Act 121, 122, 125
trade and environment 64, 141, 168
Transit New Zealand Act 121
transport policy 53, 159, 161, 168
Transport Services Licensing Act 121
transport, public 49, 107, 108, 161
transportation 157, 158
Treasury 91, 93–6, 98, 100, 106, 107, 110, 111, 116–18, 122, 123, 145, 164

Treaty of Waitangi 49, 110, 125, 166
tropical rainforests 42, 53, 66

United Kingdom 57, 58, 70, 76, 82, 91, 93, 141, 142, 162
United Nations Conference on Environment and Development 1
United States 32, 58, 63, 71, 76, 82, 86, 91, 107, 142, 162, *see also* North America
unleaded petrol, *see* leaded petrol
Upton, Simon 111
urban decay 5, 158
urban development 49, 121, 157, 158

value change 7, 31–4, 57, 67, 79, 80, 82, 87, 88, 164, 165, 167
values
  authoritarian 79, 81, 89
  cultural 17, 39
  ecological 56, 150
  economic 56, 66, 84, 161, 166
  environmental 9, 12, 15, 32, 33, 57, 68, 69, 71, 75–80, 83–5, 89, 100, 105, 106, 110, 127–9, 132, 143, 145, 150, 155, 159, 161, 164–7
  instrumental 29
  intrinsic 118, 125, 129, 131, 133, 166
  Māori 166
  materialistic 32, 33, 79, 81, 83–6, 89, 164
  postmaterialistic 7, 32, 33, 68, 79–86, 88, 89, 166
  preservationist 166
  social 22, 34, 56, 59, 150
Values Party 50, 77, 165

Waitangi Tribunal 50, 166
waste management 48, 64, 104, 121, 158
Water and Soil Conservation Act 125
water management 95
water resources 43, 44, 46, 51, 126
welfare, *see* social welfare
wetlands 5, 52, 94

whaling 65
Wildavsky, Aaron 26
wildlife 5, 40, 44
Wildlife Service (Department of Internal Affairs) 118

women and environment 49, 72, 73
Woollaston, Philip 115, 117, 122
Works and Development Corporation 119